This is a key book for understanding the profound worldview shift in all the West (not just North America, but Latin America included). Peter Jones carefully analyzes its religious underpinnings and, in light of the Scriptures, demonstrates that there are only *two* choices. I highly recommend this work as the mature reflections of a scholar who has dedicated the last 20 years to this topic.

Rev. Bill Green
Executive Secretary,
Confraternidad Latinoamericana de Iglesias Reformadas (CLIR)
Costa Rica

I have worked as a legal campaigner in Great Britain for two decades and witnessed the devastation of a politico-legal system that embraces Oneism and denies Twoism. **There is a suppression of Christianity in the public sphere, robbing our nation of what is good for all.** Peter Jones brilliantly explains how and why we are in such chaos, equipping us to speak and act relevantly in a culture steeped in old paganism.

Andrea Williams
Chief Executive, Christian Concern and Christian Legal Centre
London, England

Dr. Peter Jones' new book is spot on! His historical, theological, and cultural analysis is of the highest caliber, **inspiring both great concern for the Church of the 21st century and great hope.** *The Other Worldview* is a must read for all Christian leaders who recognize and proclaim that God is the creator and we are his creation!

The Rt. Rev. Dr. Eric Vawter Menees
Anglican Diocese of San Joaquin
Fresno, California

My good friend Peter Jones argues that the ills of modern culture stem from its denial of the biblical creator-creature distinction. Peter has made this case before, but **here he presents his most substantial, detailed, and illuminating account of this modern consciousness**, from ancient paganism and Gnosticism to such modern thinkers as Carl Jung. In the end Peter shows how the biblical gospel of salvation from sin in Christ provides the only adequate challenge to neo-pagan "Oneism," and the only way for us to know God as he really is.

Dr. John M. Frame
J. D. Trimble Professor of Systematic Theology and Philosophy,
Reformed Theological Seminary
Orlando, Florida

For over two decades, Peter Jones's work has proven indispensable for any Christian who wants to understand how to reach the pagan West with the gospel of Jesus Christ. In *The Other Worldview*, he helps readers see that there really are only two options available for how we view reality: Christianity and everything else. With the rare and enviable gift of being able to make complex ideas accessible, **Dr. Jones shows that the other worldview, in its varied expressions, cannot withstand intellectual scrutiny.**

Rev. Dr. Gabriel N.E. Fluhrer
Senior Minister, Shiloh Orthodox Presbyterian Church
Raleigh, North Carolina

The velocity and intensity of the cultural death spiral is overwhelming, yet its inevitable trajectory is affirmed in Scripture. In *The Other Worldview*, Peter Jones, with careful Biblical analysis, unfolds the inevitable embrace of paganism and its assured dissipation—**unless arrested by a God-exalting, Gospel proclamation of both common grace and redeeming grace displayed in word and deed.**

Harry L. Reeder
Senior Pastor, Briarwood Presbyterian Church
Birmingham, Alabama

If the 21st century is looking more and more like the gnostic world of the first two centuries, we should be grateful that God has also provided another Irenaeus to go with it. Peter Jones has for decades been a prophetic voice, and here he puts his wealth of wisdom and insight into something of a magnum opus, an *Against Heresies* for our time—although he would rightly insist on the singular, "heresy," instead of its plural. *The Other Worldview* is a must-read that brilliantly explains why.

Dr. Brian Mattson
Senior Scholar of Public Theology, Center For Cultural Leadership
Coulterville, California

What Francis Schaeffer did for so many in the second half of the 20th century—that is, opening eyes to issues behind the issues, the deep worldview undercurrents that dehumanize and wreak havoc on culture—Peter Jones has done for us in the first half of the 21st century. *The Other Worldview* offers probing analysis of how Romans 1—the exchange of Creator for creation worship—has taken tragic shape in Western culture. **Where many books focus on symptom-treating, Jones takes us to the disease and points us to the only possible remedy—the Gospel of Twoism.**

Dr. Thaddeus Williams
Assistant Professor of Theology, Talbot School of Theology,
Biola University
La Mirada, California

The Christian faith's battles are sometimes described as "culture wars," but Peter Jones' new book shows them to be nothing less than a war of worldviews. Peter is spot on when he identifies the *philosophia perennis* as underlying the seductive paganisms, ancient and modern, Eastern and Western. The monism and pantheism inherent in such views fail to distinguish between the Creator and the creature, the One and the many.

The Bible's worldview is quite distinct from the rest of the ancient East, and the contemporary West's entanglement with "Eastern spirituality" arises out of its rejection of the biblical paradigm. Atheistic secularism is under pressure from the innate human need for the spiritual—and this provides the opportunity for myriad spiritualities that justify any and every promiscuity under the guise of being "non-judgmental." Peter is absolutely right in his trenchant criticism of the desire to reconcile opposites and thus to obscure the difference between good and evil, right and wrong—even, perhaps especially, when this is done in the name of science.

Today, we need both a critique of the unexamined assumptions of Western culture and a competent apologetic for the Christian analysis of the human condition in a universe continually dependent on its Creator, who cannot simply be identified with it. We are in Peter's debt for providing such a critique and apologetic in this book.

Bishop Michael Nazir-Ali
President of the Oxford Centre for Training, Research, Advocacy and Dialogue (OXTRAD), and formerly Bishop of Rochester, England
England

THE OTHER WORLDVIEW

EXPOSING CHRISTIANITY'S GREATEST THREAT

THE OTHER WORLDVIEW

EXPOSING CHRISTIANITY'S GREATEST THREAT

PETER JONES

FOREWORD BY

R.C. SPROUL

KIRKDALE PRESS

The Other Worldview: Exposing Christianity's Greatest Threat

Kirkdale Press, 1313 Commercial St., Bellingham, WA 98225
KirkdalePress.com

ISBN 978-1-57-799622-4

Kirkdale Editorial Team: Brannon Ellis, Joel Wilcox, Abigail Stocker
Cover Design: Josh Warren
Typesetting: ProjectLuz.com

CONTENTS

FOREWORD

Wait just a minute. How in the world did we get to the place where we are? The sun has set on the British Empire and the grand experiment of America has blown up in the laboratory.

We can ask about the grisly impact of two world wars on Western civilization. We can look to the impact of the Holocaust, where the battle-hardened commander of the Allies, General Dwight D. Eisenhower, wept when he beheld the ghost-like, emaciated survivors of Hitler's death camps and the Final Solution to the "Jewish problem." We can read our resultant culture through the lens of Nietzsche's nihilism or Jean Paul Sartre's assessment of humanity as "Nausea" with "No Exit" in sight.

America has passed through a revolution—nay, two revolutions. The first was the revolution of the 18th century, whereby the United States secured its independence from England. We often forget that over a century and a half of colonial culture had elapsed before the Boston Tea Party was even imagined. The Revolutionary War was fought to preserve the colonial culture—its customs, mores, form of government. There was already an established American way of life that was being sorely threatened by whimsical changes in Great Britain's parliament from which the colonies were to be governed.

To be sure, America was already changing without any great assistance from England. Jonathan Edwards had already decried the declension of values, religion, and customs initiated by the Pilgrims and Puritans who settled the country earlier and who sought to establish "a light set on a hill."

The French Revolution was altogether different. It involved a self-conscious effort to turn the traditional, established national culture upside down. It was a war against the prevailing French way of life.

America's second revolution—the cultural revolution of the 1960's—was similar to the French Revolution in that its goal was to bring radical change to the forms, structures, values, and ethics of the status quo. It sought to bring in a New Age with the dawning of the Age of Aquarius.

Now the dawn of the New Age is long past. Aquarius is now at high noon. This revolution, in its inception, was relatively bloodless. But its consequences have been exceedingly bloody. In just one example, America has witnessed and sanctioned the murder for hire of over 60 million unborn babies. Living, personal beings are routinely pulled and cut to pieces in the name of women's health and liberty.

We have seen the noonday sun reveal the destruction of the sanctity of life, the sanctity of marriage, the sanctity of sex, and the sanctity of the sacred itself. The culture is not merely post-Christian and post-modern. It has become not only neopagan, but neo-barbarian.

Ideas have consequences. The ideas of the New Age, of *our* age, have their roots in ancient Gnosticism. That particular philosophy embraced a form of pantheism or monism: God is "the One"—the sum of everything. All is God, and God is all.

Of course if everything is God, then nothing is God—the very word "God" can point to nothing individuated from everything. It becomes a meaningless, unintelligible word.

Peter Jones has labored to show the distinction and impact of a zeitgeist of Oneism (monism) versus Twoism (duality). The Twoism of which Dr. Jones speaks is not an ancient form of dualism which embraced equal and opposite forces of good and evil. No, it is a cosmic duality that sees—sharply and vividly—the distinction between creature and Creator and the relationship between the two.

This is not a simple problem of arithmetic wherein we learn to count from 1 to 2. These numbers have suffixes. The suffix *-ism* is added to the 1 and the 2. The suffix *-ism* adds to a simple number an entire worldview or philosophical standpoint embraced by either.

Dr. Jones provides for us a clear map. This map traces the historical paths, the philosophical routes, and the cultural lanes that have brought us to the Age of Aquarius. It is a must-read for every concerned American—and especially for every Christian who weeps at the graveside of his culture.

R.C. Sproul
Orlando, Florida
2015

PREFACE

I recently watched the third installment of *The Hobbit* in a packed theater with my wife and one of our daughters. It was an epic adventure, to be sure, but what I noticed most was a certain *longing* underneath it all. It made me wonder if the continued popularity of C. S. Lewis and J. R. R. Tolkien represents a nostalgia for a cultural past that is no more. One keen observer sees an important difference between these two literary giants:

> Whereas C. S. Lewis tries to make us comfortable in what we already believe by dressing up the story as a children's masquerade, Tolkien makes us profoundly uncomfortable. Our people, our culture, our language, our toehold upon this shifting and uncertain Earth are no more secure than those of a thousand extinct tribes of the Dark Ages; and a greater hope than that of the

work of our hands and the hone of our swords must
avail us.[1]

These authors' vast mythical vision of the confrontation between the
forces of good and evil reveals a sense that the Christian West was
threatened by an evil that would destroy all remembrance of a culture
based on Christian principles. In the 1940s, it was easy to identify this
evil with Nazism and Marxism. These authors were no doubt concerned
as they saw the religious soul of Western culture making way for the
self-assured triumph of secular humanism.

The present book is written especially for readers one-third my
age. I write it as an uncomfortable eyewitness to a massive shift in
Western culture, where the dark forces of Sauron have taken power in
the once-Christian Shire of Western culture. First appearing as secular
humanism, these forces have now grown into a much more formidable
opponent of Christianity: a full-blown cosmology of pagan lore, seen
perhaps most clearly in Hollywood's many other religiously inspired
blockbusters—*Star Wars*, *The Matrix*, the Marvel franchise—that do not
share the worldview of Tolkien or Lewis.[2]

My plea is not a nostalgic appeal to return to the good old days of yore
but an attempt to clarify the confrontation between *the only two ultimate
worldviews*—the only two fundamental patterns of belief that underlie
how we make sense of the world. I call these "Oneism" and "Twoism."
These terms are my shorthand for what I believe the Apostle Paul is
getting at when he describes the heart of idolatry and falsehood as exchanging the truth for "the lie" and exchanging worship of the Creator
for worship of the creature (Rom 1:25).

Over the last two generations, I have watched the Oneism of ancient
paganism overtake the centuries-old Western cultural structures rooted
in basic notions of biblical truth (Twoism). The lie of Oneism is on the
rise, in large part because it is now being presented as an articulate cosmology capable of explaining the whole of human existence, claiming
to define "the right side of history," and demanding to be culturally normative. This attempt to dismantle the Christian worldview's belief in a
divinely created universe of structure and order not only undermines
right knowledge of and worship of the Creator, but severely hinders

people from hearing and understanding the Christian (Twoist) gospel at all.

In the United States, the millennial generation is the first to be immersed from birth within such a coherently antibiblical system. In many areas of the United States and in its educational institutions, this generation has been given a worldview based on the presuppositions of paganism and an outright rejection of God, the personal Creator. For many young people, these voices have drowned out serious consideration of the Christian worldview, which is now vilified—like money used to be—as the source of all kinds of evil. Thus, traditional Western culture is under siege, and the immediate casualties are the millennials, who have unwittingly been seduced by aging progressivists (my peers, mind you!).

How can one speak to a generation steeped in the old paganism dressed in new clothes? My answer to this most pressing question is unpacked in the pages below: only by a robust cosmology of God-honoring Twoism. Describing the essence of "the lie" and showing the full extent of the truth is the only way forward. We Christians need a deep understanding of both the gospel *and* the pagan system around us—the system into which the gospel speaks and which it unequivocally judges so that it may fully redeem.

I can only imagine what God will do with a rising generation of Christian millennials trained to think "antithetically" or Twoistically, as did the Apostle Paul and the early Christians who, in spite of being a small minority in a hostile pagan empire, turned it upside down for the glory of Jesus Christ.

CHAPTER 1

A TICKET TO RIDE— BUT TO WHERE?

A Map of London and a Map of Life

Three of my children live in London. Whenever I visit them, I'm amazed by the London Tube. The Underground, as it is also known, first opened in 1863 and now carries over a billion passengers each year, everywhere, in one of the biggest cities in the world. To get anywhere quickly, though, you have to know the destination of the train. Otherwise you could spend days hopping on and off, never getting where you need to go.

Some people live this way, figuratively getting on the first train that shows up, or the one the most people are taking. Few think about the destination until they end up in a station of life they do not welcome, at the end of a journey they finally regret.

A worldview contains a series of convictions and conclusions about the nature of the world that provide fundamental meaning and direction for our lives, just as the Tube map will direct a journey across London. Though our beliefs often are unarticulated inklings or unexamined hunches, we all have a worldview—the simple act of opening our mouths to speak shows a belief that life has significance and somehow fits together. Interpreting a map of life is more complicated than that of the London Underground, so we sometimes give up and hop on the next train that comes by.

Our culture, too, seems to have boarded a train headed in a different direction than the one it originally was following. Perhaps this was out of a conviction we were headed the wrong way, or perhaps we've given up on thinking about where we're finally going. But how many destinations are there, ultimately?

A Book's Origins—in a Little Autobiography

Let's begin our journey with a snapshot from my own. Influential 20th-century Swiss psychologist Carl Jung, whom we shall meet often in these pages, once described a dream in which he found himself on a rainy night in my hometown, Liverpool, England—"a sooty, dark, dirty city."[1] Thank you, Carl, for that not very flattering, though accurate, description! About 30 years after Jung had his dream, I found myself on an uncharacteristically sunny day with someone even more famous than Jung. Lunchtime had rolled around at Quarry Bank High School for Boys, and the thought of fish and chips was irresistible to my friend and me. In defiance of the school rules, we climbed over the wall and went on a 20-minute jaunt to our favorite "chippy" on Penny Lane.

"Penny Lane" probably gives it away: My old schoolmate was John Lennon, later to become a household name as one of the Beatles. He later wrote (with some exaggeration) of Penny Lane's "blue suburban skies." At the time, of course, no one could foresee his star-studded future—certainly not the headmaster, who caned us on our backsides later that day, unimpressed with either one of us.

I mention my school days with John not to gain reflected glory but because I see a certain historical irony: The same headmaster who caned John and me began each school day with Bible reading and prayer. Quarry Bank, though a state school, was typical in that regard; at that time, Christianity was my culture's accepted religion, and England was fairly representative of the rest of the West. Long after my days at Quarry Bank, I became a Christian theologian dedicated to distinguishing biblical spirituality from its many counterfeits, especially those expressed in today's versions of Eastern or New Age spirituality. I write books as an observer of the spiritual state of the contemporary West, which has changed dramatically since my high school days. On the other hand, John left Quarry Bank in 1956, when our ways parted for good, and later became a devoted follower of the Maharishi Mahesh Yogi and an impassioned spokesman of Eastern-style spirituality.

Though exposed to the same Christian culture as I was, he would try hard to marginalize Christianity. For example, in his hit song "Imagine," John asked us to conceive of a world without religions or notions of an afterlife, in which we can realize our innate personal and social potential for ultimate peace and harmony. The influence of such thinking is clear in the common quip, "I'm spiritual, but not religious." Bill and Hillary Clinton requested that "Imagine" be played on the National Mall on New Year's Eve, 2000, to usher in the third millennium.

In 1964, I came to the United States to study, arriving at Logan Airport in Boston shortly after the Beatles reached America. I came to further my education and discovered a culture even more apparently Christian than the one I had left. "Fortress America" was the epicenter of Christianity in the 20th-century world, the nation sending countless missionaries to the ends of the earth. Christianity was everywhere, as evidenced by innumerable radio and TV stations, thousands of Christian schools and colleges, scores of Christian publishers, and church buildings as far as the eye could see. I thought I had died and gone to heaven—for one thing, on Mondays, ministers could play golf free of charge, and I know that's the way it will be in heaven!

What eventually broke the spell was the Western cultural revolution of the late 1960s, for which my schoolmate was such an influential spokesperson. At the time, the revolution did not seem particularly revolutionary. It involved a handful of hippies whose influence seemed negligible. Ironically, most of the immense changes we see today have come from the convictions and assumptions—the worldview—of that handful of outliers.

"Cataclysmic" Cultural Change

I have been both a participant in and a keen observer of this tumultuous time from the Sixties through today. In my lifetime, Christianity has ceased to be the religion of heritage or choice for a great many people in the West. How could such a huge change take place in such a short time? Even as some sociological experts in the 1960s spoke of living in a "surprise-free world,"[2] an ideological revolution was actually exploding under their noses.

Elizabeth Fox-Genovese, a respected American scholar with a PhD from Harvard, quoted above, was both a Marxist and feminist voice in the Sixties. Having converted to Christianity later in life, she said of the cultural revolution in which she had participated so enthusiastically, "Within a remarkably brief period ... occurred a cataclysmic transformation of the very nature of our society."[3] Fox-Genovese is not alone.[4] A large part of my motivation in writing this book is out of my concern to explain the origin and nature of this transformation and its ongoing effects within contemporary Western culture.

The rules have changed—the trains have gone off the track. In our time, the old canopy of a more or less Christian civilization has been shredded, replaced by a new overarching structure of spiritual beliefs and practices. Many of the traditional plausibility structures that gave life meaning and significance under Christian influence in the West are unrecognizable:

1. Morality is relativized by varied (and often contradictory) personal or social convictions.

2. Honesty means being true to one's inner commitments and longings more than to external expectations or objective facts.

3. Acceptable models of sexuality and family allow various combinations of persons and genders.

4. Marriage is often functionally indistinguishable from mutually convenient cohabitation.

5. Motherhood is celebrated in the same breath with abortion on demand.

The meaning and context of spirituality and religion have undergone a paradigm shift no less fundamental. The notion of God now allows for polytheism (many gods) or pantheism (a god identical with the universe). The average millennial in the United States, for example, no longer defines a vital spiritual life as knowledge of and communion with the infinite-yet-personal Creator and Lord of heaven and earth who is revealed in the Bible. Spirituality has become a do-it-yourself life hobby that blends ancient Eastern practices with modern consumer sensibilities. If religion is merely a tacit admission that we're all grasping blindly for the same thing, then who can judge anyone else for being "spiritual but not religious"?

I may sound nostalgic for the good old days, but I'm not making a case for returning to the Western culture of the Fifties. In that era, people were just as sinful and had just as many problems, such as institutional racism and sexism—not to mention overexuberant headmasters with canes! Nevertheless, that culture, with variable degrees of success and consistency, existed under what sociologist Peter Berger called the "sacred canopy" of a basic Christian worldview, so that fundamental ideas—about God, morality, sexuality, family, marriage, motherhood, spirituality, and religion—were understood from a Christian perspective, consciously or unconsciously. People broke the rules, but everyone was assuming pretty much the *same* rules.

I have watched this "cataclysmic transformation" occur in the space of one generation. I've thought long about it, lectured all over the world on it, and written books about it. I pray that by God's grace, this reflection and research will allow me some success in analyzing what is happening now and what Christians, who are called to be salt and light, can do about it. The goal is not to recover a 20th-century Western culture, but to preach the gospel clearly in our own time and bless the culture with God-honoring living.

The changed culture in which we live is the only one young readers have known. There's nothing wrong with being young. As George Bernard Shaw is thought to have said, with obvious regret, "Youth is wasted on the young," and we all admire the energy, enthusiasm, and creativity of youth. Still, a lack of knowledge about the recent past can create problems. Current generations may accept contemporary beliefs and lifestyle choices as normal without realizing just how abnormal they were a few short years ago. Both young and old Christians may seek wisdom uncritically from the surrounding culture, whose assumptions and values are often decidedly un-Christian. While we should desire to understand our culture in order to bear witness to Jesus in it, we must avoid conforming to its expectations just to garner its affirmation.[5] Most importantly, as the church, we must call all cultures—and ourselves— in every generation to the rule that judges all other rules—the rule of faith, the law of true freedom, the Word of God.

The World of Difference in a World of One or Two

In these confusing times, I have good news for my fellow travelers: The Tube map for our life journeys is not as complicated as it seems! Contrary to our culture's assumptions, there are only two trains, moving in opposite directions and arriving at two very different destinations.

I latched onto this as I tried to understand the surprising changes in the West which emerged from the culture wars of the Seventies and Eighties. Two simple terms, "one" and "two," often surface in the contemporary debate over spirituality—I sometimes say that if you can count from one to two, you can be a theologian. The terminology of one and two will drop you in the very nerve center of the culture, like getting off the tube at Piccadilly Circus or Trafalgar Square instead of getting off in a regional substation like Plumstead or Cockfosters. If we are going to defend the gospel in our modern world, we need to understand what lies behind "the one" and "the two."

How do these simple terms describe spirituality? Peter Occhiogrosso gives us a hint in The Joy of Sects, a work that discusses all the major religions. While he does not use "one" or "two" in his title (who could resist the one he has?), he nevertheless boldly states: "...under and through each of the great traditions runs a stream ... a single stream that feeds each of these traditions from a single source ... the Perennial Philosophy."[6] He defines the Perennial Philosophy as a system that "seeks to break down duality (twoness) and return us to the unitive condition [oneness], to see that we are already one."[7] Spirituality teacher Andrew Cohen uses a similar argument in a lecture titled, "The Significance of

Non Duality: There is Only One, Not Two." Throughout the lecture he repeatedly asks, "Why is it important that there is only one, not two?"[8]

One and two also figure in discussions of the "Easternization" of the West.[9] In *American Veda*,[10] Philip Goldberg reasons that America has become Hindu, pointing to a general acceptance of the ancient Sanskrit notion of "Advaita," which means "not two." Advaita affirms that all is one. The emphasis on oneness is essential to all Eastern religions that have found fertile soil in the West, including ancient ones like Hinduism, Sikhism, Buddhism, and Taoism, as well as more recent additions like Sufism, Neoplatonism,[11] Gnosticism, and Kabbalah.

Carl Jung also explained existence in terms of one or two,[12] as has Father Thomas Keating, a Roman Catholic interfaith mystic who teaches that the high goal of spirituality is to move from the awareness of twonness (distinctions in the real world) to the nondual state of oneness.[13] The same terminology is to be found in the writings of some Protestant leaders[14] and at the heart of contemporary utopian interspirituality discussions.[15]

One or Two?—We Get One Answer

The examples above might seem arbitrary or idiosyncratic, but they actually lead us to the very center of present fascination with spirituality and the meaning of existence. Human beings have forever asked questions about this. The most essential one is: Why is there something rather than nothing? The question itself is a conundrum, for how can there be nothing if there is someone asking about it? So the second question must be: What is the nature of that something?

It might seem reductionist to insist that there are only two possible answers to these ultimate questions. However, 20th-century theologian Colin Gunton, considered one of the most important British theologians of his generation, stated:

> There are, probably, ultimately only two possible answers to the question of origins, and they recur at different places in all ages: [either] that the universe is the result of creation by a free personal agency, or that in some way or other it creates itself. The two answers are

not finally compatible, and require a choice, either between them or an attitude of agnostic refusal to decide.[16]

The nature of reality can be examined another way, by asking what controls reality. We do not control much, if anything, in our lives: Our time
and place of birth, our parents, our health, and our lifespan are out of
our control. In this vulnerable position, we have the same two choices:
to believe in impersonal fate or in personal providence.

In either case, here we reach rock bottom. Either the transcendent
Creator—one God in the unending interpersonal life and love of the
Trinity—is at the origin of everything created and sustains it all, or the
universe itself, in all its seeming variety, is all there is. And in either
case, whether we worship nature or the Maker of nature, we are dealing
with a statement of faith and an expression of worship. We cannot step
out of the universe to find an objective point of view. We must make a
faith decision between these two alternatives—and there are only two.
If God and nature make up reality, then all is two, and everything is either Creator or creature. On the other hand, if the universe is all there
is, then all is one.

This choice is exemplified in the stark separation between two
points of perspective: that of the Bible, and that of Camille Paglia, a contemporary philosopher. The Bible begins by saying: "In the beginning,
God created the heavens and the earth [i.e., nature]" (Gen 1:1). Paglia
begins her book *Sexual Personae* very differently: "In the beginning was
Nature."[17] These two views of reality have always existed, but because
we have lived for centuries in a Christian environment, the reemerging
conflict startles us. Paglia wrote what she did in conscious opposition to
the perspective on the world put forth in Genesis.

Christian thinking starts not with Paglia's view of existence but with
that of the Bible. Robert Sokolowski, a professor of philosophy at the
Catholic University of America, puts it this way:

> Christian theology is differentiated from pagan reli-
> gious and philosophical reflections primarily by the in-
> troduction of a new distinction, the distinction between
> the world, understood as possibly not having existed,

and God, understood as possibly being all that there is,
with no diminution of goodness or greatness.[18]

Such a distinction describes two completely different types of beings who can never be confused or blended—reconciled, yes, but never blended. One is totally independent, sufficient, and blessed, and would be so even if the universe had never existed. The other is totally dependent: living, moving, and having its being in the free goodness and love of another.[19]

Creator and Creature: The Bible's First and Last Word

This biblical, Christian method of thinking makes deep sense of reality. It was the essence of the faith of Israel in the Old Testament. According to the Bible, God's existence and identity is the proper frame for our own. Only from this starting point can we find true knowledge of God, creation, and ourselves. The Bible begins and ends with this assumption.

In the Beginning

Genesis 1:1 begins with the majestic declaration of difference, delivered into a world mythology that affirmed only sameness. This declaration affirms the radical uniqueness and primacy of the Creator. It establishes the indissoluble distinction between the Creator and what he has freely made out of generosity and love. After this statement, the rest of the Bible is, in some sense, commentary.

Biblical thought always begins with the affirmation of God's uniqueness, freedom, goodness, and love. In Isaiah 40, God is described as "the Creator of the ends of the earth" (Isa 40:28). Psalm 33 restates the opening of Genesis: "By the word of the Lord the heavens were made ... For he spoke, and it came to be; he commanded, and it stood firm" (Psa 33:6, 9). Psalm 104 makes similar statements from the viewpoint of a human praising the Creator, God. God's great answer to Job (Job 38–39) is not a philosophical discourse but a speech that overwhelms us with its unambiguous statement of God's lordship over all creation. Nehemiah says of God's creative power, "You alone are the Lord. You made the heavens, even the highest heavens, and all their starry host, the earth and all that is on it, the seas and all that is in them. You give life to everything, and the multitudes of heaven worship you" (Neh 9:6 NIV).

The Uniqueness of Twoness

Colin Gunton noted that this view of creation and providence was unique in the ancient world:

> Far from being one ancient myth among many, [the Genesis account] was unique in saying things that no other ancient text was able to say. ... The Bible is different, and, it might be suggested, the conveyor of a unique message, and so could not be dismissed as simply another instance of ancient myth.[20]

Before the Sixties (when it became popular to dismiss the Old Testament faith as one instance of Near Eastern religious mythology among many), even many critical scholars affirmed the uniqueness of the biblical account. For example, Claus Westermann contrasted the Genesis account with Babylonian creation myths in the following way:

> What distinguishes the [Genesis] account of creation among the many creation stories of the Ancient Near East is that for Genesis there can be only one creator and that all else that is or can be, can never be anything but a creature.[21]

G. Ernest Wright, a 20th-century Old Testament professor at Harvard —following the example of his mentor, archaeologist William Albright— taught that the difference between the Old Testament and the other religions of the ancient world was so significant that no evolutionary or developmental account of Israel's religion could make sense of it.[22] Gunton, Westermann, Wright, and Albright all highlight the difference in kind between ancient Near Eastern cosmologies and the unique message Genesis carried into the ancient world. As John Oswalt, a modern Old Testament scholar, has concluded, "[T]here are only two worldviews: the biblical one ... and the other one."[23]

Knowledge of God in Twoness

The Apostle Paul would agree. The one true God's "eternal power and divine nature can be seen in what he has made" (Rom 1:20), and what he has made expresses his transcendence and distinctiveness. All human beings get a glimpse of these characteristics of our Creator in his creation (Rom 1:20). But Paul says that "they exchanged the truth about God for [the] lie and worshiped and served the creature rather than the Creator" (Rom 1:25).[24] I read that verse many times before I realized that Paul was declaring the existence of only two ways to live and think— only two ways to believe. Human beings, he says, worship and serve either "the creature" or "the Creator." Such a simple yet profound contrast, Paul!

"Creator" and "creation" underlies all human knowledge of God and ourselves; this theme runs throughout the New Testament. Hebrews 11 explains: "By faith we understand that the universe was formed at God's command, so that what is seen was not made out of what was visible" (Heb 11:3 NIV). Paul summarizes who the true God is, the God in whom we believe, in Romans 4, saying, "[God] gives life to the dead and calls into existence the things that do not exist" (Rom 4:17). Colossians 1 sheds more light on this revealed mystery when it ties creation and its significance directly to Christ, who is also the source of our re-creation: "For in him all things were created: things in heaven and on earth, things visible and invisible, whether thrones or powers or rulers or authorities; all things have been created through him and for him" (Col 1:16 NIV).

In the End

The Bible ends with the same declaration: God is Creator. Revelation 4 quotes the citizens of heaven, with whom we will be praising God as our Maker and Lord for all eternity, saying: "You are worthy, our Lord and God, to receive glory and honor and power, for you created all things, and by your will they were created and have their being" (Rev 4:11 NIV). Clearly, our identity will always be creaturely, though glorified, and God will always be the one Creator to whom all glory belongs and from whom our glory comes. This is the Bible's first and last word.

Our Worldview Alternatives: Oneism and Twoism

I claim, with the Bible, that there are only two worldviews—one based on the ultimacy of the creation, and the other based on the ultimate, prior, and all-determining existence of the Creator. Creation and Creator are the only alternatives as divine objects of worship—the only possible explanations of the world we know. The conflict is between two mutually exclusive, antithetical belief systems. Our choice will affect the answers we give to those two important questions: Is there something rather than nothing? And if there is something, what is that something like?

For the sake of simplicity, I call these two alternatives Oneism and Twoism.[25] They are not mere variations on a general spiritual theme, but the only two timeless, mutually contradictory ways to think about the world.[26] In these two terms (Oneism and Twoism), there is a universe of difference. These are the only two destinations on the tracks we can travel; let's map them out in more detail now.

Oneism

Oneism sees the world as self-creating (or perpetually existing) and self-explanatory. Everything is made up of the same stuff, whether matter, spirit, or a mixture. There's one kind of existence, which, in one way or another, we worship as divine (or of ultimate importance), even if that means worshiping ourselves. Though there is apparent differentiation and even hierarchy, all distinctions are, in principle, eliminated, and everything has the same worth. This is a "homocosmology," a worldview based on sameness. The classic term for this is "paganism," worship of nature.

Twoism

The only other option is a world that is the free work of a personal, transcendent God, who creates *ex nihilo* (from nothing). In creating, God was not constrained by or dependent on any preexisting conditions. There is nothing exactly like this in our human experience of creating; our creative acts are analogous to God's. There is God, and there is everything that is not-God—everything created and sustained by the Father, the Son, and the Holy Spirit. This worldview celebrates otherness, distinctiveness. We only worship as divine the distinct, personal, triune Creator, who placed essential distinctions within the creation. This is a "heterocosmology," a worldview based on otherness and difference.[27] This is often called "theism."

Both of these worldviews, whether implicitly assumed or explicitly embraced, require the same fundamental certainty. In other words, if one is ultimately true, the other must be false. In the moral universe of the Bible, knowledge is never neutral. That's why Paul calls these worldviews "the truth" and "the lie" (Rom 1:25).

What's Ahead: Getting Off the Oneist Train

In the pages that follow, I show the ways that intellectual and cultural influences today are promoting a Oneist view of reality—a train headed in the opposite direction from the biblical view. I want to alert the church to the danger of adopting subtle expressions of this new spirituality out of a failure to see its underlying nature and motives.

The rapid success of Oneist thinking in the 20th-century West forces us to ask if our culture has been "given over" (to use Paul's words in Romans 1:24, 26, 28) to a traditionally pagan cosmology. If so, is there a way for our culture to step off this train and get back to the Twoist platform? What power could possibly stop the Oneist train from hurtling to destruction? There may be no return, unless it is through spiritual revival and miraculous conversion—not to a nostalgic Fifties lifestyle or to an old-time, fundamentalist, made-in-America religion, but to the heart of the Bible's Twoist worldview. Twoism is as old as history, based on the biblical witness to the person and historic achievement of Christ, who was himself "given over" for our sins and raised for our justification.[28]

I want to take you on an Underground tour, not of London, but of the deep explosive forces below the surface of our religious turmoil. The power and success of these forces is sometimes discouraging. However, by faith in the Creator, God, who has redeemed his people and revealed his purposes concerning his creation, I am confident that we will not get lost. By God's grace, we will find the map that leads genuine seekers back to the right station. Welcome aboard.

PART 1

COMING APART

In chapters 2–6 we will examine early 20th-century utopian visions of humanity based on the fundamental notion of liberation. Certain cultural leaders sought liberation from the old shackles of Western Christian values, such as monogamous sexuality and a narrow theistic spirituality based on biblically revealed religion.

Chapter 2 will deal with the great enemy of Christianity in the modern period (from the 18th to the 20th century), namely secular humanism or materialistic Oneism, and its belief that reason would save humanity—a belief that eventually led to its own decline.

Chapters 3 and 4 will look at the way that decline was enabled by the promotion of spiritual Oneism (that is, pagan mythology). We will specifically see such thinking in the optimism of Swiss psychologist Carl Jung, who envisioned the arrival of a new humanity. As Jean Houston, counselor to Hillary Clinton, would later say: "Only myth will save us."

Chapter 5 will consider how Jung's notions of sexual and spiritual liberation for healthy psyches broke out on the cultural surface during the Sixties' cultural revolution and its popular mantra, "Make love, not war." The cultural revolution was also a sexual and spiritual revolution. The optimistic hope of human progress through freedom from the past animated the Sixties' revolutionaries, who hoped to bring in a new day of human well-being, the Age of Aquarius.

Chapter 6 shows that many high hopes for a new day were dashed when free sex and cohabitation severely undermined the family structure and the moral virtues it presupposed. We will examine how Oneist thinking (deliberately) undermined the old culture by destructing "the binaries." From great optimism has come great pessimism; the liberated culture has "come apart."

CHAPTER 2

THE RISE AND FALL OF SECULAR HUMANISM

Two challenges to Western Christianity are currently contributing to the religious turmoil described in chapter 1. The first, secular humanism, is the subject of this chapter.

The Dominance of Secular Humanism—A Nonreligious Oneism

The imminent threat to Christianity in the middle of the 20th century was not perceived as an invasion of other religious systems but as the subjugation of the "Christian" West to nonreligious materialism: secular humanism, which aimed to annihilate religion altogether.

The Roots of Secular Humanism

What we call secular humanism began as plain humanism. In the 15th century, Renaissance humanism saw itself as rebirthing humanity on the ancient pagan Greek model of rational thought, well summarized in a fifth-century-BC classic statement by Protagoras: "Man is the measure of all things." The Reformation inadvertently handed humanism a key tool for its anti-tradition arsenal. The right of the individual Christian to weigh the beliefs and practices of the Roman Catholic Church against the ultimate authority of the Word of God (a good thing in itself) became for some humanists a means of replacing the Word of God with autonomous human reason.

During the 17th century, thinkers like Hobbes, Descartes, and Locke began the process of making this secularized humanistic thinking mainstream, claiming intellectual autonomy for the human mind apart from religious tradition or divine revelation. Though a deeply religious man, 17th-century French mathematician René Descartes sought to prove existence based on human reasoning alone with his famous statement, "*Cogito ergo sum*"—"I think, therefore I am." It is often claimed that Descartes laid the foundation for 17th- and 18th-century continental rationalism.[1]

Humanism's respect for intelligence and rationality gave rise in Western culture to creative, independent thought that produced countless scientific and technological advances. Such progress laid the foundation for exploits as astounding as landing a man on the moon. However, independent human thought gradually came to be seen as the only norm for *all* truth—the ultimate source of all meaning, a rationalistic Oneism. People began to conclude that belief in a world created by God and in things spiritual was merely superstitious, primitive myth to be abandoned as unthinking delusion. For the modern man, religion had to go.

Thus, roughly between the 18th and the 20th centuries, the Enlightenment, or Age of Reason, dominated the Western mind as the great opponent of Christianity. Only the ability of the human being, based no longer on faith in God but on faith in reason itself as the criteria of truth, would save us. A powerful optimism in the capacities of mankind to bring about a better world took the West by storm. Reason would replace primitive religious superstition and bring about the coming, glorious kingdom of man on earth.

This optimistic human vision as a religion of humanity is appropriately associated with the French Revolution. In 1789, the Paris revolutionaries built an altar to the goddess Reason right in the middle of Notre Dame Cathedral in Paris, the very center of European Catholic Christianity.

Intellectual Leaders of Secular Humanism

Revolutionary 18th-century philosopher Voltaire delivered a bone-chilling statement about Christianity: *"Ecrasez l'infâme,"* literally, "Crush the horrid thing." The horrid thing Voltaire had in mind was Christianity—its superstition, dogma, institutions, ethics, and view of man. Voltaire's theme became the battle cry of the 18th-century Enlightenment, a cry directed against Christianity itself.

Atheist humanism took over the intellectual elite of Europe. Emperor Napoleon Bonaparte I asked Pierre-Simon Laplace, a great French scientist who helped develop mathematical astronomy and statistics, about the place of God in his work. Laplace reportedly replied, "I have no need of that hypothesis."[2]

Many serious social observers and philosophers in the 19th century predicted the final victory of secularism and the disappearance of religion altogether:

- Ludwig Feuerbach, a 19th-century philosopher, called Christianity a delusion and God "a gigantic human projection,"[3] essentially "man writ large."[4]

- Charles Darwin further drove faith in God as Creator from the scientific track with another variation of secular humanism. He posited the theory that all creatures were produced from a common ancestor by an unguided, impersonal process of natural selection worked out through randomly occurring variations. Most of his later followers have held that life on earth came about by mere chance, and man is "the result of a purposeless and natural process that did not have him in mind."[5] Darwin thereby effectively made God superfluous and the creation (including humanity) a purely physical, self-generating, but mindless mechanism.

- Karl Marx dismissed religion as the "opiate of the masses." Marx saw religious belief as a sign of a wrongly ordered society. He believed that once society had been rationally organized the need for faith would disappear.[6] "Man," said Marx, "is the supreme divinity."[7]

- Friedrich Nietzsche, a 19th-century German thinker, considered life to be a strictly this-worldly phenomenon, rejecting the notion of a world beyond. He took opposition to divine truth to its logical extreme, going so far as to declare, "God is dead."[8] This theme would reappear in Western thinking in the Sixties, espoused by a number of leading theologians.

At the end of the 19th century, popular atheism started to influence the new science of psychology. Sigmund Freud, in *The Future of an Illusion*, referred to himself as a "godless Jew" and is reputed to have said, "The more the fruits of knowledge become accessible to men, the more widespread is the decline of religious belief."[9] As a psychologist, he went on to argue that religion (including Judaism) is a "mass delusion" or "collective neurosis" which formally enshrines our "infantile" longing for an all-powerful protective (but also threatening) father figure. He thus considered religion a serious pathological condition, the great obstacle to mental health, from which the future world would doubtless be healed. This emphasis has not disappeared. Richard Dawkins, one of the New Atheists, defined faith as "a kind of mental illness" in 1976, an argument he still uses.[10]

Among many sophisticated intellectuals of the 20th century, it became axiomatic that religion would eventually give way to the evident "truth" of secular humanism. One example is British writer Evelyn Waugh. Raised within the upper-class British educational system, Waugh attended a preparatory school for boys that was based on "sound principle and sound knowledge, firmly grounded in the Christian faith." At the age of 17, he recorded the following in his journal: "In the last few weeks I have ceased to be a Christian. I have realized that for the last two terms [of the school year] at least I have been an atheist in all except the courage to admit it myself."[11] Waugh recalled that his tutors assigned books that were generally subversive of faith, and "[W]e were left to suggest our solutions and encouraged to be unorthodox." He remembered that half his class "were avowed agnostics or atheists."[12] This occurred in a school system that was ostensibly Christian.

Waugh's testimony is representative of a period of about two centuries during which the secular humanist program was an immense success. Even the church was invaded in full force and began seeking to reinterpret the Christian message in anti-supernatural terms. In the 19th century, secularism in Christian dress, known as theological liberalism, became a powerful factor in the Christian movement, in particular influencing scores of seminaries, divinity schools, and other institutions for the education of the ministry to make as their goal the revising of the Christian faith to reflect the secular humanist spirit of the modern age.

Liberalism was motivated by the desire to redefine Christianity according to the sensibilities of modern people. It reinterpreted the gospel as social justice and saw Jesus only as an example, not as a divine-human Savior. The New Testament message was often described as an ancient version of Marxist theory, in which Jesus was a revolutionary like Che Guevara but in ancient Palestine, seeking radical change in the social and economic power structures of his time.

In the late 1960s, when I studied New Testament at Harvard, demythologization was a popular topic. It sought to transform the old Christian faith into 20th-century psychology. Traditional beliefs and key biblical events were emptied of their historicity. Skeptical scholars wrote books denying the miracles in the Gospels, including Jesus' physical resurrection, thus tearing the heart from the Christian gospel and eliminating the faith of many in the mainline churches.

With the appearance of the "death of God" movement in the Sixties, the disappearance of traditional Christianity seemed strangely confirmed, even in "Christian" America. American theologians like Thomas J. J. Altizer, Gabriel Vahanian, Paul Van Buren, David Miller, and William Hamilton celebrated in the new world the final triumph of Nietzschean deicide. Rational man had come of age, no longer needing "the God hypothesis." As my fellow theological students and I studied this radical "Christian" theology in the late 1960s, we saw it as the final triumph of liberal, secular humanism.

Predictions of the disappearance of Christianity have seemed to be confirmed by its demise as the dominant social force in Western society.[13] This is new; there was a time in recent Western history, in spite of the dominance of secular humanism among the intellectual elite, when hardly anyone openly put the existence of God into doubt. For instance, in 1890, the Supreme Court of the United States defined religion as "one's views of one's relation to his Creator, to the obligations they impose of reverence for his being and character and obedience to his will."[14] There was no other definition of God but that of a personal transcendent Creator! Thanks in large part to secular humanism, this is no longer the case in public discourse.

The New Secular Humanism

So, what is secularism or secular humanism, and what has it become? It is now known under other names. As an intellectual discipline it is called philosophical materialism; as a social movement it is known as modernity; as a somewhat religious expression it is described as atheism; as a political theory it is practiced as Marxism; and for many people, it is an un-thought-out, default way of living as if God did not exist. All these expressions of secularism reject the supernatural as a holdover from superstitious, primitive faith systems. Without any reference to God, secularism attempts to describe rationally the whole of existence from a this-worldly materialistic perspective with the human being at the center of existence. Thus, all these expressions of secular humanism can be called Oneist (though not of the "spiritual" kind) because they seek to describe the world by the world, using this-worldly human reason, with no reference to an external, transcendent Creator. Making reason ultimate is a form of worship.

This secular humanist view still often influences Western universities. Some readers will recognize a description of professors who exhibit in their classrooms a ferocious antagonism to spirituality. Secularism has affected all areas of Western society, claiming for itself exclusive access to reality. The scientific mind, committed to naturalism, is the only way of knowing anything. But this is not the whole story. Something strange happened on the way to the 21st century. Despite the secularists'

confident prediction of the "withering of religion," it is secular humanism that has recently been withering.

The Death of Secular Humanism?

Against all expectations, modern science itself has contributed to the
demise of all-knowing secular humanism. The Enlightenment belief
in a human rationality capable of plumbing the deepest secrets of the
natural world has been undermined by discoveries like quantum physics and Heisenberg's uncertainty principle, which states that observing
subatomic particles prevents the ability to know the true nature of their
physical reality. Richard Feynman, a Nobel Prize-winning physicist, believed that no one *really* understands quantum physics, with its notions
of indeterminacy and nonlocality.[15]

Perhaps an even stronger argument against secularism, however, is
its catastrophic fruits. Its optimistic belief in humanity and profound
self-confidence fostered two world wars that claimed untold millions.
Its emphasis on social justice supported totalitarian fascism, eventually ending in massacres by the likes of Stalin, Hitler, and Pol Pot. Its
overemphasis on human supremacy and progress ultimately produced
hyperindustrialization and a series of ecological disasters. Its focus on
individual self-realization promoted soulless consumerism that ignored
an absolutely essential aspect of human existence: spirituality.

Postmodern Critique

"Rationalism, the Enlightenment's path to earthly salvation, has reached
a dead-end," said Christian philosopher Vishal Mangalwadi. "Therefore
many sensitive people are hoping that nonrational mysticism might
enlighten us."[16] The culture is at the end of the line with no spiritual re-
sources to face the deep problems of life. Secular humanism has proven
inadequate to provide for all of life's dimensions, many of which are not
merely rational.

In our day that intellectual challenge has been particularly difficult
for the rationalists. Recent philosophy has called philosophy itself into
question. The movement or mood generally known as postmodernism
has deconstructed the secular religion of reason and progress. Many of

the children of the secular humanists have chewed up the legacy of their intellectual parents and spat it out. Human reason, once considered our contact with the objective meaning of the universe, is now rejected as a futile exercise in subjectivity. This critique of reason argues that we cannot escape our limited, human situation as temporal, thinking bodily beings. We are miniscule elements in a seemingly infinite cosmos, unable to stand outside it to make true statements about its essential nature. Postmodernists are not rejecting thought as such. They only reject rational thinking and objective observation as the only sure means of grasping the meaning of reality.

The Wizard of Is

Postmodern thinkers argue that so-called rational truth, like all truth, is "socially generated." Truth is a subjective opinion with no infallible relationship to the way things actually are. As Bill Clinton memorably said, "It depends on what the meaning of the word 'is' is."[17] As a philosophy, postmodernism deconstructs the validity of the claim of rational discourse to be an objective account of the true nature of things. Truth, taken in this sense, is merely personal power that one person or social group attempts to impose on others or to employ for selfish ends. A rational explanation has become impossible.

French postmodern philosopher Michel Foucault is a classic example of this trajectory in the recent history of philosophy. In the 1950s he was a paying member of the French Communist Party and a convinced secularist. He left it when his suspicion grew that Marxism was just one more ideology of power with no relationship to the way things actually are. Foucault argued that truth claims were merely power grabs; others' condemnation of his homosexuality was only the straight majority view, powerfully and arbitrarily imposed on a victimized homosexual minority for purposes of social control.

In 1959, Foucault received his doctoral degree on the basis of a thesis published two years later as *Madness and Unreason: History of Madness in the Classical Age*.[18] Foucault accused Descartes (who coined "I think, therefore I am") of being able to doubt everything except his own sanity. In other words, Descartes held on to his reason as his chosen anchor to reality only by denying a very real possibility, namely his own insanity. Descartes was not as objective as he thought himself to be after all.

Though secularism is still influential, the postmodern way of thinking is firmly entrenched in our culture, and its critique of modernist hubris makes sense. Since postmodernism is not a passing fad, the demise of secularism, which it so mercilessly criticizes, is highly likely. One postmodern writer speaks, for example, of "the embarrassing intolerance of atheism."[19] Atheistic secularism's complete dismissal of the value of religion is embarrassing to postmodern intellectuals who have become convinced of the subjective character of all worldviews. For them, tolerance has become one of the great values to be respected, even the tolerance of religion and spirituality.

Beyond the postmodern critique, two other factors have seriously dented humanist self-confidence. First, in spite of the popularity of New Atheism,[20] atheism is under intellectual pressure from various expressions of theism. Antony Flew, one of the most renowned of the 20th-century atheists, became a theist toward the end of his life; he believed in some sort of personal creator god, though not necessarily the one who reveals himself in the Bible. He was unable to account for the mystery of the personal, thinking, planning, self-critical, and self-conscious human being, who cannot be explained purely from physics or chemistry. He stated, "It is simply inconceivable that any material matrix or field can generate agents who think and act. Matter cannot produce conceptions and perceptions ... such a world ... has to originate in a living Source, a Mind."[21] In spite of Flew's hesitations, the only true candidate for this role is the personal, Trinitarian, transcendent God revealed in Scripture.

Second, atheism is under spiritual pressure, since many, recognizing that the material world is insufficient in and of itself, are simply hungry for spirituality—whether as an explanation for the way things are or as an answer to the longings of the human soul. That includes those who say they are "spiritual but not religious," who are turning away in droves from the religion of secular humanism and its profound sense of futility and alienation between humanity and the rest of the universe. People understandably long for wholeness. As one spiritually hungry atheist, Sam Harris, grants, "There is more to understanding the human condition than science and secular culture generally admit."[22]

A new way of thinking that began to incubate in the first part of the 20th century sought to find in the "primitive superstition," long rejected by secularists, the very answer to the deepest needs of modern man. Rationalism is, therefore, not only criticized for its inability to give a satisfactory justification of its own significance. It is also criticized for making man—via reason and observation—the norm of everything and thereby eliminating any spiritual or religious dimension to life that reason and experimentation can't master.[23]

The Rebirth of Religious Oneism

The Death of Postmodernism, Too?

We are not simply witnessing the waning of secular humanism. As Richard Tarnas, a progressive spiritualist, notes, the end of secular humanism is also the end of postmodernism. As a reasonable critique of rationality, postmodernism is, in some ways, the "last gasp of enlightenment philosophy [which] presupposes a metanarrative of its own, one perhaps more subtle than others, but in the end no less subject to deconstructive criticism."[24] Postmodernism is circular because it must presuppose its own rational thinking in order to criticize the rationalism of secular humanism. The gaping irrational hole produced by deconstructive postmodernism cries out to be filled by a new paradigm, a new, unifying, nonrational principle, a metanarrative, a *grand récit*—a mythical world that can bring mind and spirit together.

There is a future for the postmodern mindset, since it is adaptable to the great spiritual changes in contemporary society. Its focus on the personal and on individual and communal experience fits perfectly with the rise of this new sense of mystical spirituality. From this perspective, one group of scholars, the Bible and Culture Collective, describes a bright future in postmodernism: "[Postmodern] deconstruction appears atheistic and anarchistic to many. Others have noted a *mystical* tendency in postmodern deconstruction, and have argued that deconstruction is amenable to mysticism and negative theology[25] in Jewish-Christian thought."[26] David Tacey, a Roman Catholic theologian, sees a particularly happy fit between Buddhism, the mysticism of Meister Eckhart, and the postmodern consciousness.[27] Postmodernism contributes, to the future of human development, its emphasis on pluralism, complexity, and ambiguity, but Tarnas notes that these emphases "are precisely the characteristics necessary for the potential emergence of a fundamentally new form of intellectual vision."[28] He intimates that human development needs help from other sources.

The Death of God

David Miller provided a hint of this move from secular humanism—weakened at its core by postmodernism—to a renewed fascination with spiritual Oneism. Miller occupied a key leadership position on the publications committee of the Society of Biblical Literature but was also associated with the "death of God" theologians of the Sixties. As mentioned above, when my Christian professors, fellow students, and I studied the "death of God" theology, we were convinced that it marked the triumph of secular humanism. This was seemingly affirmed by one of this theology's proponents, T. J. J. Altizer, who taught that God had so completely incarnated himself in the world that by the act of dying on the cross he liberated man from any alien, transcendent divine power.[29] This inventive reading of Christian theology was surely the final triumph of atheistic humanism!

But—not so fast. David Miller described the death of God not as the victory of secular, atheistic humanism but as the return of spiritual paganism; not as the death of any notion of divinity but as the death of the specific transcendent God of biblical Twoism. His book *The New Polytheism* predicted with surprising assurance: "[A]t the death of God we will see the rebirth of the gods and goddesses of ancient Greece and Rome."[30]

What did Miller know that few others realized at the time? Long after my student days, I discovered that Miller was a lifelong follower of Carl Jung and had taught Jungian psychology in clinical programs worldwide, including the Jung Institute in Switzerland and at Pacifica Graduate Institute in California. (The importance of Miller's fascination with Jung will be clearer in the next chapter, where I will trace the significance of

Jung in shaping modern culture.) Miller understood that the death of God was the death of the Twoist God of the Bible, a demise that would not herald the victory of secularism but a celebration of the liberating rebirth in the West of the Oneist pagan gods from faraway places and ancient times. Miller's celebration of the death of the biblical God in the 1960s thus signals a number of seminal events for our own time:

1. The *coup de grace* of Western Christendom as a significant so-cial and cultural force—we are now on the defensive, not for our truth claims but as a force for good within the culture[31]

2. The demise of secular humanism—most unexpected and still not widely noticed

3. The rebirth of the old pagan belief in the divinity of nature and humanity

Following secular humanism, the rebirth of ancient paganism is the second great challenge to historical Christianity in our time. We are just beginning to see its power. In order to understand the changing direction of our society, all Christians (especially millennial Christians, for whom secular humanism has begun to fade in influence) need to meet Swiss psychologist, Carl Gustav Jung, the creator of transpersonal psychology.

CHAPTER 3

CARL JUNG'S DREAM FOR A "NEW HUMANITY"

Cultures, ours included, do not emerge from nowhere, nor do they remain static. The West has been transformed through the influence and determined efforts of Carl Jung and leaders like him. Whereas many people passively ride the rails of history, Jung laid his own tracks. But who in the world was Carl Jung? He is not a household name like JFK or John Lennon.

Who Was Carl Jung?

We all know the *Star Wars* series and are accustomed to thinking of a dark side, a light side, and the need to balance them. Along with that basic idea, Jung also developed the concept of the inner self, which many now evoke to describe their deepest feelings. It was Jung who coined the terms "extrovert" and "introvert." The Myers-Briggs personality type indicator, the most popular of all personality tests, was developed from his theories. If you have sat opposite a counselor rather than lying on a couch, you have Jung to thank. He has influenced twelve-step programs, video games, novels, movies, and educational materials.

Jung is often considered the father of the New Age movement, which has deeply and directly affected the contemporary world. Jungian psychology opened popular culture to Indian spirituality. Jung was deeply moved by Indian guru Vivekananda and his teaching on the divine self. When he traveled to India, Jung was impressed that Indian thinkers could join good and evil without any pangs of conscience. So while his name is not commonly known, Jung influenced philosophy, archaeology, anthropology, literature, and, most of all, popular psychology and spirituality—all by psychologizing religion. His theories on this subject have profoundly affected the soul of Western Christianity as well.

During the early 20th century, general optimism surrounded the new science of analytical psychology developed by Sigmund Freud and his young associate, Carl Jung. Here was a new discipline based on objective scientific analysis that would rationally explain and solve the problems of human behavior, making the world a better place. Jung and his colleagues spoke of a new day in human affairs when individual behavioral dysfunctions would be healed by psychology and wisdom culled from all the world's cultures, drawing mankind together in a new era of human flourishing.

Indeed, Jung saw himself as the architect of a "new humanism"[1] and the creator of "a new ordering of human affairs."[2] He developed not only a widely accepted therapy for tortured minds but also a religious blueprint for the future of humanity. In the 1950s, Jung claimed, "We are only at the threshold of a new spiritual epoch."[3] He believed that he was developing "the world's final, unitary religion."[4] This heady futurist vision to bring all people and all religions together provided Jung and his disciples with clear and driving goals. The goal was staggering. Some 70 years ago, Jung predicted a new global Christianity adaptable to all other religions:

> I imagine a far finer and more comprehensive task for
> [psychoanalysis] ... I think we must give it time to infil-
> trate into people from many centers, to revivify among

intellectuals a feeling for symbol and myth, ever so gen-
tly to transform Christ back into the soothsaying god of
the vine, which he was, and in this way absorb those ecstatic instinctual forces of Christianity for the one purpose of making the cult and the sacred myth what they
once were—a drunken feast of joy where man regained
the ethos and holiness of an animal. That was the beauty
and purpose of classical religion.[5]

In spite of Jung's positive take on the future, all was not rosy in the
emerging field of psychology. Jung and Freud parted ways in the first
quarter of the 20th century.[6] While Jung proposed a version of psychological healing based on spirituality, Freud dismissed religion as an
illusion, an illness needing healing. This split was an early sign of the
eventual victory spirituality would win over humanistic materialism.
The future belonged to Jung.[7]

However, few people, whether secular or Christian, understood the
true nature of Jungian thinking. Jung's plan to restore "classical religion"
and "transform Christ back into a soothsaying god of the vine" indicates
that there was more to Jung than scientific theories about psychological
personality types.

Will the Real Carl Jung Please Stand Up?

A Secret Persona

Jung's success was partly due to the mysterious persona he projected
to the general public. His vision for the future of mankind involved
deconstruction of biblical Christianity and the promotion of pagan
spirituality, but he knew that his invitation to mysticism could never
be accepted in a mixed culture of secular humanism and Christian
theism, both opposed—for different reasons—to nature worship. This
"priest"[8] therefore adopted scientific jargon.[9] Such intellectual subterfuge was exposed in an explosive biography of Jung by Richard Noll,
a psychologist and history of science professor at Harvard. By careful research of Jung's published materials, Noll developed the thesis
that Jung deliberately obfuscated his meaning to the public while

developing his true theories in his private circle of fellow researchers and practitioners.

Noll's books *The Jung Cult: Origins of a Charismatic Movement*[10] and *The Aryan Christ: The Secret Life of Carl Jung* were not popular among committed Jungians, many of whom had based their own careers on the teachings of their master. Jung's followers were offended at Noll's boldness in stating, for example:

> This 20th century mask [of scientific research] was constructed deliberately, and somewhat deceptively, by Jung to make his own magical, polytheist, pagan worldview more palatable to a secularized world conditioned to respect only those ideas that seem to have a scientific air to them.[11]

In public lectures and writings, according to Noll, Jung was careful always to speak and write "in code."[12]

Though vilified in academic psychology, Noll was ultimately vindicated by Jung himself. Almost fifty years after Jung's death, the Philemon Foundation published the *Red Book*, a folio-sized, 371-page, bright red volume that contained Jung's accounts of his own occult experiences at key times in his life. Noll had never seen the contents of this volume. In the *Red Book*, we discover Jung's true thoughts about the period after his split from Freud, when he suffered a number of years of depression and engaged in tortured self-analysis. During this time he had "psychotic fantasies" and experienced "numerous paranormal phenomena."[13] He became immersed in "the world of the dead" and wrote the book *Seven Sermons to the Dead* under the name of gnostic writer Basilides. In the *Red Book*, Jung gives details of what he calls "numinous" experiences, which included his relationship with a spirit-guide, Philemon, of whom he said, "Philemon represented a force which was not myself. ... It was he who taught me psychic objectivity."[14] The same spirit-guide, Philemon, addressed Jung as "Christ."[15]

Though rejected by most Jungians, Noll's thesis was confirmed not only by the *Red Book* but also by Jung's personal friends, such as Jungian academic June Singer, who observed that Jung had "two personalities: one, the rational and scientific; two, the one that made him really great, the transpersonal [i.e., paranormal] one."[16] She also claimed that Jung had "more than a little interest in the occult."[17] Jung himself stated: "This step beyond science is an unconditional requirement of ... psychological development ... because without this postulate I could give no adequate formulation of the psychic processes that occur empirically."[18] Jung further admits the importance of his psychic/numinous experiences with the spirit world during the years 1914 to 1930, when he "pursued ... with the help of alchemy ... the inner images ... that threatened to break me."[19] Everything he wrote after these experiences was, as he put it, the "outer classification" of them. At the end of his life, Jung became more open as to the true meaning of his theories, stating: "We can no longer practice any psychology that ignores the existence of ... parapsychology [paranormal phenomena]."[20]

For Jung, the future of psychology lay in the development of paranormal spiritualism. This becomes evident in the *Red Book* and in his own sense of "Christ consciousness," or what Noll calls "the Aryan Christ"—saving Christianity from the Creator, the God of the Old Testament.

Jung's Background

Knowledge of Jung's early background helps unveil the real man. Jung did not hail from a conservative Christian family. His paternal grandfather was Grand Master of the Swiss order of Freemasons, and his maternal grandfather was an occultist and spiritualist. His maternal grandmother was a seer who "fell into a three-day trance at age twenty, during which she communicated with spirits of the dead and gave prophecies."[21] Carl's mother was a medium who spent long periods "enthralled by the spirits that visited her at night."[22] For many years, Jung attended séances with his mother and two cousins.[23]

Carl's father was a Lutheran pastor. Though this meant that Jung was exposed to a form of Christian orthodoxy, his father's faith was pure formalism, so Jung turned away from it and openly rejected Christ in his youth. He said, "'Lord Jesus' never became quite real for me, never quite acceptable, never quite lovable ... 'Lord Jesus' seemed to me in some ways a god of death. ... Secretly, his love and kindness, which I always heard praised, appeared doubtful to me."[24] Knowing only a stiff, theologically liberal brand of Christianity, Jung was able to add various forms of liberal Christianity to his developing pagan spirituality.

Pagan Myths for Western Psychology

Jung's therapy depended on a belief in myth that was not always admired in the "Christian" West at the beginning of the 20th century. For example, during Charles Darwin's 1832 voyage to the Galapagos Islands, Darwin witnessed naked aboriginals dancing themselves into delirium and was shocked, finding the display "a most rude, barbarous scene."[25] Around 1900, W. H. Auden criticized W. B. Yeats's work on Hinduism as a "deplorable spectacle of a grown man occupied with the mumbo-jumbo of magic and the nonsense of India."[26]

However, values changed. Carl Jung was driven by the idea that pagan myth reflects the worldwide search to understand and heal the self by discovering that all the gods are found within us. His ideas influenced death-of-God theologian David Miller to predict in the early 1970s that "at the death of God we will see the rebirth of the gods and goddesses of Greece and Rome."[27] Jung was not just proposing a theory of psychological therapy, but a worldview by which all could reach higher levels of personal liberation.[28]

Jung stated, "The decisive question for man is: Is he related to something infinite or not?"[29] However, he answered that key question not with Christian truth but with a different source of ultimate meaning and psychological health. Transpersonal psychology was based on Jung's own experiences of the paranormal and on newly-rediscovered pagan traditions. His original doctoral dissertation was titled "On the Psychology and Pathology of So-Called Occult Phenomena,"[30] in which he associated these phenomena with psychological health, available to all.

Stop and reflect: The modern view of psychological health is based in large part on a paganism-inspired account of the way the world works.

Mythological Archetypes as a Frame of Meaning

Jung sought to liberate the Western psyche from its Christian presuppositions by refurnishing the mind with what he called archetypes—organizing principles of religion from time immemorial.

According to Jung's theory, the subconscious is the spiritual depths of the human being, where fantasies are interpreted as mystical experiences of the "real" spirit world. Jung believed our instincts are based on spiritual archetypes (explanatory myths) from all the world's religions and the spirit world that inspires them.

Jung had a vast knowledge of the world's religious traditions and mythologies and sought to employ their common, recurring spiritual themes in his understanding of therapy. He identified scores of archetypes, including the Übermensch (Nietzsche's superman), child, great mother goddess (either good or terrible), shadow (the essential place of evil), self (the ultimate unity of the personality), hermaphrodite (a male/female, symbolized by the circle), wise old man, *anima* in man, and *animus* in woman. He based others on the gamut of human instincts and fantasies or on universal notions such as the rebel, lover, creator or dreamer, jester, sage, and magician or shaman. These were to function as "the fundamental determining structures of human experience,"[31] the new philosophical "universals" to bring the world together in a satisfying synthesis.[32]

This list, though incomplete, appears broad and diverse. However, like global interfaith gatherings, which celebrate diversity but agree on one common view of the cosmos as divine, and like ancient worshipers of the goddess Isis, who confessed the deity as one yet also saw Isis as the goddess of "a thousand names,"[33] so Jung's archetypes actually express *only one way* of looking at ultimate reality. Significantly absent from this list are notions like the innate knowledge of God as Creator (Rom 1:10–21) or the law of God written on every human heart (Rom 2:15). The archetypes seem intended to steer people to the heart and source of pagan religion.

Joining the Opposites

That pagan heart was the ideal of joining opposites, the very key to Jung's method of healing the subconscious. The importance of this joining is present throughout Jung's work, expressed as *coincidentia oppositorum* (the union of opposites) or *mysterium coniunctionis* (the mystery of joining). Mircea Eliade claimed this notion has been an essential element in all world religions, especially Hinduism, in which abolishing the contraries and reuniting the parts is known as the "royal Way of the Spirit."[34] Jung integrated this notion into modern psychology.

The ultimate goal of individuation or maturation, as Eliade explained, is the removal of opposites.[35] For Jung, therefore, good and evil are only relative. The mature or individuated self is the self that has come to terms with, assumed, and finally silenced the various inner contradictions.[36] Male and female are nonexclusive options for whatever fits your fancy. This idea has fueled present-day ideas of omnigender sexuality. Such joining, it is claimed, brings healing from guilt, breaks the malevolent chains of biblical law and heterosexual monogamous marriage, and produces liberty for the unified individual. It eliminates the notion of God behind guilt.

The practical concern for human psychological liberation has theological implications. Or, to put it another way, one's definition of God determines everything else. For Jung, God joins the opposites too. Jung preferred the gnostic God, "Abraxas, half man, half beast, as a God higher than both the Christian God and Devil, that combines all opposites."[37] As W. B. Yeats claimed for his motto: *"Daemon est deus inversus"* (the devil is the other side of God).

Jung often used the ancient symbol of the *ouroboros*—the tail-eating snake—found in ancient paganism and Gnosticism. For him, it was an archetype of maturation and a dramatic symbol of the integration and assimilation of the shadow self, the dark side. The feedback process from the head to the tail is also a symbol of immortality, since the *ouroboros* sheds its skin in death, then brings itself to life again. The circle formed by the snake symbolizes a singular, ultimate unity with the cosmos, and the reconciliation of the opposites.[38] This scientific expert of human behavior therefore based his understanding of the world and human reality on pantheism.[39]

Such a way of thinking leads to radical conclusions. Maria Molzer, a colleague of Jung who analyzed members of some of America's wealthiest families (the Rockefellers and McCormicks), echoes Jung's idea of joining: "I too think that God and the Devil are two manifestations of the same principle, and that one necessitates the other ... We must learn to value the Devil again. The Christian religion expelled him. He asks for his rights again."[40] In the Jungian world, evil becomes your friend. Such rationalization is demonic.

As we noted above, the *Red Book* reveals Jung's deeply held beliefs. In it, he described his "frequent exercises in the emptying of consciousness" to "seek what was beneath the threshold of consciousness."[41] He sought to understand psychology by penetrating deep into "classical Chinese philosophy [and] the mystical speculations of India and Tantric Yoga."[42] He was deeply involved in the occult, and there met his spirit-guide, Philemon, whom he described as a "pagan" old man with the horns of a bull and the wings of a bird.[43] As Jung began to encounter many parapsychological events, Philemon introduced him to Abraxas, the devil-god of Gnosticism.[44]

Founding a New Religion

Jung and his followers were spiritual pantheists opposed both to the biblical tradition and to secularism. They anticipated a "postsecular age" and the end of secularism (which treated Jungian notions of spirituality as primitive, nonscientific superstition) and Christianity (which failed to integrate the dark side and to recognize the validity of the god within).[45] Jung charmed the secularists by claiming his work was scientific. He charmed the church by claiming his theories represented a new form of Christianity.

However, Jung was neither a scientist (in the strict sense of the term) nor a Christian. In 1922, he recorded in the *Red Book* the conversations he had with his soul, a resolution of his self-doubt. His soul told him: "The great work begins ... you must go to a higher level of consciousness ... to no longer be a Christian." He asked, "But what is my calling?," and his soul replied, "The new religion and its proclamation ... a new ordering of human affairs."[46] On the back cover of the *Red Book* is written in embossed gold type:

> The years, of which I have spoken to you, when I pursued the inner images, were the most important time of my life. Everything else is to be derived from this ... my entire life consisted in elaborating what had burst forth from the unconscious and flooded me like an enigmatic

stream and threatened to break me. That was the stuff
and material for more than only one life. Everything later
was merely the outer classification, the scientific elaboration, and the integration into life. But the numinous
beginning, which contained everything, was then.[47]

Jung saw these inner experiences of enlightenment as the source for all
his later opinions, including the reconciliation of opposites as a hope for
the future of mankind. For him, the united archetypes pointed to "the
sphere of the *unus mundus*, the unitary world ... the ultimate ground of
the universe,"[48] where the divine and the human meet and merge. His
vision was of a future society which would "transcend type and sex."[49]
According to Noll, Jung believed he "had been initiated into the most ancient of mysteries and had become a god. The gods had shown him the
mysteries of life and human history, visions of the future and of a New
Man. ... He could save the world. Having been blessed with the direct
knowledge of the divine, who better than he to be prophet of a new age?"[50]

Jung's Legacy

Why Such Success?

How did Jung's ideas infiltrate our culture? Jung proposed a technical, psychological model that described healthy human behavior as connection
with one's subconscious and with archetypes. Sexual and spiritual liberation were essential for the therapeutic health of the subconscious. His
approach was received as the latest scientific word on the human psyche,
and his psychospiritual healing methods appealed to scientific rigor. This
became the last word on health and spirituality for many 20th-century
Westerners. Understanding and applying his theories, his followers claim,
will help an individual to reach a stage of individuation or maturity
through a journey of transformation, eventually meeting one's true self
and also the divine. In spite of the complexities of Jung's system, with its
semi-scientific terminology, his emphasis on the subconscious had down-
to-earth ramifications that caught on and still persist.

Jung received enormous help from the church. Whereas Freud
was dismissed as an atheistic humanist, Jung was viewed as a man of

the spirit and hailed by some as the first Christian counselor.[51] Jeffrey Satinover, a psychiatrist and former president of the Jung Foundation of New York, noted "the truly astonishing number of clergy who have become Jungian analysts."[52] He added, "It is no exaggeration to say that the theological positions of most mainstream denominations in their approach to pastoral care, as well as in their doctrines and liturgy—have become more or less identical with Jung's psychological/symbolic theology."[53]

Wealthy families like the Rockefellers, the McCormicks, and the Mellons financially supported Jung's vision.[54] The women in these families were early clients of Jung's therapy, and their money introduced the English-speaking world to Jung, bringing him worldwide influence.

How many of those who accepted Jung's therapeutic, liberating methods would have repudiated his message had they known the source and true meaning of Jung's thinking? For many, the damage had been done. A Polish Roman Catholic scholar tells of a German priest, Eugene Drewmann, who began as a professor of dogmatic theology and through "a reduction of theology to psychology ended up with New Age and Buddhism. For him, Sigmund Freud and Carl Jung became more important than Jesus and Saint Paul."[55] The consequences of these decisions are now clear. "Only now," said Satinover in 1994, "at a time when Jungian and Jungian-related spirituality, with its emphasis on gnostic 'wisdom,' sexual freedom, Eastern mysticism, pantheism, goddess worship and accommodation with evil, has infiltrated deeply into the church, has the veil at long last begun to be lifted."[56]

The Dominance of the Subconcious

For centuries, the West was taught a generally biblical cosmology. However, as the power of Christianity waned in the West because of secular humanism, many found Jung to be a godsend. He provided both a spiritual and therapeutic mechanism for the individual's subconscious to be liberated from the ethical demands of holy living and the pain of guilt. With external moral and spiritual demands relativized and thus eliminated, the sense and even the very notion of sin could be dismissed as an irrational emotional disorder not welcomed in the sophisticated

20th century. Personal desire, even fantasy, became the route to science-based psychological wholeness and human maturity.

Jung perfectly expressed this vision for a new humanism in his justification of an extramarital affair with a young student. Writing to a friend, he said, "Nothing matters but the completion of the self."[57] Jung died in 1961, but his views lived on in a motto of the Sixties: "If it feels good, just do it." An original member of Jung's circle expressed Jung's vision as "free love will save the world"—which became a battle cry of the Sixties sexual revolution. In the 1940s, Harvard psychologist Henry Murray and his mistress, Christiana, as a tribute to Jung, made an engraving which read:

> We give homage to the Old Man for his great conception—Animus-Anima [male and female combined], which started us in righteous understanding along our path; [and] for his teaching that the erotic problem in our civilization had never been faced and that its solution was the highest quest for the spirit.[58]

Jung's therapy caught on. Today the subconscious trumps every other authority and provides truth that cannot be challenged. Our inner self has the last word. TV personality Dr. Phil, in a bestseller called *Self Matters*, argues that we must create our own life through the discovery of the inner self. Christopher Lasch, a keen observer of modern times, titled his own book on our culture *The Culture of Narcissism*.[59] Our culture is addicted to fantasy—just look at the success of the porn industry. The utopia we have been conditioned to envision is built on the pure fiction of our instincts. The term "fantasy" derives from "phantom," something existing solely in the imagination but often mistaken for reality. It is the lie. Jung exploded the foundations of the long-standing edifice of Western biblical Twoism, rebuilding them with a "new humanity" based on religious Oneism.

The Measure of the Man

How can we estimate the importance of such a seminal thinker as Carl Jung? When Richard Noll sought to find a figure in history whose influence would correspond to the importance of Jung, he chose the fourth-century emperor, Julian the Apostate, who was raised a Christian but chose to return to paganism:

> Jung ranks with the Roman emperor, Julian the Apostate, as one who significantly undermined orthodox Christianity and restored the polytheism of the Hellenistic world in Western civilization ... for a variety of historical and technological factors—modern mass media being the most important—Jung has succeeded where Julian failed ... the patriarchal monotheism of the orthodox Judeo-Christian faiths has all but collapsed, and filling the void, we find Protestants, Catholics and Jews adopting alternative, syncretistic belief systems that often belie a basis in Jungian "psychological" theories.[60]

The urgency of understanding our recent past in order to speak truth to our present time is reflected in *Lord of the World*, written in 1907 by a Roman Catholic monsignor, when Jung had just entered the prime of his career. The author, Robert Hugh Benson, described an elderly statesman explaining the spiritual situation of that time to a young priest:

> "First, you see, there was Materialism, pure and simple that failed more or less—it was too crude until psychology came to the rescue. Now psychology claims all the rest of the ground; and the supernatural sense seems accounted for. That's the claim."
>
> "No, father, we are losing; and we shall go on losing, and I think we must ever be ready for a catastrophe at any moment."[61]

Was the young priest right to fear an imminent spiritual catastrophe? Certainly the Sixties, in adopting Jungian notions of sexual and spiritual liberation, represented a cataclysmic transformation of the old Christian civilization.

CHAPTER 4

THE PERENNIAL PHILOSOPHY—THE ORIGIN OF CONTEMPORARY SPIRITUALITY

We doubtless have little understanding of the new spirituality's origins if we are only now, in the 21st century, noticing its arrival. We are not, as some may think, entering uncharted territory. Spirituality always grows from deep roots. Jung's use of ancient pagan archetypes in psychology was only new because of its application to modern therapeutic techniques.

Many people today identify themselves as "spiritual but not religious," but where did that come from? Catherine L. Albanese, former president of the American Academy of Religion, calls this new spirituality "American metaphysical religion"—something beyond the material but not specifically Christian. She says, "In its own way, American metaphysical religion has been as vigorous, persuasive, and influential as the evangelical tradition that is more often the focus of religious scholars' attention."[1]

Journalist Tony Schwartz spent six years in the 1990s researching marginal spiritual groups and leading gurus who claimed to have discovered the god within through altered consciousness. He asserted that he had stumbled across "an emerging American wisdom tradition," originating in the New Age phenomenon of the Sixties but having more "balance."[2] In light of the highly visible position of Christian orthodoxy in Western culture, we have not noticed the growing presence of another spiritual alternative that differs from both secular humanism and Christianity.

The Sleeping Giant of Western Paganism

What Jung and his circle promoted in the first half of the 20th century and what David Miller predicted in 1974 as the rebirth of the gods is now appearing on the surface of our culture as what it really is—the return to the West of an elaborate, extensive, impressive paganism that in one form or another has flourished throughout the entire course of human history.

"Pagan" doesn't refer here to ancient tribal religions or immoral, "godless" people, as the term is sometimes used to mean. Paganism comes from the Latin word *paganus*, which means "country dweller." It originally referred to rural common folk, but, by extension, it came to refer to people who held onto their traditional folk religions after the arrival of Christianity, which usually appeared in towns before taking hold in rural regions. Those who call themselves pagans or neopagans nowadays do so for a similar reason: They deliberately worship the earth or themselves as aspects of the divine and do not accept Christian orthodoxy's claims regarding the uniquely self-existent God of creation and salvation. Indeed, pagans are usually conscientiously opposed to organized religion in any form. There is an almost limitless variety of expressions of paganism, but all pagan religions are ultimately Oneist.

Jung made no pretense about preferring paganism to Christianity, as we discovered in the last chapter. He was a careful interpreter who wove together the common threads of ancient Gnosticism, Hinduism, Buddhism, medieval alchemy, and 19th-century German mysticism into a single tapestry for the modern world.

For many centuries, especially in the West, such spirituality was driven underground by the triumph of early Christianity. Isis had lost; Jesus had won. Paganism became a secretive, underground stream persisting in Western beliefs, known mostly to secret initiates through esoteric books and specialized language. Therefore, let the reader beware: We are not dealing with some marginal cult or a new theory that can be resisted with a little effort and goodwill by the American heartland. The ancient pagan giant is stirring. The formidable beast of thought and practice that dominated the ancient world is now at our door, demanding authority in our homes, laws, and even churches. Needless to say, it is essential that contemporary Christian believers understand the true nature of this opposing—and recently reappearing—spirituality.

As British playwright George Bernard Shaw said, "There is only one religion, though there are a hundred versions of it."[3] What is this "one religion"? The expression that put everything together for me in the last few years of my research on paganism is the classical, coded term, "perennial philosophy" (*philosophia perennis*), sometimes also called *philosophia occulta* or *magia*.[4] The phrase was coined in the late 17th or early 18th century by mathematician and philosopher Gottfried Leibniz,[5] but the idea goes back into the mists of time. The term was made famous by Aldous Huxley, author of *Brave New World*. In his book *The Perennial Philosophy*, Huxley defines the term:

> [The perennial philosophy recognizes] a divine Reality substantial to the world of things ... and finds in the soul something similar to, or even identical with, divine Reality. ... Rudiments of the perennial philosophy may be found among the traditionary lore of primitive peoples in every region of the world, and in its fully developed forms it has a place in every one of the higher religions.[6]

This is a perfect, sophisticated definition of paganism.

In chapter 1 we met Peter Occhiogrosso, author of *The Joy of Sects*, who has argued that in spite of the many antagonistic expressions of the world's religions, they share a deep level of agreement "which is not spoken of by their mainstream purveyors."[7] He calls this, as the reader will recall, "a single stream that feeds each of these traditions from a single source ... the Perennial Philosophy."[8] A modern Jungian, Stanislav Grof, has compared the experiences of North American, Mexican, and South American shamans with the spiritualities of Vipassana, Zen and Vajrayana Buddhism, Siddha Yoga, Tantra, and the Christian Benedictine order. He draws connections between all these and experiences described in literature on the perennial philosophy.[9]

Other key visionaries of our present culture include mythologist Joseph Campbell, a committed disciple of Jung, who saw in the perennial philosophy the basic pagan myth,[10] and Huston Smith, hailed by some as the greatest living scholar of world religions, who says that Huxley's *The Perennial Philosophy* "converted me from naturalism to a mystical view of reality."[11] Smith calls himself a "Perennialist with a capital P."[12]

The term "perennial philosophy" has popped up in the strangest of places—including the British royal family. His Royal Highness Charles, Prince of Wales, a highly influential environmentalist, gave the opening address at a conference on the subject of tradition and modernity in September 2006.[13] He tells us of what tradition he speaks. In his address, Charles mentions the work of the Temenos Academy, which, he points out, "has long been committed to the perennial philosophy."

A Philosophy of Many Names

The perennial philosophy goes by other names as well. Wiccans speak of the "Old Wisdom," encapsulated in the phrase, "as above, so below," a phrase one finds both in Freemasonry ("Let that which is below be as that which is above")[14] and in ancient Gnosticism (as in the *Gospel of Philip*: "I came to make [the things below] like the things [above...]").[15] It also recalls ancient Hermeticism, which has recently been revived by Rhonda Byrne in her bestselling book *The Secret*. In her introduction, Byrne speaks of the "Great Secret" of past spirituality and cites the so-called Emerald Tablet from 3000 BC, on which is etched—you guessed it—"As above, so below."[16] Such teaching is found in Sufism (Islamic mysticism), especially among modern Sufis, and was used by George Gurdjieff to create the Enneagram, a nine-pointed circle designed to

bring nine different personality types and their vibrations to a consciousness of the One.[17]

The perennial philosophy is also called the "Eternal Script,"[18]
"Enlightenment," the "Forgotten Truth," or "Primordial Tradition,"
which its followers believe goes back to the Tower of Babel.[19] The *arca-
num arcanorum*, the "mystery of mysteries," like all these terms, refers
to one ultimate secret that lies behind all astrology, magic, and forms of
the occult. Some contemporary pagans speak of their practices as the
"Old Religion."[20]

The same fundamental belief in the divinity of nature is found
in medieval alchemy, of which Carl Jung was a committed follower.
Jung wrote:

> For the alchemist, the one primarily in need of redemp-
> tion is not man, but the deity who is lost and sleeping
> in matter. ... Man takes upon himself the duty of car-
> rying out the redeeming *opus* and attributes the state
> of suffering and consequent need of redemption to the
> *anima mundi* [Latin, "soul of the world"] imprisoned
> in matter.[21]

One leading theosophist, Alice Bailey, said of the future: "...there is a
great and glorious unfolding plan for the destiny of the nations ... [God's]
plan for the evolution of humanity, and the preparation of teachers to
guide it, called within the esoteric traditions the Great Work."[22]

This terminology of the Great Work was found in sects like the
Rosicrucians and spiritual alchemists of the Middle Ages. Long before
that, the term was used similarly in ancient Hermeticism, which became popular at the time of the Renaissance.[23] Later traditions of the
Hermetic variety used the term "Great Work" in this same way. Eliphas
Levi, a 19th-century leader of the Hermetic Order of the Golden Dawn,
stated, "The Great Work is, before all things, the creation of man by
himself, that is to say, the full and entire conquest of his faculties and
his future; it is especially the perfect emancipation of his will."[24]

This sounds suspiciously like Jung, as does a further definition by
Aleister Crowley, another member of the same Hermetic Order and
who was featured on the cover of the Beatles album *Sgt. Pepper's Lonely*

Hearts Club Band. For Crowley, "The Great Work is the uniting of opposites ... the uniting of the soul with God, of the microcosm with the macrocosm, of the female with the male, of the ego with the non-ego."[25]

This same vision reappears with Jung's term "opus" in a popular book on the environment, *The Great Work: Our Way into the Future.*[26] The author, Thomas Berry, was a Catholic theologian who, following his apostasy, called himself a "geologian." He stated that the "historical mission of our times is to re-invent the human—at the species level ... by means of ... shared dream experiences."[27] Berry thus referred to the work done in ancient "shamanic times"[28] and believed that our contemporary calling to be carrying on "the Great Work of the First Peoples ... [who] established an intimate rapport with the powers that brought [America] into existence."[29]

The perennial philosophy, the great tradition, the old religion—all are iterations of the underlying worldview we've been calling Oneism. The prevalence of such philosophies and spiritualities in all their variety suggests that there is a highly significant contingent of cultural influencers—from common Wiccans to the next in line to the British throne—who identify with ancient pagan traditions and even promote them as the hope of the future.

Prophesying the Pagan Moment

The reappearance of a variety of Oneist spiritualities that have caught the imagination of multitudes of Westerners was strangely prophesied as *the* coming world religion by certain perceptive observers. I say "strangely" since at the time that such predictions were made, secular humanism and Christianity dominated the scene. To everyone else, such a mystical spirituality did not seem to stand a chance.

Early Prophets of Paganism

Toward the end of the 19th century, Friedrich Nietzsche predicted that his ideas about the death of God and the inversion of values would one day be commonplace. What Nietzsche predicted, one commentator perceptively notes, was not just one more "competing form of religion,"[30] over and against Christianity, but its very antithesis—a "transvaluation" of biblical theism; not heresy but apostasy. Nietzsche saw, in the place of God, the coming of the Übermensch—the truly free new man for whom nothing is forbidden except what obstructs his desire and ability for self-realization. Serious historical work on Nietzsche suggests that part of his motivation for overturning biblical values and for redesigning "man" was his penchant for homosexuality.[31] The carefully chosen words of his German biographer are worth citing:

> A new ideal confronted him—the ideal of the Übermensch, the Superman, a throbbing creature of health and pulsating *joie de vivre*, a creature for whom he yearned as the lover yearns for his distant beloved. Nietzsche's passion for this masculine idol became the core of his thought. Classical Greece, with its ideal of bravery in battle, its worship of physical beauty and the mysteries of its cult of sexuality, became the model for his own life.[32]

In his time, Nietzsche was dismissed as a lone, raving lunatic who died insane in the arms of his doting sister. Now his "ravings" are echoed in a revived pagan spirituality and in the cultural goals of leading thinkers who find his ideas to be totally normal.

In 1920, years after the death of Nietzsche, Jessie Weston, author of 11 books on the Holy Grail legend, predicted an imminent day of revelation. She was sure that "the grail is a living force, it will never die; it may indeed sink out of sight ... but it will rise to the surface again, and become once more a theme of vital importance."[33] For Weston, the Grail represented the mystical quest of human beings for divine self-realization. The Grail theme and the perennial philosophy surfaced as a worldwide phenomenon in Dan Brown's *Da Vinci Code* with the claim that spiritual truth is common to both paganism and Christianity. Long suppressed but now rising to the surface, this "truth" concerns the death of the God of the Bible and the divinity of Mother Nature and humanity.[34]

In 1930, another Mason, Foster Bailey, husband of Alice Bailey (cited above), spoke of a new mystical age. He declared with uncanny confidence: "a new day is dawning ... The Piscean Age is passing; the Aquarian Age is coming on."[35]

The Prophecies Come to Pass

Carl Jung, with his self-identification as a modern gnostic, fits in this same esoteric tradition. Jung predicted in the 1950s, at the dawn of the Sixties revolution, that "we are only at the threshold of a new spiritual epoch."[36] He saw himself as a modern Joachim of Fiore, the charismatic monk who at the end of the 12th century prophesied the age of the coming of the Spirit, following the age of the Father (from creation to the coming of Christ) and the age of the Son (from Christ's coming until Joachim's own day). The monk's teachings were eventually rejected, but Jung believed that his own theories about the unconscious were finally ushering in the age of the Spirit in an even more radical way than Joachim of Fiore had imagined it. Jung's spirit age would signal "the end of the Christian aeon" by "the invalidation of Christ."[37]

Beginning in the 1960s, such prophecies began to be fulfilled. The underground perennial philosophy, known and cherished by initiates, rose to the surface of Western culture in Jung's vision of a new humanity. Since then, this spirituality of "going within" (searching for the god within) has been rising in public visibility. Jung created the momentum and the occasion, but he was clearly part of a long tradition of esoteric spirituality. He simply passed it on.

The current revival of spiritualism, ushered in through therapeutic psychology and popular mysticism, has roots deep in the long and troubled history of Creator-denying paganism. The origin and nature of this spirituality helps reveal the true identity of these influences, being adopted since the middle of the last century by people who assume such ideas and practices are perfectly normal and good for the soul, a breath of fresh spiritual air.

CHAPTER 5

THE SIXTIES SPIRITUAL AND SEXUAL REVOLUTION

A Spiritual Tsunami

What began as a barely visible "cult"[1] has become a spiritual tidal wave. The open, though somewhat marginal, expression of this overwhelming wave first occurred in the cultural revolution of the Sixties. Perhaps at the time, the term revolution may have seemed a little overdramatic. Wasn't it merely a typical generational rebellion against the rules of its parents? The term is appropriate, however, because a revolution is a movement that deliberately makes a sharp break from inherited social and cultural structures. In 1789, the French Revolution sought a total break from its Christian past. It guillotined thousands of Roman Catholic priests, installed a statue of the goddess Reason on the altar in Notre Dame Cathedral in central Paris, changed the 7-day week into 10 days, and renamed all the months of the year. *That* was a revolution!

The Sixties brought both a spiritual and a sexual revolution. This chapter will explore the explosive spiritual ideas stemming from Jung's theories and then examine their sexual implications. Though seldom openly violent, the cultural changes of the Sixties were just as world-changing as those of the French Revolution—they entailed a break with Western culture's Christian roots, seeking a new spiritual base in the religious heritage of the East.

This was the essence of a hit Bob Dylan song of 1964 in which he declared that "the times, they are a-changin'," a change which parents "can't understand."[2] Dylan doesn't evoke the typical tensions between one generation and the next—his song evokes a departure, a rupture. The hippies went East while the gurus came West. The Beatles went East to Rishikesh, India, in 1968, and in 1970, their guru, Maharishi Mahesh Yogi, came to the United States. When a generation feels that the Bible on one hand and science and technology on the other cannot ultimately provide meaning, what is left? Colin Campbell has affirmed this trend, noting that "the decline of both religious and secular theodicies ... created a cultural vacuum that only an Eastern outlook would be able to fill."[3] During the Sixties, we discovered in the West an atypical, seemingly spontaneous spiritual phenomenon with no clear precedents in Western history—the beginnings of the so-called New Age.

It should come as no surprise that Jung, though he died in 1961, was one of the main popularizers of the Age of Aquarius and the New Age movement. As early as 1940, Jung wrote, "1940 is the year when we approach the meridian of the first star in Aquarius. It is the premonitory earthquake of the New Age."[4] In the 1950s, he stated, "We are only at the threshold of a new spiritual epoch,"[5] believing that his theories about the unconscious were ushering in the age of the Paraclete, which would signal "the end of the Christian aeon" by "the invalidation of Christ."[6] In speaking of the Age of Aquarius, Jung predicted a reinterpretation of Christianity's view of God via Hindu Vedantic pantheism and the victory of a self-realizing spirituality[7] (which, interestingly enough, included the now-widespread practice of yoga).

My readers may or may not recall the lilting mega-hit song from 1969, "Age of Aquarius." I used to sing it and loved the music but, like most people, had no idea of the meaning of the lyrics:

> When the moon is in the Seventh House
> And Jupiter aligns with Mars
> Then peace will guide the planets
> And love will steer the stars.
> This is the dawning of the Age of Aquarius.[8]

Those few who understood knew that if Aquarius was here, the Age of Pisces (Age of the Fish or the age of Christendom) was on the way out. Songwriter Don McLean caught the importance of the moment with his plaintive 1971 song "American Pie," in which he asks:

> Did you write the book of love,
> And do you have faith in God above,
> If the Bible tells you so?

He seems to see the end of Christianity, up to that point as American as apple pie, and especially with the words:

> And the three men I admire most,
> The Father, Son and Holy Ghost,
> They caught the last train for the coast,
> The day the music died.[9]

McLean stated in 2009 that "American Pie" was "a big song ... that summed up the world known as America."[10]

During that period we witnessed New Age prophetess and Hollywood actress, Shirley MacLaine, who wrote a best-selling novel, *Out on a Limb*, and made the outlandish announcement in a television special: "I am God." Many of us wondered when that limb would break, but it never did, and the New Age tree has taken over much of the West.

In fact, the Sixties were but the dawning of the Age of Aquarius. Sociologist Christopher Partridge described it as the time of "the re-enchantment of the West." David Horowitz and Peter Collier, Marxist leaders of the Berkeley Students for a Democratic Society in the Sixties, later wrote a book about their experiences titled, *Destructive Generation: Second Thoughts about the Sixties*.[11] Fearing the worst, these men had come to understand that the inspiration at the heart of the revolutionary changes they helped foment was the destruction of the entire worldview of recent Western civilization.

Pagan Revival

As paganism was making its way into our culture through the attractive principles of transpersonal psychology, the popular pagan revival in the United States was bolstered by Joseph Campbell, a close friend and admirer of Jung and a popularizer of Jung's ideas about mythology. This college professor—who was raised Roman Catholic but later renounced Christianity—made these ideas known through wildly successful books and a 1988 PBS television program, *The Power of Myth*. The production became one of the most popular TV programs in the history of public television.

What was Campbell doing? Along with journalist Bill Moyers, he was putting Jung's esoteric language of transpersonal psychology into layman's terms: Inner problems and inner mysteries need the guideposts that myths provide. These myths are the search for meaning by human beings throughout the ages. Myths are not to be seen as mere purveyors of rational meaning; rather, they create the experience of being alive.[12]

Another ex-Roman Catholic spiritualist and enthusiastic Jungian, Mark H. Gaffney, describes what was happening against the background of the larger canvas of ideas. He describes "a serendipitous confluence of events"[13]—an unforeseen but delightful turn of happenings—that included both the decline of Christianity and secularism and the growth of alternate spiritualities. Part of that turn of events in the Sixties was the publication of the gnostic texts discovered at Nag Hammadi in 1945, which Jung promoted and of which Gaffney became a skilled interpreter. The gnostic texts made a heretical form of Christianity available to those seeking alternate forms of the old faith. James Robinson, the editor of the 1977 translated and published English version of the Nag Hammadi texts, understood their appropriateness to the cultural changes he saw taking place: "The focus ... has much in common ... with Eastern religions, and with holy men of all times, as well as with ... the counter culture movements coming from the 1960's."[14]

Gnosticism is just one expression of ancient mythology. As the hippies went East and the gurus came West, scores of alternative spiritualities proliferated. Evidence of a pantheistic spiritual revival is seen in such movements and expressions as the Native American vision quest, the Akashic records, Ayurvedic medicine, chakras, Eastern meditation of all kinds, Eckankar (soul travel), feng shui, Hare Krishna, karma, mandalas, mantras, reincarnation, shamanism, Sufism, Tai Chi, Tantrism, and *I Ching*—to name just a few. These methods are becoming a dominant source of religious truth in a culture that once thought of the Bible as God's supreme revelation.

Hindu America?

Jung was fascinated with yoga, Hindu spirituality, and the culture of India, where he travelled in 1937 and 1938. He was obviously impressed; he declared in 1932, "We have conquered the East politically [but now] the spirit of the East is really *antes portas* [before the gates]."[15]

When I first discovered "Christian" America in 1964, I never thought America could be called Hindu. If you feel this label is extreme, I would encourage you to read a book by a Western intellectual convert to Hinduism, Philip Goldberg, called *American Veda: From Emerson and the Beatles to Yoga and Meditation: How Indian Spirituality Changed the West.* Goldberg reminds us that in 2009 even *Newsweek* recognized the shift: "We Are All Hindus Now ... large numbers of Americans have arrived at the worldview of Hinduism, where 'Truth is One, but the sages speak of it by many names.' "[16] According to Goldberg, "America is engaged in a reconfiguring of the sacred, comparable to the Great Awakenings of the 18th century."[17]

Another, even more impressive study makes the same point. Colin Campbell, documenting the "Easternization of the West," argues:

> ...a plausible case can be made for the claim that there is a process of Easternization currently occurring in the West ... quite unlike anything previously experienced ... it concerns fundamental changes in the dominant worldview that prevails in the West ... in all areas of life, including religion ... medicine, the arts, political thought and even science ... it also concerns what has been lost. [18]

"What has been lost"—namely, faith in Christianity and in "the power of reason to usher in a better world."Now I think I'm beginning to understand the perceptiveness of a chant I heard from many hippie students in the Sixties, "Hey! Ho! Wha'd'you know? Western Civ has got to go!" They weren't just trying to get out of class!

In certain respects, American culture has undergone a religious conversion. The Sixties revolution produced a "spiritual reawakening" not just for the hippies: We all now experience the effects in our everyday lives, whether we realize it or not. Our thinking and vocabulary includes concepts like mantra, avatar, and karma. The health care profession offers traditional Eastern approaches to healing and physical illness, such as healing touch, Ayurveda, and meditation.[19]

We must understand that though techniques like yoga and mindfulness[20] seem innocent enough and may even accomplish some pragmatic ends, the worldview and assumptions undergirding them are Oneist. In the light of the determined effort to promote Hinduism as a religion, how much is our present fascination with alternative techniques subtly drawing the 21st-century West, including many Christians, into a non-biblical worldview? Do yoga and mindfulness draw us subtly into the spirituality of some of the many forms of Oneism?[21]

For example, Hindu convert Dr. David Frawley, otherwise known as Pandit Vamadeva Shastri, stresses the place of yoga within this ancient religious sensibility:

> [Hinduism] represents the native and pagan traditions of the world that contain the key to the older and more experiential spirituality of humanity that so many people are looking for today ... the world would be a kinder and more understanding place to live in with yoga and meditation as the foundation of human life and culture.[22]

The invasion of Eastern spirituality means that, far from disappearing as some thought it would, the New Age movement has gone mainstream, morphing into the various and complementary expressions of its essentially god-within spirituality.

Spiritual Interfaith

In addition to our culture's fascination with ancient myths and spiritualities, most of the major religious communities and almost all the mainline churches in the contemporary West seek interreligious unity and interspiritual practice. The phenomenon Jung had anticipated is here: "Our world," he said, "has shrunk, and it is dawning on us that humanity is *one*, with *one* psyche ... [this] should prompt Christians, for the sake of charity—the greatest of all virtues—to set a good example and acknowledge that though there is only *one* truth it speaks in many tongues."[23]

This is where we must situate mainline Christian interfaith efforts. Roman Catholic theologian Heather Eaton is representative when she argues that the Christian faith must exhibit openness to reinterpretations of its teachings in light of "the myriad religious traditions, and [show] a willingness to be transformed by inter-religious dialogue." The modern religious person needs to encounter the many religious perspectives and spiritual sensitivities and be transformed by this process. From this perspective, Christianity is just one of many paths to discover religious truth.[24] What church father Hippolytus saw in the second century AD as gnostic apostasy is now seen as Christian maturity.[25]

The religious and spiritual changes Jung predicted and that began to flourish in the middle of the 20th century are now noticed by a number of scholars as a significant factor of the modern West:

- Sociologist Christopher Partridge states: "There is some evidence to suggest that 'a rising tide of spirituality ... is producing a re-enchantment of the world.'"[26]

- Historian of religion Wouter Hanegraaff speaks of the "profound transformation of religion" in the West, away from traditional Christianity towards "magic."[27]

- Philosopher Richard Tarnas believes that "we are living in one of those rare ages, like the end of classical antiquity or the beginning of the modern era, that bring forth, through great stress and struggle, a genuinely fundamental transformation in the underlying assumptions and principles of the cultural world view."[28]

The runaway train of contemporary Western humanity, derailed by disenchantment with secular humanism, the hollow hope of postmodernism, and ultimately by its rejection of biblical Twoism, cannot be put back on track. In fact, it does not need repair, but redemption! The historic Christian church needs to take a long look at what has happened from the beginning of the 20th century to the beginning of the 21st in order to recognize a number of important things:

1. The old enemy, secularism, is on the way out.

2. A new spiritual enemy has appeared—paganism.

3. Christianity no longer occupies a privileged position in Western society.

4. Some Christians, mesmerized by the success and apparent beauty of this cultural spiritual movement, fail to see that its basic religious vision stems from a deliberate attempt to undermine the Christian faith and the civilization it helped to engender.

5. This new religious option is massive in its conception and breathtaking in its intentions. It is bent on seizing ideological power—all, of course, "for the good of humanity."

6. Leaving Bible tracts on park benches, referring to "the old, old story" or having pleasant but shallow conversations with our neighbors will not be sufficient witness in a post-Christian cultural situation of widespread antagonism toward the gospel.

7. Understanding our culture's deep commitment to Oneism and developing an appropriate Twoist response is essential both for evangelism and for cultural renewal. (This will be addressed in part 3.)

This spiritual phenomenon is variously called the "Fourth Awakening," the "Great Emergence," the "Great Shift," the "New Pentecost," the "present fundamental transformation," or "a new alignment." It is not simply the addition of a few useful spiritual insights or of some unfortunate heterodox deviations; on the contrary, we are facing a paradigm shift. The old is in the trash, like last month's freezer-burned leftovers. A new dish is in preparation, seductive in appearance but laced with poison, and will be the only dish on the menu.

Since the early days of the virtually unknown "Jung cult," Jung and his followers have succeeded in creating a modern world in many ways seduced by one or another of the various Oneist spiritualities. And the seduction, this time also thoroughly sexual, is far from over.

A Sexual Tsunami

Although it was not widely known at the time, the group around Jung was involved in various extramarital relationships; they remained married for the sake of appearances, but as time went on, they began to experiment with more radical sexual activities on the basis of Jung's theories that the human being was made up of both an *animus* (the male element) and an *anima* (the female element). Jung and his followers were determined to have, as Noll put it, "the courage to sin."[29] (Later, certain radical feminists would pick up on these ideas, calling their sisters to become "sinarticulate," to "liberate the inner slut," and to "reestablish the consciousness of the Sacred Prostitute."[30])

When, 70 years ago, Jung looked into the future, he realized the enormity of the challenge to bring about the spiritual and sexual liberation he and his cohort were already enjoying in a culture that was still under the influence of Christian public morality. "The ethical problem of sexual freedom is really enormous and worth the sweat of all noble souls. But 2000 years of Christianity can only be replaced by something equivalent, an irresistible mass movement."[31]

Liberated Heterosexuality

What could be more irresistible for a mass movement than a sexual liberation for our psychological and spiritual health?

Our culture now claims the right to erotic freedom for the purposes of self-fulfillment and self-realization in an even more pronounced way. But when Jung's convictions about sexual expression empowered the Sixties cultural revolution, it was a unique moment in the West, following many centuries of deep Christian influence. The Christian notion of sexual restraint out of respect for creational boundaries—and the

Creator's revealed will—became identified as psychologically repressive and unhealthy. The exploration and satisfaction of sexual desires began to be seen as intrinsic to one's personal identity and growth.

The merging of sexual liberation and the new psychology is exemplified in the writings of Marxist thinkers associated with the Frankfurt School, founded in the 1930s in Germany, which later relocated to the United States. Herbert Marcuse, a leading intellectual in this circle, proposed "polymorphous sexuality," "life instincts," or "free gratification of man's instinctual needs" as the means of social engineering to produce a liberated, revolutionary utopian world.[32] The book was a huge hit among students in the Sixties; I once heard him lecture in person.

Though Marcuse focused on Freud, he appreciated Jung's insistence on the liberating power of fantasy,[33] believing that psychology had entered the realm of politics to make social revolutions possible.[34] This change in the value and scope of sexual relations was supposed to help lead the way to a disintegration of the whole social structure organized around the "monogamic and patriarchal family,"[35] necessary to make way for the Marxist utopian alternative. Thus sexuality entered politics in the Sixties with a bang as well.

Other sources contributed to the still-heterosexual revolution, popularized by, for example, sex researcher Alfred Kinsey[36] and Hugh Hefner, the founder of *Playboy* magazine. They openly celebrated and marketed unlimited sex as a human right. However, Jung's promotion of sexual self-realization and fantasy, Kinsey's research, and the efforts of many others pushed the revolutionary consequences beyond the bounds of heterosexual relationships to their logical—and spiritual—conclusion: They denied any personal identity and social structure rooted in objective, created realities and moral restraints. Thus the liberation of the subconscious has progressed in our day to the outer boundaries of the queer and the weird in unbounded expressions of Oneist sexuality.

Liberated Homosexuality

A Building Revolution

The first signs of the coming homosexual revolution appeared with the Stonewall riots of June 28, 1969, celebrated annually today as Gay Pride

Day. Few took notice at the time. Its claims soon appeared more openly in the *Gay Liberation Front Manifesto* in the 1970s. The *Manifesto* reflects incredible prescience and consistency of vision:

> Equality is never going to be enough; what is needed is a total social revolution, a complete reordering of civilization. Reform ... cannot change the deep-down attitude of straight people that homosexuality is at best inferior to their own way of life, at worst a sickening perversion. It will take more than reforms to change this attitude, because it is rooted in our society's most basic institution—the Patriarchal Family.[37]

Though the ideas were present decades ago, it is only in our time that homosexuality has taken such a prominent and visible role in contemporary culture and media. A number of authors have documented this process.[38] They note that in 1988, 175 leading gay activists held a "war" conference. The next year, Marshall Kirk and Hunter Madsen, who were present, wrote *After the Ball,* a book that identified the AIDS epidemic as the occasion to "establish ourselves as a victimized minority." Their intention was to:

> ...convert the average American's emotion, mind and will through a planned psychological attack in the form of propaganda fed to the nation via the media ... using the mechanism of prejudice to our own ends—using the very processes that made America hate us to turn their hatred into warm regard.[39]

This deliberate attempt to develop fear and hatred of biblical Christianity seems to have succeeded, as the endless characterization of traditional Christians as homophobic now shows. In 1999, speakers at a Gay, Lesbian & Straight Education Network (GLSEN) Conference on education said: "If we do our job right, we're going to raise a generation of kids who do not believe the claims of the religious right."[40]

Kirk and Madsen also used a demonstrably false statistic, claiming that 10 percent of the population is homosexual, according to the theory that "when it comes to fighting the charge that homosexuality is statistically abnormal hence immoral, there is strength in numbers."[41] A Gallup poll found a majority of adults believe the percentage of gays in the population is 25 percent, and that millennials put the figure at 30 percent.[42] Actually, on July 15, 2014, the government's National Center for Health Statistics (NCHS) released a study indicating that 1.6 percent of Americans identify as gay or lesbian, while 0.7 percent identify as bisexual. Almost 98 percent of the 35,557 survey respondents identified themselves as straight or "not gay."[43]

Shifting Opinions

Nevertheless, the switch in public opinion toward supporting gays and lesbians as a victimized minority and shaming biblical Christians as bigoted and intolerant has been a stunning success. The speed and extent of this change in attitude toward homosexuality has been noted:

- "In 1988 ... only 12 percent [of Americans] agreed that gay couples should be allowed to marry and 73 percent disagreed." In 1996, 28 percent supported same-sex marriage. By 2013, support had risen to 52 percent.[44]
- 74 percent of millennials (the generation born between about 1980 and 2000) accept homosexuality as normal, approving of marriage equality.[45]
- 80 percent of Catholic students support same-sex marriage.[46]
- 44 percent of young evangelicals now favor marriage equality.[47]

These major shifts are not the result of new facts or serious conversations. The popular media has manipulated public opinion by being either openly supportive or else wary of any engagement on the issue. Kathryn Montgomery, an expert in media communication, writes:

> Although a number of lobby groups have campaigned
> for exposure on the airwaves, the gay lobby has been by
> far the most organized and best coordinated ... gaining
> a reputation as "the most sophisticated and successful
> advocacy group operating in network television."[48]

Already in 1996, gay writer David Ehrenstein could say that "[t]here are openly gay writers on almost every major prime-time situation comedy you can think of." He concluded: "In short, when it comes to sitcoms, gays rule."[49]

Yesterday's radicals are not only today's media trendsetters but are leading government officials as well. For instance, championing gay rights has become official United States foreign policy. In April 2013, the United States Agency for International Development (USAID), with little fanfare, committed to spending $11 million of taxpayer money to train activists, to raise up international lobbyists for same-sex marriage, to fight anti-discrimination laws, and to promote homosexual rights around the world. The "enlightened" United States government—in a deeply ironic expression of cultural imperialism—is coercing majority world countries into accepting this Western religious agenda.

Sexuality without Boundaries

Queer theory insists that "all sexual behaviors ... and identities, and all categories of normative and deviant sexualities, are social constructs, [rejecting] the idea that sexuality is an essentialist category ... determined by biology or judged by eternal standards of morality and truth."[50] For this to happen, though, the key eternal standard of what is good and what is evil has to go. The truth to be overcome is moral.

Jung's father was a Lutheran minister, but Jung's conception of sin departed so dramatically from that of his upbringing that he came to believe that doing evil could actually have a beneficial effect on the personality by freeing the individual from what some call "one-sidedness," putting one in touch with "instinctual being." Noll has described Jung's beliefs: "The shackles of family, society, and Deity must be broken."[51] Here, the libido is god. In such a view it was easy—indeed, noble—to move on from the narrow confines of past heterosexual license to the broad Elysian fields of contemporary pansexuality.

The attitude of millennials shows this outlook's progress. The schoolbooks and media of this generation implicitly or explicitly endorse the notion that there are no inherently distinct male or female identities and roles in society, and that sexuality is an expression of choice. How far can this dissolving of distinctions go? In 2000, Virginia Ramey Mollenkott, an ex-Presbyterian professor of literature who is now an out lesbian spiritualist, offered a radical paradigm for the future liberation of sexuality: an omnigender society of "allosexuality [other sexuality] ... an arrangement of many erotic patterns in no particular hierarchy"[52] by which virtually all sexual choices are normalized. The choices Mollenkott suggests include:[53]

1. The intersexual or hermaphrodite (people with both sets of sexual organs)[54]

2. The transsexual (those who have undergone a sex change operation)

3. The transvestite (or cross-dresser)

4. The drag queen and king (cross-dressing performance artists)

5. The transgenderists or bigenderists (those who engage in cross-dressing or cross-living part or full time)

6. The androgynes (those with both male and female gender identity and roles at the same time)[55]

7. Heterosexuals

8. Homosexuals

9. Bisexuals

10. Those who enjoy various fetishes (such as group sex, sadomasochistic sex)[56]

11. The autoerotic (sex focused on oneself, such as masturbation)

12. The asexual

13. The pansexual (an "all of the above")

14. The pedophile (who, Mollenkott suggests, is not as bad as people think.)[57]

The Marriage of Sexuality and Spirituality

Why were Hollywood and the media so eager to manipulate the rising generation on the crucial issue of sexuality in recent years? Was pansexuality a mere pretext for a much larger agenda? What ideology are these elite opinion-makers, graduates of the Sixties cultural and sexual revolution, really normalizing? The sexual agenda is just a visible symbol of a powerful, century-long deconstruction of the Christian worldview and its replacement with a pagan Oneist cosmology, of which sexuality is a sacrament.

Oneist Spirituality and Sexuality

The religious understanding of sexuality was clearly expressed by a close friend and passionate disciple of Jung, June Singer, who was at his bedside when he died. In her 1977 book, *Androgyny: Toward a New Theory of Sexuality*, Singer applied Jungian theory, arguing that the spiritual Age of Aquarius was also the sexual Age of Androgyny. The new humanism of this age required a new view of sexuality, androgyny—the conflation of male and female genders in one person.[58] "We have at hand ... all the ingredients we will need to perform our own new alchemical *opus* ... to fuse the opposites within us."[59] (Remember the "Great Work" we saw in chapter 4?) Cultivating this erasure of sexual boundaries is crucial to realizing the coming new age: "The androgyne participates consciously in the evolutionary process, redesigning the individual ... society and ... planet."[60]

Androgynous priests were associated with the worship of the goddess Ishtar in the Sumerian age (1800 BC).[61] It is recorded of the Canaanite goddess Anat: "Her priests dressed up and wore make-up like [women]."[62] At the beginning of the fifth century AD, the cult of the goddess Cybele continued to have success. Augustine, in his *City of God*, describes firsthand the public display of homosexual priests (*galloi*):

> They were seen yesterday, their hair moist, their faces covered in make-up, their limbs flaccid, their walk effeminate, wandering through the streets and squares of Carthage, demanding from the public the means to subsidize their shameful life.[63]

Singer traced the nature of the androgynous human Self, which implies homosexuality, all the way back to the true underlying nature of the cosmos:

> The archetype of androgyny appears in us as an innate sense of ... and witness to ... the primordial cosmic unity—that is, it is the sacrament of monism, functioning to erase distinction. ... [This was] nearly totally expunged from the Judeo-Christian tradition.[64]

Notice Singer's reference to "monism"? Oneism is simply a more literal term for that basic concept. If in "primordial cosmic unity" there is no Creator/creature distinction, then in this-worldly sexuality there is no male/female distinction.

The sexual boundary-breaking and excesses of today's culture are not simply due to factors like Hollywood seeking ever-greater box office success or the widespread availability of Internet pornography. There is more beneath the surface. People in our culture, as in every other, act upon temptations to express their sexuality sinfully—but what is considered an expression of sinful sexuality today is often different than what would have been considered sinful historically. We openly celebrate what would have shamed many previous generations. This change is best explained by the direct expression of the resurgence of an ancient, yet still powerful, Oneist worldview behind many of today's excesses—a worldview with a close connection between spirituality and sexuality that the Bible understands very well.

Biblical Sexuality and Spirituality

The Apostle Paul's teaching on homosexual practice is a great example of the biblical understanding that though sexual sin is indeed an issue of immoral behavior, it's even more an expression of a religious commitment, even if many do not realize it. Sexual inversion of the created order is an embodied manifestation of Oneist worship and cosmology. Paul introduces his teaching on homosexuality in Romans 1:26-28 with the words "for this reason" (Rom 1:26). Homosexual behavior is religious, described clearly in Romans 1:26-27 as the worship of creation in place of the worship of God the Creator.

Think of it like this: Sexuality and spirituality inevitably meet; they are not watertight compartments of human reality, but are intertwined aspects of the image of God. If in your heart and mind you collapse God

and creation, good and evil, you will eventually collapse male and female in a physical expression of your religious reality, and—in good
Jungian thinking—liberate your subconscious fantasies.

This logic can be seen in the current cultural pressure regarding
same-sex marriage. Marriage is now about mutual love and voluntary
commitment, undergirded by personal expression and self-affirmation.
It is no longer a calling to reflect the image and will of the Creator and
Redeemer in our sexuality. There is, therefore, no inherent limit on
what, who, or how many can be married—why limit an important aspect of human self-realization to one man and woman, or to only two
consenting adults?

Rod Dreher writes of Philip Rieff, an observer of the Sixties sexual revolution:[65]

> In classical Christian culture, [Rieff] wrote, "the rejec-
> tion of sexual individualism" was "very near the center
> of the symbolic that has not held." He meant that re-
> nouncing the sexual autonomy and sensuality of pagan
> culture was at the core of Christian culture—a culture
> that, crucially, did not merely renounce but redirected
> the erotic instinct. That the West was rapidly re-pa-
> ganizing around sensuality and sexual liberation was a
> powerful sign of Christianity's demise.[66]

Even in some sectors of the evangelical world we are enjoined to
"[e]mbrace the feminine side of Jesus" as we discover the feminine side
of ourselves.[67] The contemporary belief of some in the church that there
are no categorical sexual and gender distinctions fails the test of biblical
faithfulness. It tramples over Genesis 1:27 (male and female in God's image), which grants deep religious meaning to sexual distinctiveness and
complementarity.[68] It disastrously fails to promote the goodness and
health of human sexuality as created good by God, to be enjoyed on his
terms. The revolution Jung and his followers desired has today liberated
sex and rediscovered religion—but not the Truth of Christianity.

CHAPTER 6

A DESTRUCTIVE GENERATION

Are we really "coming apart"? The phrase sounds too extreme to describe the effects of Jung's long vision for a new humanity. But as Peter Collier and David Horowitz observed in *Destructive Generation: Second Thoughts about the Sixties*, the old régime needed to be destroyed before utopian progress towards the new humanity could be made. So we must ask: Has this destructive part of the project succeeded, thereby imposing the new ideas of egalitarian progress on our culture? After all, things have never been better! Through technological advances in medical science, deadly diseases have been eradicated. Millions have been lifted from poverty and have gained access to education and health care, leading to longer, more prosperous lives. Awareness and protection of human rights has increased tremendously. Thanks to the miracle of computers and the Internet, the ideals of freedom and democracy have spread around the world, and people are increasingly recognizing the oneness of humanity. There is also growing awareness of the importance of a clean, green environment. In many ways, the last half century has seen great progress and positive change.

Some are, therefore, upbeat about the future. Wayne Baker, in *United America*, is optimistically surprised to have discovered that Americans are solidly bound together through 10 core values, on which "we can build, improve and sustain the nation."[1] In his endorsement of the book, Brian McLaren hopes for an "outpouring of positivity" and a national unity "around a sense of wider connectedness."

Other social commentators are not so sanguine. Indeed, the title of a recent article by Stanford scholar Deroy Murdock is veritably apocalyptic: "The United States of Decline: America Unravels at an Increasingly Dizzying Pace." For him, the "decline is breathtaking, and the prognosis is dim," since in the areas of economic, cultural, and foreign policy, "the American people have been betrayed."[2]

Patrick Buchanan announces similar prospects in *The Death of the West*. He identifies this cultural death with the loss of historic Christian identity. Buchanan does not see much hope in common beliefs, as argued by Wayne Baker. He notes that while we remain attached to the same principles of government, those principles are not enough to hold us together. The South was "attached to the same principles of government" as the North, but that did not stop a four-year bloody war between brethren.[3] For Buchanan, the "coming apart" is both religious and geographical: He cites a *Washington Post* journalist who stated after the 2000 United States presidential election, "We have two massive colliding forces. One is rural, Christian, religiously conservative. [The other] is socially tolerant, pro-choice, secular, living in New England and the Pacific Coast."[4]

Some objective elements indicate an implosion of culture due to the liberation movements arising out of the Jungian vision of a new humanity and its first popular expression in the counterculture of the Sixties. No one can truly question the fundamental implosion of the family and traditional marriage since the 1960s. The judgment is somber: As commentator Mark Steyn notes, "Much of what we loosely call the Western world will not survive the twenty-first century."[5]

Dim Prospects

The millennial generation consists of the adult children of parents who were themselves young adults in the Sixties. You might expect to see the positive effects of a liberated new humanity on family structure and morals, but don't hold your breath. As one commentator observed in June 2014, "The sexual revolution that began in the 1960s has borne its fruit: single-parent homes, absentee fathers, overwhelmed mothers, poverty, and children who roam the streets instead of study in class."[6]

A sociological study titled *unChristian* by two Christian millennials leaves little hope for the future.[7] These authors take their generation's critique of the church so seriously that they affirm, in the title of their bestseller, that it is "unchristian," yet they fail to see the implications of their reasoning. They quite rightly show that the dramatic cultural changes are not due to ordinary generational shifts—they argue that this generation's world, like none other, "is coming unglued."[8] If they are right, then can the authors put faith in the unglued spiritual and moral judgments made by a generation growing up in such an "unglued" state of affairs? Can millennials judge any more objectively than their forefathers what Christianity should look like?

The authors of *unChristian* portray this generation as exposed to more violence, dissolving family structures, pornography, and sex before and outside of marriage. The book further points out that substance abuse and addiction are widespread; that STDs, AIDS, teenage pregnancy, single motherhood, absent fathers, and abortion are common;[9] that profanity is normal; that one in six millennials is in debt; that one in four is divorced; that suicide is the third leading cause of death; and that they are a fatherless generation.[10] Of the 20-somethings from Christian homes, 60 percent no longer have any connection to church.[11]

The Death of Marriage

It gets worse. The trumpeted humanity-affirming freedoms of the modern world are far from evident. The seemingly malevolent chains of heterosexual monogamous marriage (as Jung saw it) have been exchanged for a public celebration of an individual act of mere self-expression, with no long-term commitments, buttressed by no-fault divorce.[12] Nearly half of all American marriages now end in divorce.[13] Freedom from family structures has created disappointing results, especially for children. Sociologists show that the proportion of single parents has more than tripled in American households since 1960.[14] Single mothers earn half the income of married mothers, and problems are compounded by work and family conflicts, marital instability, health problems for the entire family, and poor educational outcomes for children.

Many have given up on formal marriage with the added insecurities that follow. The Centers for Disease Control and Prevention reports that 50 percent of all women are living with a man to whom they are not married, a sharp increase from 35 percent in 1995.[15] These cohabiting couples often leave childbearing until it is too late, resulting in record levels of infertility. Since cohabitation usually does not last, many of those women with children become single mothers, needing government assistance. Medical doctor Ben Carson notes that 73 percent of African American babies are born out of wedlock; when this occurs, the educational pursuits of the mothers are terminated in most cases, and the babies often are doomed to a life of poverty and deprivation, which makes them more likely to end up in the penal or welfare systems.[16] Some observers claim we are quickly approaching the point of no return from the damages of casual sex, cohabitation, and single motherhood.[17] When there are no fathers, half-families can become entirely dependent on the state.

Historian Lawrence Stone has said, "At no time in history, with the possible exception of Imperial Rome, has the institution of marriage been more problematic than it is today."[18] As W. Bradford Wilcox has noted, "Middle Americans are on the verge of losing their connection to marriage."[19] Emotional health is in steep decline as the family collapses in North America. Suicide has now surpassed car crashes as the leading cause of death for Americans. More American soldiers died last year by suicide than in combat. One third of America's employees suffer chronic and debilitating stress.[20]

Despite the initial optimism of the "I'm Okay, You're Okay" generation of their parents, millennials face 16 percent unemployment, crushing debts for sometimes worthless degrees, a 20 trillion dollar government deficit they did not create, and oppressive taxes. To turn their fate around, millennials face the painful task of delaying their lives. In order to pay off their student loans or just to survive, marriage, children, and homes of their own will have to wait until a solid economy comes back.[21] Little wonder that nearly half of Harvard's incoming freshmen in 2013 admitted to cheating on homework, exams, or other assignments in their young academic careers. The survey by the university's student newspaper concluded that for these students, getting ahead is worth more than being honest.[22] The moral fabric of this generation is coming apart.

The Plague of Pornography

The sexual freedom Jung advocated was certainly given to young people born after the Sixties revolution. They have access to limitless sexual fantasy in free pornography, woven into the fabric of our culture. As the network of Roman roads made possible the rapid spread of the gospel in the early church, the new "roads" of the Internet are often used for evangelism, but pornography also roars down those highways at top speed, pouring pornographic content into millions of personal computers and smartphones. Internet users become entangled in the expanding web of sexual degradation. In 2012, over 43 percent of adult industry executives believed mobile devices would become consumers' primary porn-viewing and "sexting" devices. By 2015, they predicted, users of mobile adult video on tablets would triple.[23] In this age of streaming video and widespread Internet access, pornography use has become increasingly widespread—among both men and women.

A contemporary expert in the study of pornography states: "Nearly half a century after the sexual revolution of the 60s, we are still experiencing its aftershock"[24] as a result of the "sense of sexual entitlement"[25] that has come from this revolution. This expression of instant sexual gratification is a derivative of the Jungian "therapy" of liberated fantasy. In spite of Jung's and the Sixties' optimism that such fantasy would produce human maturation, it seems to have produced the opposite. Instead of freedom, sexual libertarianism has produced slavery to empty images and impersonal shells of sexuality.

The pornographic shortcut to the God-given desire for sexual intimacy has deep and binding physiological effects on the brain. Brain specialist William M. Struthers explains, "Men seem to be wired in such a way that pornography hijacks the proper functioning of their brain ... rewiring it ... and has a long-lasting effect on their thoughts and lives ... seared into the fabric of the brain."[26] Struthers notes that this addictive drug creates men whose mental life is "over-sexualized and narrowed" (and the same is true, though in different ways, for women). Such men can no longer look at women without mentally undressing them,[27] reducing women to mere sexual objects. Sexual violence thus becomes normative; scenes portrayed by the porn industry often contain forms of physical aggression against the female partner.[28] It is little wonder that pornography's effect on marriage is devastating.

Struthers feels confident that those caught within the trap of pornography are "given over to the desires of [a] twisted and depraved heart."[29] How long can such a society survive? One commentator says, "We are, admittedly, approaching the tipping point beyond which we may be powerless to prevent our implosion"[30]—I might add, especially in the area of sexuality. The immoral misuse and decline of heterosexual sex and marriage has inevitably created conditions in which many now support same-sex marriage, which represents a new definition of the human being.

The Rise of Homosexuality

In its scale and velocity, the moral revolution we are witnessing on the issue of homosexuality is without precedent in human history. We are not looking at a span of centuries or even the length of one century. This revolution has taken place within a single generation. Although one is sympathetic if constitutionally guaranteed rights are prejudicially refused to individual homosexuals, even non-Christian thinkers understand the enormous cultural repercussions of rewriting our definition of human sexuality and spirituality.

In the last chapter, we met Sixties-era sociologist Philip Rieff, who said that "the West was rapidly re-paganizing around sensuality" and that "sexual liberation was a powerful sign of Christianity's demise."[31] But he was among a small minority who saw just how liberated sexuality was becoming. Today there is no "normal" sexuality. Indeed, any attempt to say so is criminalized as discriminatory bullying.

Rod Dreher, whom we also met in the last chapter, highlights a cover story in *The Nation* in 1993, noting that if the gay-rights cause, which was then still "a small and despised sexual minority," was to survive and eventually succeed, it needed to invent for itself "a complete cosmology." Dreher continues, "[P]ut bluntly, the gay-rights cause has succeeded precisely because the Christian cosmology has dissipated in the mind of the West."[32] Charles Taylor, in his religious and cultural history *A Secular Age*, observes, "The entire ethical stance of moderns supposes and follows on from the death of God (and of course, of the meaningful cosmos)."[33] Identifying the essence of this "new" cosmology, Dreher adds: "To be modern is to believe in one's individual desires as the locus of authority and self-definition."[34] This contemporary self-definition is exactly the basis of Jungian psychological theories that touted a new humanity in the first half of the 20th century. Based on promising notions of "liberation," these theories were actually derived from a pagan understanding of existence, and their implementation has ultimately produced social and personal implosion.

Coming Apart: The Sociological Reality

In his well-documented sociological analysis titled *Coming Apart: The State of White America 1960–2010*, Harvard political scientist Charles Murray shows—without any reference to recent religious or sexual movements yet with hundreds of charts and an immense amount of quantitative data—that since the 1960s America has become deeply divided. A new lower class has all but abandoned four principles of the cultural success of America's founding—honesty, industry, marriage, and religion, which Murray calls "virtue" and on which all segments of the population once agreed. This new lower class is separated from the new upper class, "a hollow elite" that has profited from the founding values without retaining the conviction to insist upon them.

Just a few examples of losing the classic sense of virtue include:

- The Presbyterian Church (U.S.A.), in its 2014 general assembly, supported same-sex marriage and the ordination of homosexuals while turning down support for "pro-life" principles and favoring abortion (even of live babies who survive the abortion process).[35]

- The National Cathedral in Washington, DC, in a special Sunday service marking Lesbian, Gay, Bisexual, and Transgender (LGBT) Pride Month, hosted the Rev. Dr. Cameron Partridge, who was born a woman but who now identifies as a trans-man. Partridge was joined by homosexual bishop Gene Robinson.[36]

Charles Murray never seriously considers the issues of morality he raises, but his conclusion is nevertheless devastating: "All is lost. ... the American project is dead"—unless a civic "Great Awakening" takes place among the "hollow elite" to rediscover and put into practice the founding principles.[37] But if this is all we can expect, then truly all is lost. Robert Webber, in *Who Gets to Narrate the World?*,[38] agrees that "the more noble features of the [American] story—hard work, self-sacrifice, personal integrity—have given way to laziness, greed and narcissism ... a downward spiral of self-indulgence."[39]

The public interest or the common good are meaningless unless we have a common measure, an agreed-on principle of justice and a concept of human flourishing. Pragmatism can only take us so far. We need convictions about moral truth, and we no longer have them. Robert Reilly takes the issue of the loss of virtue much further. He sees recent court cases justifying same-sex marriage as "the progressive abandonment of the idea of virtue traditionally held to be necessary to a free people,"[40] in the rejection by the legal authorities of the nation of the very notion of natural law and rights bequeathed by the Creator. America, at its deepest level, has come apart.

But not only America; on a larger scale, what has come apart is the old Christian consensus. John Adams once said, to the chagrin of progressives through the ages, "Our Constitution was made only for a moral and religious people. It is wholly inadequate to the government of any other."[41] On April 9, 1967, Martin Luther King, Jr., gave a speech entitled "The Street Sweeper," in which he said:

> I'm here to tell you today that we need God. When I think about God, I know his name. "I Am" sent you. This is the God of the universe. And if you believe in him and worship him, something will happen in your life. You will smile when others around you are crying. This is the power of God.[42]

Professor Walter E. Williams of George Mason University states: "Customs, traditions, moral values and rules of etiquette, not laws and government regulations, are what make for a civilized society ... people behave themselves even if nobody's watching. Police and laws can never replace these restraints on personal conduct so as to produce a civilized society."[43]

Even self-described "Amazon feminist" Camille Paglia, speaking of the elimination of sexual distinctions, has said, "What you're seeing is how a civilization commits suicide."[44] British journalist Melanie Phillips notes that "at its most profound level it [the attack on contemporary culture] is an attack on the creed that lies at the very foundation of Western civilization."[45] And I would add that the creed is (or should be): "I believe in God the Father Almighty, Maker of Heaven and Earth."

On June 3, 1953—over 60 years ago—as a young teen, I watched Elizabeth, Queen of England, give her assent to the coronation oath administered by the Archbishop of Canterbury. The questions to which she gave an affirmative answer, under oath, read:

> Will you to the utmost of your power maintain the Laws of God and the true profession of the Gospel? Will you to the utmost of your power maintain in the United Kingdom the Protestant Reformed Religion established by law?

In July 2013, almost exactly 60 years later, Queen Elizabeth II gave her royal stamp of approval to a government law legalizing homosexual marriage. Politics oblige. Though her approval was a legal formality (and I don't intend to question the Queen's faith), the symbolism of her act is powerful. A constitutional bulwark of the Christian faith meekly surrendered, legalizing a relationship that woefully rejects the image of God in man as revealed in Genesis 1:27: "God created man in his own image ... male and female he created them." Around that time, the same decision was made in France and in New Zealand. It is hard to imagine the eventual global cultural implosion this overturning of the defining essence of human life will entail.

A leading British theologian wrote to me on April 2, 2014, as Parliament formalized same-sex marriage, with the following message:

> The Rainbow Flag flew over Whitehall this past week-end, and our Deputy Prime Minister urged us to raise a glass in celebration. *The Times* carried an article about the upcoming marriage of two women who will be known as "Mrs and Mrs". ... Romans 1:32 is now, it seems, official government policy. When the waters of Oneism that have been beating the shoreline for many years come fully in, the house on the cliff top collapses with apparent, but not real, suddenness.

Busting the Binaries

This old "Christian" world is indeed coming apart. Behind multisexual liberation is the effectively systematic promotion of ideological Oneism and the determined elimination of the binary structure of theistic Twoism, which Scripture teaches is the way the world was made. Remember—Oneism is the belief that all Is One and that the difference between the Creator and the creature must be eliminated along with all the distinctions that Creator placed in his creation. What I call Twoism is the belief that there are two kinds of existence—God, and everything else (all of which is created). These two are the only two possible religious options.

Oneists describe what seem to be civic or political issues, but which hide a deep spiritual program below the surface. Here are some of the phrases that you may already have met in public life and that describe aspects of Oneism:

- Transgressing or denying boundaries
- Denying the subject/object distinction
- Breaking taboos
- Abolishing "either/or"
- As above, so below (no distinction between the divine and the human)
- Non-duality
- Oneness—all is one

Oneists feel the necessity of obliterating the Twoist distinctions God has placed in creation, and they do it partly by using terms that evoke human rights and global oneness. The theistic view of reality is being essentially erased from public consciousness at all the crucial levels of human experience.

Destroying Spiritual Binaries

On the edges of evangelical orthodoxy, Brian McLaren—in defending an interfaith approach to religion—has stated, "We need to move beyond our deadlock, our polarization, our binary, either/or thinking."[46] Church historian Diana Butler Bass calls for a "religionless" and "creedless" Christianity,[47] announcing the arrival of an age of pure inner experience, with the godhead "defined in less dualistic terms."[48] Bass advocates praying to God as "our Mother ... the nourishing spirit of mother earth."[49]

A clear example of contemporary Oneist thinking is the refusal to use the term "evil." Professor Michael Boyle of La Salle University took to the pages of the *New York Times* to condemn any reference to ISIS or the Islamic State as "evil" or a "cancer."[50] Boyle wants to avoid the gross simplifications of moralistic language in describing the acts of jihadists who, in front of the camera, behead eight-year-old Christian girls and secular American journalists, sell captive women as sex slaves, and plan to eradicate all Christians and Jews. If that's not evil, then there is no evil—which is precisely what Oneists want. To use the term "evil" would force them to admit that some things cannot be included in the union of all things. Moral clarity has thus no place in this utopia.

Jung joined the binary of good and evil to produce a deeply relativized view of morals, allowing the individual to decide what is good or evil. Choices such as indulging in pornography or aborting a baby are relativized because there are no distinct boundaries for sexual stimulation or between a mother and her baby. Endless sexual permutations are all valid; a baby and the mother have the same needs, and all is swallowed up by the One. As the Center for American Progress puts it, "[C]hildren belong to all of us."[51]

For many today, even in evangelicalism, there is neither paradise nor the fall, neither heaven nor hell. Indeed, no one is left behind, as Rob Bell concludes in his book, *Love Wins*.[52] However, eliminating a final hell eliminates an absolute Judge, thus obliging the human race to create its own set of morals and to enforce them. This produces hell on earth. There is no ultimate justice or accountability with regard to real evil— only the values imposed by human power.[53]

Naturalistic evolution allows neither qualitative distinction between humans and animals nor the ultimate distinction between Creator and creation. Transhumanism sees the end of biological evolution in favor of the evolution of the mind, as the human and the machine are joined.[54] Scientific teams and laboratories around the world are grappling with the logistics, science, and morality of merging technology with biology. Engineering and medical students' absorption of Oneist principles is sure to affect future decisions made in this field.

Destruction of Cultural Binaries

Political correctness denies any distinctions between cultures, religions, or value systems. Thus, politically correct multiculturalism dominates the public square and the university campus and affects domestic and foreign policy. Christiana Figueres, Executive Secretary of the United Nations Framework Convention on Climate Change, opened the 2011 Cancun meeting by praying to the pagan Mayan goddess Ixchel.[55]

Destruction of the gender binary began with radical feminism's rejection of patriarchy and the ultimate patriarch, God the Father. We have moved on. "M" and "F" are being eliminated from birth certificates and passport applications, as are the terms "mother," "father," "husband," and "wife." Instead, we have "Parent A" and "Parent B." While even some evangelicals say there are no hard and fast sexual categories because we are all human beings God loves,[56] the fatherhood of God is an essential element in God's revelation of his love for creatures and is prominent in the message of Jesus.

Homosexual leaders call for deconstruction of the gender binary, and this destruction is often set in motion on college campuses, which serve as a sort of laboratory for future social life. College educators Genny Beemyn and Sue Rankin ask: "Can We Put an End to the Gender Binary?" They argue that "there is no one way a person should be."[57] On its website, Dartmouth says that it "seeks to provide a living environment welcoming to all gender identities; one not limited by the traditional gender binary."[58] Oberlin College, which was founded by two Presbyterian ministers and headed by Charles Finney, describes "transgenderism as the transgressing of gender norms ... finding a space that ... defies the binary in our society ... that you were assigned."

Signs at gay rallies say it all: "Are you a boy or a girl? No," and "Infants Rage against the Gender Binary." On November 8, 2012, the *New York Times* ran an article, "Can a Boy Wear a Skirt to School?," describing this generation as the "forward-thinking cohort" of the population, for whom "gender fluidity ... is a creative playing field." *Elle* magazine featured a model who publicly declared herself transgender. This was called "pushing the boundaries of gender roles for models." The model herself, Andreja Pejic, asks for all to understand that this massive transformation is no big deal: "My recent transition hasn't made me into a different individual. Same person, no difference at all, just a different sex ... I hope you can all understand that."[59]

Individual sexual identity is being undermined by radical feminism and LGBT principles. The binary of heterosexual marriage was severely undermined by the feminist rejection—in the name of radical equality—of marriage itself. The distinctive roles of the husband and the wife disintegrate as women are liberated from bondage to their traditional roles, and men are freed to express their more sensitive, nurturing, and feminine side. This is also clearly happening in the growing acceptance of same-sex marriage where sexual binary distinctions have been eliminated. David Kupelian observes: "In this fuzzy utopian fantasy, society was supposed to evolve into a great big happy androgynous paradise where everyone is equal to everyone else in every way."[60]

Ironically, such an approach betrays the very Oneist worldview that has tried to create a smooth-running engine for society in all areas of human life. But some are not equal; instead of utopian harmony, the wheels are coming off.

Conclusion

Charles Murray counted on a civic Great Awakening to take place among "the hollow elite" on whom he counted "to rediscover and put into practice the founding principles" based on virtue. In his book *On Character*,[61] social commentator James Q. Wilson defined virtue as "habits of moderate action; more specifically, acting with due restraint on one's impulses, due regard for the rights of others, and reasonable concern for distant consequences."[62] Today's elite has given up on those founding principles, a tradition so deeply tied to the cosmology of the binary, and are committed to a deeply spiritual civilization without God, based on the Lie. For the new to come, the old must "come apart." As in all successful revolutions, the old must be destroyed in order for the new day to arrive. In the French Revolution, heads had to roll before the new society of *liberté*, *fraternité*, and *égalité* could be realized. Thus, in the West, the destruction of the binaries and the systematic elimination of Christian influence in the public square have been a necessary prelude to the realization of a transformed, new society.

But nothing has really changed. The new is not new. Old Testament scholar John N. Oswalt, in *The Bible among the Myths*, makes an important statement about ancient paganism. In a section titled "Denial of Boundaries," he states that in the ancient world, boundaries between realms (humans and gods, gods and nature) were eliminated. All the boundary-crossing behaviors of the ancient world (such as cult prostitution, incest, and homosexuality) are not "primitive behaviors ... or unfortunate aberrations ... They are theological statements, necessary expressions of the worldview of which they are part."[63]

The new "complete cosmology" is applied to everyone. At its heart, it makes man a god, joins opposites, rejects the moral order of good and evil, and dismisses the objective reality of created human nature. Its present effect is to erode the old humanity of the (admittedly imperfect) Christian civilization, which is indeed coming apart. The new humanity, trusted to save us, is based on the Lie. To this seductive falsehood our modern culture is being given over for its inevitable undoing, both present and future.

> And since they did not see fit to acknowledge God, God *gave them* [*over*] to a debased mind to do what ought not to be done ... [for them] there will be wrath and fury. There will be tribulation and distress for every human being who does evil (Rom 1:28; 2:8–9; emphasis mine).

Already the reassuring stick figures of men and women on separate bathroom doors in public places like airports are being replaced by "gender open" signs.[64] As I write, many believe that the United States Supreme Court is about to declare same-sex marriage constitutional. The brave new world of the new humanity is at the door!

PART 2

GIVEN OVER

You can see why a bullet train can travel at 200 miles per hour once you understand the principles of physics behind its speed. All the other elements—its shape, its luxury, its lines, even its color—seem to fit once the power source has been unveiled and understood. Likewise, you understand something of the power of the spiritualist movement in our time once you reckon with the deep source of that power, as we did in part 1 of this book. We examined the engine of our culture—which, once constructed on a largely Christian consensus, has come apart through secularism, Jungian psychology, the cultural changes of the Sixties, and the appearance of Eastern religions in the West. We noted the determined effort to undermine the binary principles of a culture deeply influenced by biblical values of life-affirming differences. We admitted that such destructive thinking has, in large part, succeeded. From great optimism has come great pessimism. The old culture has come apart. It is off the rails—and who will put it back on the tracks?

We must now examine the systematic worldview that affirms wholesale the implications of what the Apostle Paul called a "debased mind" and what Robert Reilly calls a comprehensive rationalization. Reilly argues that we have reached a point of crisis:

The power of rationalization drives the culture war, gives it its particularly revolutionary character, and makes its advocates indefatigable. It may draw its energy from desperation, but it is all the more powerful for that. Since failed rationalization means self-recrimination, it must be avoided at all costs. This is why the rationalization is animated by such a lively sense of self-righteousness and outrage. ... This necessarily becomes a group effort. For them to succeed in this, everyone must accede to the rationalization. ... Since the necessity for self-justification requires the complicity of the whole culture, holdouts cannot be tolerated, because they are potential rebukes.[69]

Although we situate this problematic worldview in ideological thinking, ideology always affects behavior. The subject is vast, requiring a major study on its own, but we note, if only in passing, the fact and depth of the "rationalization" described by Reilly. The human being is made up of mind, body, and spirit, which are inextricably intertwined. The articulation of a pagan cosmology is necessarily accompanied by a significant change at the deep level of sexual behavior, which becomes engraved on the functioning of the brain.

The above is just one example of how our culture is being "given over" (Rom 1:24) to a cosmology that justifies all actions, answers all probing questions, and silences all objections. Willful moral defiance is a woeful expression of rebellion against God the Creator and will receive his judgment. This culture has created a wholesale rationale for disobedience in a systematic and coherent exposition of the Lie and has drawn close to the logical end of rebellion. It is surely the time of Romans 1:32: "Though they know God's righteous decree that those who practice such things deserve to die, they not only do them but give approval to those who practice them" (Rom 1:32).

CHAPTER 7

A COSMOLOGY OF RADICAL EGALITARIANISM

A New Wisdom Tradition?

In chapter 6, we saw Charles Murray's hope in the appearance of a "Great Awakening" of the American spirit to return American culture to the virtues of its founders, and we noted an attempt to undermine the culture by a programmatic destruction of the binaries. Tony Schwartz, researching various New Age groups, uncovered a different kind of awakening, a liberating rejection of the original founding virtues, a new vision based on pagan spirituality. Schwarz triumphantly announced his discovery of what he called an "emerging American wisdom tradition" that would save humanity.[1]

How odd! America was once a sender of missionaries spreading the Truth of the Christian gospel in the modern world. But we now see the awakening of a potent, virulent, and consistent Oneist cosmology. America has become the creator and incubator of a worldview that joins

Eastern spirituality with Western pragmatism. It is promoted as a new wisdom tradition of Western shamans for the salvation of the entire planet. Christian believers must understand the systematic character of this wisdom tradition, both in order to speak the gospel clearly to it and also to avoid subtle temptations to compromise.

To thrive, the church needs to identify current pagan influence and understand this movement's deliberate plans for a systematic reprogramming of the 21st-century Western mind. The Christian world needs such insight if it is ever to wake the sleeping giant of Christian orthodoxy.

Powerful pagan worldviews are not new. One writer says of ancient Babylon: "Babylonians made pagan religions fashionable ... they incorporated art, drama, and music into religion until the pagan ideas were attractively represented as the highest expressions of their culture."[2] The glory of pagan Rome had the same effect. One is reminded of the hilarious conversation between two Jewish freedom fighters against the Roman occupation of Palestine in Monty Python's The Life of Brian: One freedom fighter asks, "All right, but apart from the sanitation, medicine, education, wine, public order, irrigation, roads, the fresh water system and public health, what have the Romans ever done for us?" A voice from the crowd shouts: "Brought peace?" The freedom fighter replies: "Oh, peace, shut up!"[3]

It is true, the Pax Romana of imperial Rome brought peace, and its provision of panis et circensis ("bread and circuses") was an attractive combination—unless you were a slave, a Jewish freedom fighter, or a Christian. A new global empire of peace and prosperity is the seductive promise we are offered, not just for individual mystical experiences but for a redefinition of life on a peaceful, unified planet. Hindu guru Deepak Chopra is offering a million dollars to any skeptic who can disprove the reality of the spirituality found in the "world's wisdom traditions" which are, he claims, "just as precious as science."[4] Here, the new spirituality and serious science are proposed as two equally important areas for the human experience of liberation, neatly packaged in a totalizing pagan cosmology.

The New Age Grows Up

In the Sixties, during the postmodern deconstruction of secular human-ism, an odd spiritual phenomenon with no real precedents in Western history arose, calling itself "the New Age." A stream of Eastern spiri-tuality merged with a brook of Western esoterism (the search for the true divine self) to become, in a few short years, a flood engulfing what had been for over two centuries a historically theistic/Twoistic culture. During that period, the Beatles went East and the gurus came West, while Shirley MacLaine became a "god" on primetime TV. Conservative Christian apologists in the 1980s and 1990s were greatly concerned by the appearance of this unusual spirituality but called it the latest reli-gious cult, which would doubtless go the way of all spiritual novelties. They were wrong, as I attempted to show in my first English book,[5] *The Gnostic Empire Strikes Back.*[6]

Philosopher Steve Bruce was also wrong when, in 2002, he pre-dicted its demise;[7] he saw New Age spirituality as a "shallow ... diffuse religion ... with little social impact." In the same way, sociologist Paul Heelas characterized the New Age as "self-spirituality ... that lacks the typically secular grounding in critical enquiry."[8] Christopher Partridge dismissed this spirituality as an exotic egotistical focus on the spiri-tual well-being of the self, pointedly asking in 2004: "[W]here are the New Age schools, nurseries, communes, colleges, ecological housing as-sociations, subsistence farming centers, criminal resettlement houses, women's refuges, practical anti-racism projects and urban renewal pro-grams?"[9] Strangely, while the term "New Age" has virtually disappeared, the reality has not. Why?

First, the marginal New Age movement went mainstream, reappear-ing behind today's spiritual mantra, "I'm spiritual but not religious." Those who say this reject formalized expressions of religion for inner enlightenment, precisely what the New Agers had already done. Many now adopt practical, seemingly harmless routes to spirituality: holis-tic health, yoga, and such stress reduction techniques as mindfulness meditation.[10] For many, the interest does not rise above issues of prag-matic usefulness.

Second, *the* New Age has begun to grow up, developing into a search for something beyond personal individualistic enlightenment. Andrew Cohen, a New Age pioneer, sees a change in contemporary spirituality:

> This shift from narcissism to humility to big Self is, and always has been, the journey of the mystic and the realizer. The bigger our self becomes after we've transcended the crippling effects of narcissism, the more powerfully and creatively we will be able to live our precious human lives. Because we've gotten over our small selves, we will be living for a higher purpose. And that's what changes everything.[11]

The new spirituality movement has become a full-orbed worldview with its eye on a future transformed humanity. This second version of the New Age—the creation of a cosmology to explain everything—deserves our full attention. Remember the story in *The Nation* that noted if the gay rights cause (then "a small and despised sexual minority") was to succeed, it would need to invent "a complete cosmology"?[12] It did, and "succeeded precisely because the Christian cosmology has dissipated in the mind of the West."[13] In 1977 June Singer spoke of the necessity to keep alive her friend Carl Jung's vision of a "new humanism":

> What lies in store as we move towards the longed-for conjunction of the opposites ... [is the question,] can the human psyche realize its own creative potential through *building its own cosmology* and *supplying it with its own gods?*[14]

Serious attention is being given to building out this holistic view of existence. Significantly, the term "cosmology" also appears in the work of a disciple of Thomas Berry, Mary Evelyn Tucker, a professor who intended to introduce a systematic pagan vision into her environmental work at the United Nations. As part of the drafting committee of the Earth Charter, a document the United Nations hopes will determine future life on the planet, she repeats the same earth-shaking theme, saying that the solution lies in developing "a new cosmology."[15] She was seeking to develop her mentor's goal of "solutions ... comprehensive enough ... to support a new pattern of human presence on the planet ... our great work."[16]

A Pagan Cosmology for All

I insist on the term "cosmology" because seemingly unrelated elements in modern culture are actually held together as organic elements of a coherent worldview. Indeed, the development of a full-scale pagan cosmology represents the second birth of the New Age, now devoted to the "great work" of a clear articulation of paganism. Instrumental in that new birth is philosopher Ken Wilber.

Deepak Chopra calls Wilber one of the most important pioneers in the field of consciousness in this century. Robert Kegan, of the Harvard Graduate School of Education, considers him a national treasure, and Emergent Church leaders like Rob Bell and Brian McLaren are avid Wilber supporters. Ken Wilber, reared in a conservative Christian church and now a major proponent of Buddhist mysticism, proposes, as the title of his book indicates, *A Theory of Everything*.[17] Clearly, Wilber is not limiting his search to New Age seminars, sweat lodge trances, or hypnosis sessions, intended for personal spiritual growth. His vision is a far-reaching cosmology:

> ...to include matter, body, mind, soul and spirit as they
> appear in self, culture and nature: a vision that attempts
> to be comprehensive, balanced and inclusive ... that em-
> braces science, art, and morals; that equally includes
> disciplines from physics to spirituality, biology to aes-
> thetics, sociology to contemplative prayer; that shows
> up in integral politics, integral medicine, integral busi-
> ness, integral spirituality.[18]

Here, in nascent form, are all the elements—"schools, nurseries, communes, colleges, ecological housing associations, subsistence farming centers, etc."—that Partridge found lacking in the first iteration of the New Age. In this full cosmological embrace, Wilber dismisses the postmodern rejection of "metanarratives" as "so yesterday" and fallaciously self-referential.[19] His book title indicates his intention to approach all thinking from an "integral vision," joining everything, including all the opposites, based on Buddhist understanding of Oneism. Wilber speaks of "a strong desire around the world to find a more balanced and comprehensive integral politics."[20] His integral paradigm has been used at the World Economic Forum at Davos, Switzerland, as well as at the United Nations and at the United Nations Children's Fund (UNICEF). There are also many Integral institutes—Integral Business, Integral Medicine, Integral Education, Integral Yoga, or Integral Psychology. Wilber is determined to create a functioning, totalizing worldview that will eliminate once and for all the voice of Twoism in the culture.

Am I exaggerating? Actually, in 2000, I observed this innately religious pagan utopianism in the making. I attended a weekend conference in Berkeley titled, "Transforming World Views for the Planetary Era," organized by the California Institute of Integral Studies, honoring Thomas Berry and his book *The Great Work*, conceived under the dominant influence of Carl Jung.[21] How interesting—"worldviews" and "cosmology" in our postmodern era, the era that was going to end all worldviews and metanarratives? Some of the speakers had already helped integrate their ideas into the Earth Charter, mentioned above.

I again saw evidence of this new-looking spirituality in a 2011 online forum called "Beyond Awakening: The Future of Spiritual Practice." I realized immediately that "beyond awakening" could also be stated as "beyond personal experiences of enlightenment." Within a few weeks, this forum had enrolled 35,000 participants. Hailed as "the most important conversation for the planet today," the program consisted of interviews with early prophets of the New Age—Jean Houston, Barbara Marx Hubbard, Surya Das, Ram Dass, and Michael Murphy—along with younger players like Ken Wilber. "Beyond Awakening" intends to create a functioning world community in which, no doubt, a very spiritual, pagan Caesar will rule as lord.

Such visionaries are present at many global meetings and organizations and have increasing influence among the world's cultural and political leaders. Today's second-generation spiritualists call themselves "cultural creatives," "progressives," "brights," or "integral spiritualists." The webcast claimed a following of 50 million cultural creatives in the United States and 80–90 million in the European Union who plan, with their well-defined blueprint for the "new human," to take over US and Western culture by AD 2020. Essential to this takeover is worldview, which, because of its breadth, can silence objectors and make falsehood look perfectly acceptable.

A Cosmology of Liberated Politics

Modern "Purificationism"

Secular sociologist Ernest Sternberg recognizes the importance of this growing cultural movement, calling it "world purificationism."[22] As a specialist in urban planning and disaster preparedness at the University at Buffalo, Sternberg focuses entirely on the sociological and political aspects of what he sees as a powerfully world-transforming movement. He concludes that "[w]e are in the midst of the worldwide rise of a non-religious chiliastic [apocalyptic] movement, preaching global human renewal and predicting apocalypse as its woeful alternative."[23]

World purificationism, according to Sternberg, is a vast alliance of social movements that look ahead to a new era of social justice and sustainable development, in which diverse cultures will end discrimination and harmoniously share the earth. Predicting a government of grassroots organizations, purer than past democracies, the movement has a decidedly globalist vision: "As old nation-state boundaries fade away, communities will coordinate with each other globally by means of rectification cadres called non-governmental organizations."[24] As an example of the movement's power, Sternberg cites the World Social Forum, which met in January 2009 in Belém, Brazil, and hosted 113,000 participants from 114 countries, representing 5,800 organizations, with 2,500 journalists in attendance.

Sternberg himself does not buy into world purificationism—calling it a myth comparable to the "new man" of old Marxism. The modern myth believes that "it is possible now, amid present corruption and degradation, to build a glorious New Rome."[25] Sternberg speculates that current utopian ideology will become a new totalitarian system whose current enemy is the toxic empire of declining Western Christian civilization.[26]

This contemporary movement has roots in modernism. The purificationist view of the future is committed to a view of the state that can produce an earthly utopia. If the old empire viewed both the human be-ing and the state as fallen and flawed (needing limits and controls), the new vision sees the human being and human institutions as perfectible. It counts on political power as the means of utopian social transforma-tion. The goal is to continue the process of collectivist transformations, begun with 19th-century Marxism, to arrive at the equal distribution of all things human—though, as Orwell wrote, "some are more equal than others."

However, the new left has long included the erotic as well as the eco-nomic, and liberation embraces both the social and the psychological.

Political Liberation and Psychological Liberation

In the 20th century, the Frankfurt School and thinkers such as Antonio Gramsci, Herbert Marcuse, and Saul Alinsky promoted a revised version of 19th-century Marxist liberation in Western Europe and the United States. These men took Marxist analysis through its logical next steps.

Gramsci was one of the most important Marxist thinkers of the 20th century and a key thinker in Western Marxism. Gramsci advocated forming workers' councils and refused violent revolution, urging his fellow Marxists to establish "ideological hegemony" by stealth—staging a "long march through the institutions" such as the news media, aca-demia, and political parties. He believed a Marxist revolution could be achieved peacefully by getting people to think and act in Marxist terms without the labels. The state would then become Marxist through the democratic process. His ideas deeply influenced Marcuse and Alinsky.

By the Sixties, Herbert Marcuse had become an American citizen and sought to redefine Marxism for the new world. He believed that the new levels of economic and social freedom achieved by modern-day capitalism had hypnotized "the worker" into "voluntary servitude" and self-imposed ignorance. As already noted, Marcuse, following Jung and Freud, called for "polymorphous sexuality" and the activation of "repressed or arrested organic, biological needs,"[27] what he called "life instincts."[28] This new Marxism sought to transform not only the work-ing conditions of the disenfranchised but the imprisonment of the human psyche in the chains of divinely-created cosmic structures.

Though they may remain largely unnoticed for the moment, contemporary hard-left progressive Americans have the political and cultural wind in their sails. "We are the Underminers, and this is our time," declare the radicals who are working to "remake America" into a "new society."[29] Here is the important definition of their immediate goals: "To undermine something is to weaken its very foundation in order to bring about its eventual collapse."[30]

The guiding book of this new movement is *Imagine: Living in a Socialist USA*,[31] hailed by the author of *Marxism in the United States*, Paul Buhle,[32] as "the best, most insightful, and most lively work on socialism to appear in a long time."[33] Among the authors is Frances Fox Piven, a prominent theorist of both socialism and community organizing. In the 1960s, with Richard Cloward, she devised a plan to provoke chaos by deliberately overwhelming governmental systems to the point of collapse, paving the way for state intervention and an eventual collectivist system.

Piven was a former mentor to the young Barack Obama,[34] and, later, his professor at Columbia University. With him, she was a member of Chicago's "socialist" New Party, which closely followed the playbook of neo-Marxist Saul Alinsky by deliberately avoiding revolutionary buzz words.[35] *Imagine* states clearly that socialism is not just an economic program for income redistribution but a social agenda of radical egalitarianism.[36] This version of neo-Marxism, which carefully avoids the very term, is "neo" because it goes beyond the anticapitalist liberation of the worker, which it still includes, to a liberation of the psyche and of sexual fantasies. It is a cosmology, and thus it includes views on sexuality, which, it states quite openly, is a wholesale program of human "identity politics."[37]

> ...our conception of socialism is not limited to restructuring work and economic activity. It embraces altering the full range of social, cultural, political and familial structures and power relations ... all the institutional forces that affect our lives.[38]

David Horowitz was the son of Jewish Communist party members, and, as a committed Marxist at Berkeley in the Sixties, he nevertheless saw how the violent means employed by the radicals had failed to produce revolution. With the purity of radicals, "we in the 1960s didn't want to pretend to be democrats ... That's why we failed ... That's why [present Marxists] have succeeded now."[39] He observes that the contemporary new left had learned the "technique of stealth," due in large part to the influential teachings of Saul Alinsky, a deeply committed Marxist from Chicago and an expert in camouflage and linguistic deception.

A Cosmology of Nature Worship

Care for the environment is good and necessary, but it can also serve as an occasion for the extension of radical utopian thinking. Environmentalist Paul Hawken, in Blessed Unrest, claims there are at least one million, possibly two million, environmental organizations,[40] which constitute "the largest social movement in all of human history,"[41] largely backed by the millennial generation. What is the ideological nature of this "largest social movement"? It tends towards collectivist political solutions, and its religious inspiration is the worship of nature.[42] Hawken affirms that the heart and soul of the environmentalist movement is spiritual—and not just any spirituality; it is "indigenous culture and native spiritual practices"[43] plus Buddhist ideas that eliminate the concept of external divine authority and "rigid categories."[44] This replaces biblical revelation with classic Oneism. The stealth approach seems to have succeeded in bringing many unsuspecting members from the rising generation into the new cosmology.

The ecospiritual agenda is introduced on campus through "sustainability," which is now defined more broadly than ecology to include elements of a multicultural sustainability of pansexuality, socialism, and interfaith. Life will only be sustainable when we are all one and all distinctions are eliminated.

Cooperation undoubtedly merges into religious syncretism for the vast body of youthful converts already introduced to the nature-worshiping spirituality of contemporary deep ecology—what is called, you remember, the perennial philosophy,[45] which will save the earth. Aging New Agers, now the cultural creatives, have a motivation that outstrips the Sixties discovery of "enlightenment" and now exhort their followers to total dedication. Andrew Cohen, founder of EnlightenNext magazine and an important mover and shaker in the transformation of conscious-ness movement, has said:

> When we begin on the spiritual path, more often than not, it's all about ourselves. But if we stick with it, eventually we cross a threshold where ... we come to recognize that our own development has always only been for the sake of the evolution of consciousness ... That's where I be-lieve a new moral context is going to come from.[46]

This new resolve for personal mysticism, collective social justice, and egalitarian politics is, perhaps, the beginning of a new, all-encom-passing seductive religious vision. Utopia will elude humans because sin inevitably causes dystopia,[47] but our God-given yearning for utopia can never be erased, and we will try in our own strength to give it one more chance.

A Cosmology of Comprehensive Sexual Liberation

In the contemporary push for a classless egalitarian society in which all privilege must be cast aside, gender distinction is the final bulwark of difference and thus must be eradicated. Since the worldview we are examining has pagan roots, it will naturally idealize homosexuality, as pagan tradition has always done.

Homosexuality is now the defining issue for a general program of human transformation into a Oneist reality. First presented as civil rights issue, this seemingly noble request hid the intent to challenge and change the presumption of heteronormativity and thus to redefine the very notion of sexuality for everyone. As noted in chapter 5, the 1970 Gay Revolution Party manifesto said, "The gay revolution will produce a world in which all social and sensual relationships will be gay and in which homo- and heterosexuality will be incomprehensible terms."

From a Twoist understanding of life, one can readily see that the vari-ous aspects of this pagan cosmology complement one another as aspects of the same worldview. If socialism is not just an economic program for income redistribution but a social agenda of radical egalitarianism, we will see the following changes as the program progresses:

- traditional norms of male and female will be things of the past;
- LGBTQ people will have the same access to "all cultural, social, political, and economic structures"; and
- marriage will be for all, with no special privileges attached to it.

This sexual agenda is an essential element of an apocalyptic transformation of human society and a utopian remaking of human identity in which all binary distinctions and all "-isms" (e.g. classicism, racism, sexism, machismoism, heterosexism, and ageism) have been eliminated, and in which all sexual expressions are normal. At the highest state level, in July 2014, President Obama signed an executive order legitimizing the sexual preferences all federal workers who claim to be LGBT. There is no reason to think that this list will not grow or that these four categories are superior to the expanded list, LGBTQQIAAP.[48] Indeed, there seems to be no reason to limit further expansion from including pedophilia, zoophilia (bestiality), and all forms of sexual sadism—all in the name of civil rights.

In 1997, gay activist Paula Ettelbrick clearly outlined the aims of the gay movement: "Being queer is more than sleeping with a person of the same gender ... it means transforming the very fabric of our society ... the goal [is] radically reordering society's view of family."[49]

A Cosmology of Complete Egalitarianism

The push for homosexual rights is not a concession we throw to a tiny percentage of our population in a compromise that will bring no real harm to society. Pushed with ethical fervor through appeals to anti-discrimination, equal rights, equality legislation, and the checking of privilege, this social movement deconstructs foundational social concepts like the family, gender, and social achievement. There's no "live and let live" when faced with advocates of this agenda. The Employment Non-Discrimination Act, which demands that homosexuality be treated as a normal lifestyle choice, would federalize civil litigation against Christians and threaten every person who lives in a God-honoring way with expensive civil rights lawsuits. Advocates of the cosmology we are discussing will push until the government imposes coercive sanctions on anyone who fails to affirm the moral goodness of gay unions.

The American mind, naturally sensitive to racism because of the North American history of slavery, responds to the contemporary rallying cry for equality by bringing white privilege to an end and denouncing "sustainable racism."[50] But racism is immediately associated with the religion of the white founders of America, Christianity. The progressives understand that the depth and power of traditional Christian culture must be undermined and eliminated if total equality is to be achieved. Progressive author Paul Kivel describes the old culture as a Christian hegemony, that is, "the everyday, pervasive, deep-seated, and institutionalized dominance of Christian values, Christian institutions, leaders, and Christians as a group, primarily for the benefit of Christian ruling elites."[51] From this perspective, same-sex marriage is an issue of critical political and ideological importance.

Thus the Constitution is labeled as a male document of white privilege, the evil incubator of capitalism and heteronormativity. This anti-Constitution ideology becomes the spearhead of future social justice in a coming classless society, in which all forms of privilege—racial, sexual, social, religious, and economic—will ultimately be eliminated.[52] Interestingly, Alinsky taught "that the task of the radical is to turn middle class people against themselves, to make them instruments of their own destruction."[53] This is the final form of multiculturalism by which the Constitution will be demonized and eventually changed via the euphemistic process known as progressive constitutionalism. According to this approach, the Constitution is a dynamic document in need of interpretation in the light of the progressive tradition.[54]

We begin to see why the progressive vision is so radical. An indication of how far this leveling could go is shown by the complaint by Ivy League students against the Dartmouth College administration for its institutional and structural "micro-aggression" and violence. They denounced its "racist, classist, sexist, heterosexist, transphobic, xenophobic, and ableist structures" and called "for more 'womyn' and people of color [on the] faculty; covering sex change operations on the college health plan; censoring the library catalog for offensive terms; and installing 'gender-neutral bathrooms' in every campus facility, specifically including sports locker rooms," all in the name of equality.[55]

Spiritual Implications

This utopian vision has a long spiritual history. The ideal of the alchemists of the Middle Ages involved "the uniting of opposites ... the fusion
of male and female, good and evil, life and death—whose union, they
believed, eventually creates the perfected and completed, ideal personality called Self."[56] The utopian cosmology in question understands how
deeply the Christian faith has molded Western culture and intends to
destroy the "bourgeois" Judaeo-Christian culture as the first step toward a better world. To accomplish this, its advocates must weaken the
culture systematically in its economy, its military, its psychology, and
its morals. They also know what it will take to establish a revived pagan
cosmology and will not tolerate half measures. They want all or nothing.
The goal is the complete remaking of human identity.[57]

We cannot see into the future to know if the agenda will succeed, but
we need to face squarely the movement that is attempting to wrest our
culture from its tenuous grip on Twoist principles. At this point, such a
powerful cosmology takes on an unmistakably religious character. One
is reminded of the goal of the occult Hermetic Order of the Golden Dawn,
already quoted in chapter 4: "The Great Work is, before all things, the
creation of man by himself, that is to say, the full and entire conquest
of his faculties and his future; it is especially the perfect emancipation
of his will."[58]

Sternberg's analysis of "world purificationists" is right but does not
go far enough. Like Murray's sociological analysis mentioned in chapter 6, it fails to capture the true power of the movement: its possession
of a new liberating cosmology, including not just politics and economics but sexuality and spirituality. The sociological analysis, joined to the
ideology of revolutionary sexual and spiritual liberation, forms a powerfully influential movement, determined to reinvent the world. Indeed,
as politics becomes more all-inclusive, it becomes more religious, claiming to answer all human aspirations, physical and spiritual, and to usher
in a better world.

To articulate an effective Christian response, a full understanding of
what lies in store is essential. The era that such thinking introduces into
Western history is no longer simply post-Christian or postmodern, but
goes by another, surprising name—postsecular.

CHAPTER 8

PAGAN COSMOLOGY OF SYNTHESIS: THE JOINING OF REASON AND SPIRIT

Every good story has a happy ending. The coming era, which is upon us, is neither post-Christian nor postmodern, but postsecular. This new day in spirituality involves "a renewed openness to questions of the spirit while retaining the secular habits of critical thought."[1] It signals the end of materialistic secular humanism and a final synthesis of mind and spirit in a cultural affirmation of Oneist untruth.

We are facing the establishment of a worldview that seeks to banish as an outmoded intellectual and spiritual superstition the worldview that created Western civilization. After decades of undermining the West's Christian heritage, the new utopian, totalitarian vision, empowered by a sense of historical destiny, is using selective tolerance to make it obvious that in the future there will only be one way or the highway.

The Great Synthesis: Spirituality and Science

In 2009, Mike King, a one-time research fellow at London Metropolitan University, published a book with an intriguing title, *Postsecularism: The Hidden Challenge to Extremism*,[2] in which he outlines the major features of a new way of thinking.[3] Postsecularism, he argues, traces a middle path of wisdom between two now-defunct ways of living and thinking. King seeks to show that postsecularism "does not accept that reason must rule out religion," but, like all self-respecting multiculturalists, he opposes religious extremism. By "religious extremism" he means either extremist theism ("the old religion" of the Bible, which is dismissed as "superstition") or extremist atheism (which is dismissed as the self-assured dogmatic rationalism). King confirms:

1. The demise of secular humanism
2. The retreat of Christianity as a major cultural force
3. The explosion of spiritualism

In other words, the postsecular era can claim to be on the right side of history in representing the triumph of a pagan cosmology over both materialistic secular humanism and biblical faith. It opts for a spiritual cocktail of ingredients, from the religious left to the new science to mature New Age spirituality and deepening mysticism.[4] This is the kind of thinking endorsed by the Dalai Lama, who calls for a rediscovery of spirituality "beyond religion" and for the convergence of spirituality and science.[5] Spiritual mythology (of a decidedly non-Christian bent) is now considered a valid field of exploration for formerly critical intellectual secular humanists. Richard Tarnas seeks to engage the allegiance of the old rationalists by describing this new intellectual openness to spirituality as the high point of human evolution—the moment when "the human intellect is ... reaching a highly critical stage of transfiguration ... as an authentic expression of nature's unfolding."[6]

Jung's Influence

For this contemporary synthesis between intellect and spirit, Jung rises from his grave. His psychological and scientific theories of the unconscious are crucial to this new construction, seen as the essential bridge into the postsecular era. Tarnas observes:

> Indeed the modern psyche appeared to require the ser-
> vices of [Jungian] depth psychology with increasing
> urgency, as a profound sense of spiritual alienation and
> other symptoms of social and psychological distress be-
> came more widespread. With the traditional religious
> perspectives no longer offering effective solace, depth
> psychology itself, along with its numerous offspring,
> took on characteristics of a religion—a new faith for
> modern man, a path for the healing of the soul bringing
> regeneration and rebirth, epiphanies of sudden insight
> and spiritual conversion.[7]

By "traditional religious perspectives," Tarnas means Christianity. For him, Jungian depth psychology opens the possibility of a new synthesis which will include the old scientific methodology, now "strengthened and often stimulated by the reemergence of and widespread interest in various archaic and mystical conceptions of nature."[8] Tarnas leaves no doubt as to what will be included in the new synthesis: "Platonic and Pre-Socratic philosophy, Hermeticism, mythology, the mystery religions" ... Buddhis[m] and Hindu[ism] ... Gnosticism and the major esoteric traditions ... Neolithic European and Native American spiri-tual traditions—all gathering now on the intellectual stage as if for some kind of climatic synthesis."[9] Note the total absence of any mention of re-ligious Twoism.

This is happening even in mainline churches. Justifying the holding of an Islamic prayer service in the National Cathedral in Washington, DC, on November 14, 2014, Cathedral Dean Rev. Gary Hall characterized the biblical views of God and Jesus as "extremist Christianity," stating: "I have much more in common with progressive Jews, Muslims, Hindus and Buddhists than I do with certain people in my own tradition, with fundamentalist Christians."[10] Mike King also explicitly underlines the postsecular dependence on Jung by using the example of transpersonal psychologist Stanislav Grof, a postsecularist who journeyed from athe-ism, scientism, Marxism, and Freudianism into spirituality via the psychology of Carl Jung.[11] Because his spirituality is claimed to be scientific, Jung becomes an essential factor in the postsecular merging of the old enemies of science and spirituality.[12] Again, with postsecularism, we see the emerging parameters of the new human openly embracing Eastern spirituality as scientific truth (a subject to be discussed in the following chapter).

Grof shows the flawed logic of the secular mind. He speaks with indignation against the "current contemptuous dismissal" by secularism (what he rightly calls "monistic materialism"[13]) of spiritual, paranormal states, which he describes as a "sense of numinosity" belonging to "a superior order of reality." He believes that such states are "objectively" or "directly experienced" and thus rationally demonstrated.[14] Today some intellectuals call for a rediscovery of additional ways of knowing, in order to engage with the mystery of the universe.[15] The human mind has more cards than it has been playing in the past and needs to seek these equally valid, spiritual ways of knowing.[16]

It must be said, as we noted above, that both Jung and certain contemporary Jungians were forced to admit the extrascientific character of Jungian theory. Remember that Jung said his work did not finally "allow for scientific proof" because it was "beyond science."[17] In the *Red Book* he stated that the experiences of paranormal phenomena (the occult) represent the "most important time of my life. ... Everything later was merely the outer classification, the scientific elaboration, and the integration into life."[18] So the postsecular intellectuals will be "scientists" like Jung.

Science Meets Spirituality

The new science[19] is a perfect opening for the new spirituality. Quantum physics, with its disorienting notions found in the subatomic world of quantum indeterminacy, quantum holism, and quantum nonlocality, do not exactly fit the Enlightenment rationalist project,[20] with its outdated image of a "clockwork universe" and of "man as machine." In quantum physics, it is believed that the human being unconsciously helps run the machine, "joyously co-extensive with and co-creator of the cosmos."[21] Physicist Fritjof Capra argues that science proves that "living nature is mindful and intelligent."[22] Thus there is no need of the old creationist notion of a specially created universe "with overall design or purpose."[23] Another physicist, Amit Goswami, argues in *The Self-Aware Universe* that "science proves the potency of monistic philosophy over dualism—over spirit separated from matter."[24]

According to astrophysicist Dr. Frank Stootman, Heisenberg and Schrödinger (both Nobel Prize-winning fathers of quantum mechanics) were inclined to understand quantum mechanics through a more Eastern metaphysical worldview. Along with many of their contemporaries, Schrödinger "expresse[d] a belief in the Hindu Vedanta," and Heisenberg believed in "a central order, or One, to which all religions pointed."[25] According to Stootman, however, they interpreted quantum mechanics using Eastern mysticism rather than objective science. He argues that the difficulties in giving adequate expression to quantum reality rather "seem to imply a limitation of knowledge and of reductionism as a philosophy rather than offering ultimate support for the veracity of monism."[26]

Nevertheless, such difficulties have made possible the joining of science and spirit as the essence of postsecularism. "Science," says Stootman, "has recently moved comfortably into monism with the rise of the new Romanticism."[27] This joining has seen a further recent transformation, which is part of the postsecular era, namely, "the evolutionization of spirituality." This is the perfect expression of the postsecular—evolution as "true science, blended with deep spirituality ... a spiritual new worldview that can meet the demands of the twenty-first century,"[28] based on "fact,"[29] evolving toward ultimate Oneism for some kind of final synthesis. Western romanticism and Eastern mysticism are rejuvenated by evolutionary science; optimism is evident.[30]

At the Berkeley conference I mentioned in chapter 5, the roster of speakers included Richard Tarnas, whose book *The Passion of the Western Mind* is read in the history and philosophy departments of many Western universities. John Sculley, former CEO and Chairman of Apple computers, states that Tarnas's work is "[p]owerful ... will serve us well into the next millennium."[31] Tarnas believes we have reached a pivotal breaking point in the development of Western culture so that the future of the planet and the future of the human spirit now hang in the balance.

The intelligence and deep spirituality of the modern human must finally come together—here again are the alternatives—rejecting both theism and atheism to embrace postsecular pantheism. Human history is culminating in a great synthesis of the two tendencies of Western history: the autonomous mind of scientism and the wild spirit of the Romantics (the spiritualists). According to this account, Christianity will disappear from history. This immense thesis culminates in a breathless final description of our source and destination: "[T]he deepest passion of the Western mind has been to reunite with the ground of its being" (the birthing womb of Mother Nature). In this final synthesis, theism has been completely eliminated.

The collective psyche seems to be in the grip of a powerful archetypal dynamic in which the long-alienated modern mind is breaking through, out of the contractions of its birth process, out of what Blake called its "mind-forg'd manacles,"[32] to rediscover its intimate relationship with nature and the larger cosmos.[33] Richard Tarnas senses the arrival of a "powerful crescendo"[34] as "many movements *gather now on the intellectual stage as if for some kind of climactic synthesis.*"[35] This marriage of the Western mind and the Eastern animistic spirit is the very essence of much postsecular spirituality. It constitutes the ultimate union of the rational with the mythical, the normal with the paranormal, the material with the immaterial, the human with the divine.

The New Pantheism and Secular Atheism—Blood Brothers

Is this marriage plausible? Physicist Steven Hawking—like Einstein—has identified God with the laws of nature. Einstein himself endorsed the god of Spinoza, a 17th-century Jewish philosopher/scientist who believed in pantheistic Oneism.[36] Sam Harris, who, in *The End of Faith*, excoriates organized religion as dangerous and absurd, has said, "We need a positive statement of ... spiritual experience ... [though without] any endorsement of divisive superstitions."[37]

This deep connection between secular humanism and pagan spirituality is further demonstrated by the ideas of Mitchell Silver, an atheistic philosopher who teaches at the University of Massachusetts Boston. In his book *A Plausible God*,[38] Silver sees a profound compatibility between these two systems. He examines classic atheism and the "new" Jewish spirituality as expressed in various mystical techniques such as Kabbalah. Silver argues that secular atheists and new spiritual believers are two groups of moderns who accept the same literal description of reality. The new god of modern spirituality (based on ancient pagan spirituality) "is so thoroughly naturalistic that a godless nature can be expected to perform about as well as a godly one."[39] Both are equally plausible because, essentially, they describe the same thing—nature—using different terminology. He concludes, "When the messiah arrives (or after the revolution), there will be those singing god's praises and others whistling a secular song, and neither need be out of tune."[40]

As Silver shows, the synthesis is eminently possible—not just between secularists and spiritualists but between all the religions and large portions of the church—by jumping on the trains of interfaith and interspirituality. According to Jung, Jesus, Mani, Buddha, and Lao-Tse would all be singing "god's praises" as "pillars of the spirit." As Jung said, "I could give none preference over the other."[41]

So the postsecular era is also the interspiritual age. Roman Catholic mystic and monk Wayne Teasdale predicted a coming synthesis that would include the churches: "We are at the dawn of a new consciousness, a radically fresh approach to our life as the human family in a fragile world ... Perhaps the best name for this new segment of historical experience is the Interspiritual Age."[42] The ecumenical movement was first an attempt to draw Christian denominations together for fellowship and world evangelism. It then began to engage in interfaith conversations with other religions for the sake of understanding. It next moved into interfaith pluralism, celebrating common beliefs between all the religions. Now mainline churches and leading non-Christian religions engage in spiritual communion, celebrating the Interspiritual Age.

The Coming Interspiritual Age, a collection of essays in honor of Wayne Teasdale,[43] celebrates his prediction that "spirituality would become the global spiritual view of our era, [since] ... the real religion of humankind can be said to be spirituality itself ... A planet-wide enlightened culture."[44] Many mainline Christian churches have adopted this vision, discovering the power of this new pagan cosmology—including the practice of Oneist spirituality, utopian globalism, relativized morality, and liberated sexuality.[45] In many cases, these "churches" show no sign of following the biblical Twoist cosmology, instead jumping onto the Oneist train. They constitute a kind of pagan Trojan Horse in the larger Christian movement.

This rising spiritual cosmology includes churches as it seeks to take the whole of existence into account. According to Andrew Cohen:

> It's urgent that we begin to define a new moral, philo-
> sophical, and spiritual context that will ... embrace
> the multidimensional nature of the human predica-
> ment in all its complexity at the beginning of the 21st
> century. ... Something within has been let loose. ... The
> invasion of a new awareness, irresistible and uncon-
> trollable ... has swept away everything.[46]

The title of a lecture Cohen gave in 2012 sums up the essence of the new cosmology, based on Oneism: "The Significance of Non Duality: There is Only One, Not Two."[47]

Jean Houston,[48] another influential visionary, has had a long career as a teacher and author in human development through mythical spiri-tuality. She studied religion with theologian Paul Tillich. Houston says that she "learned that beneath the surface crust of consciousness, we all seem to be encoded with this vast mythic and symbolic universe—the internal imaginal reality."[49] She also has mentioned the similarity between her discoveries in probing the human psyche to those discov-ered by Carl Jung, Joseph Campbell, and Stanislav Grof.[50] Her vision of a coming utopia is an expression of the cosmology we've been describ-ing—and it would make Carl Jung most proud:

> I believe that the Earth herself is weaving a new species,
> a new humanity, and a new scenario of what the world
> may be. The signs of the new growth are everywhere.
> There are three million voluntary associations connect-
> ing fields of ideas for greening the social agenda, and
> fostering greater community responsibility and inven-
> tiveness. Many millions of what used to be called "cul-
> tural creatives" are adopting voluntary simplicity and

putting economics back where it belongs: as a satellite to the soul of culture, rather than the field of culture being a satellite to economics.

A new appreciation and celebration of our relationship to nature is rising in this new integral culture. I think this is where we are everywhere given the opportunity to release old habits and toxicities, as we prepare to participate in this next stage of biological governance and social well-being ... and that is why we have an opportunity to play a role in the greatest transition drama the world has ever seen.[51]

This vast vision for a spiritually-transformed world "that exceeds our imagination"[52] necessarily includes the transformation of sexuality. As Houston notes, "I'm finding more and more gays and lesbians have a deep and beautiful spirituality. I see my work as trying to be a bridge for consciousness for the gay community."[53]

Conclusion

We're witnessing a return to, and modern embrace of, principles originally found in the ancient spirituality of the pre-Christian, pagan world. This is happening just the way Richard Noll described it—as we saw in chapter 3, he showed that Jung had succeeded where the Roman emperor Julian the Apostate had failed. We are being "given over" to this seductive but false cosmology.

The cultural changes aren't simply driven by Hollywood producers pushing the envelope for box-office success but are the inevitable result of reinterpreting the very nature of human existence. We can speak reasonably of the rise of a worldview that claims to be the spiritual culmination of the long flow of Western history. And Christians must understand the basic nature of this vision, which, as an overarching cosmology, is applied to all areas of human behavior. Its optimism surely won't pan out. Will those who seek to eliminate the notion of right and wrong have the character and ability, let alone the desire, to establish a truly just and humane society that shows respect and tolerance?

The answer is becoming obvious—the train's destination is in sight. *New York Times* writer Josh Barro tweeted that "anti-LGBT attitudes are terrible ... we need to stamp them out, ruthlessly."[54] The term "ruthless," used in this way, ought to squash any realistic hopes for a fair and just utopian society. Nevertheless, the ideology behind this journalist's opinion is proposed as the new *morality,* the right thing to do. It is being incorporated into public policy because it is no longer considered the free expression of individual behavior; it has become a generalized cosmology, followed by everyone who wishes to be on the right side of history. The growing marginalization and silencing of Twoist thinking will lead to its criminalization; it will be stamped out in the wake of a new definition of justice. This process has begun.[55]

We've already seen a sea change in cultural expressions of this agenda within a single generation.[56] Its goal is clear: To remake America, you must undo it. Tony Perkins of the Family Research Council believes that religious liberties are under assault "more than at any point in our nation's history."[57] It's worth restating Melanie Phillips here: "The attack on Western civilization at its most profound level is an attack on the creed that lies at the very foundation of that civilization."[58]

That creed—antithetically opposed to the Oneist antithesis—is the subject of the next chapter.

CHAPTER 9

SALVATION BY SHAMAN

One day your child may ask you: "What is a shaman?" A shaman is a magician, medium, or healer (often of ambiguous or androgynous sexual orientation) who owes his or her powers to mystical communion with the spirit world. Sometimes called a "witch doctor," "spiritual guru," or "medium," the shaman is a spiritually alert human being, in touch with and in control of departed spirits and the spirits of animals; able to see into the past and predict the future; and diagnose, cure, or even cause human suffering. Shamans claim the ability to travel in the upper and lower worlds and are thus intermediaries between the natural and spiritual world. For these reasons, they've always occupied a place of great authority in pagan religion.

Roads to Modern Shamanism

This concept might sound ancient and primitive, with little relevance to the great issues of our time. But after wandering through the wilderness of secular materialism, today's pilgrims are thirsty for spirituality.

Even non-Christian pilgrims are eager for the practical benefits that spirituality offers, such as stress reduction, relaxation, and a sense of belonging and wholeness. It also offers deeper benefits, such as the apparent experience of discovering of one's true self and even the possibility of saving humanity by creating a future utopia of peace and cooperation. Deep in the heart of this upbeat utopian cosmology, however, is a spiritual power deriving from the dark world of shamanism.

Most of us would agree that the world is in a mess, and the desire in the human heart to create a better culture is indomitable. To create something as deep and complex as a human utopia demands a long process. The first steps taken in that process come from a choice of possible paths, so even those first steps are crucial. Spiritual disciplines like meditation or yoga seem to offer ways of making the world a better place, but the path of contemporary spirituality leads down a slope right into paganism. And one of the most common roads into pagan spirituality today is—believe it or not—yoga.

Yoga: Serious Spirituality

"Yoga is harmless!" I hear you protesting. "Why should the devil have all the good moves? Besides, everybody does it, so it must be okay." A few years ago a secular journalist spoke of a "wave of unprecedented yoga mania" and mentioned a program, "Yoga in the Hood," endorsed by the mayor of Los Angeles.[1] Yoga will hopefully solve even the gang problems of urban LA. In many cases, such practices as meditation and yoga are not promoted as religious techniques but as neutral tools for self-improvement. Who doesn't want to be skinny and mellow while maintaining individual identity as a Jew, Catholic, Buddhist, or evangelical Christian?

Christian yoga programs have risen in popularity and acceptability.[2] Such programs often have names like "Yahweh Yoga," "Holy Yoga," and "Outstretched Inc."[3] Yoga is one of the first small steps Westerners often take into the vast and exciting ocean of altered consciousness, discovering a refreshed view of themselves. The bestseller *Eat, Pray, Love* by journalist Elizabeth Gilbert (and its movie version, starring Julia Roberts) celebrates good Italian food, exciting sex, and Eastern meditation, all of which combine to produce the new, satisfied, holistic Westerner.[4] Now the practice of yoga is going global, spreading Hinduism (by proxy) throughout the world.[5]

This activity for toned bodies and stress-free minds seems a long way from shamanism, yet yoga's key principle, says a *Los Angeles Times* journalist, is "union among all living beings."[6] In an article titled "Inner-Peace Movement," another states that some involved in yoga "are taking the next step: exploring the spiritual underpinnings, visiting Buddhist temples or retreats or developing a relationship with a swami."[7] Yoga takes you beyond healthy bodies.[8] After all, in Sanskrit, "yoga" means "union with God" or "yoked to God." The goal of yoga is to promote the union of Atman (the individual soul) with Brahman (the greater soul), which is not a personal being but a spirit force, what the Hindus call "deities."

We are a long way from shamanism, right? Not really. There are various forms of yoga, a dozen or more. Jung was fascinated specifically by Kundalini Yoga. "Kundalini" means "serpent power"; the experience is called the awakening of the Kundalini, a sexual-spiritual energy that rises up through the seven chakras, or energy centers, in the body to elevate the soul beyond the body into the point of maximum focus and concentration—called *bindu* in Hinduism—where duality is compressed into a singularity, a state of Advaita ("not two"). This is a direct experience (*gnosis*) of a nondual or unitive reality— the goal of all yoga techniques, the liberation from the opposites. Seeing yoga as an essential part of his therapy, Jung noted, "Yoga is a method by which the libido is systematically 'drawn in' and thereby released from the bondage of opposites."[9] This union of the opposites is also the spiritual goal of the shaman.[10] I'm not, of course, arguing that everyone who practices yoga is a shaman—but I *am* warning that yoga can be the first step into an entire alternative spirituality. This is also true of "mindfulness meditation."

Mindless Meditation

Meditation is another technology of the sacred, which, like yoga, has become part of the spirituality *du jour* in the once "Christian" West.[11] Mindfulness meditation is a Buddhist technique for the suppression of desire. Though its ostensible goal is to help practitioners pay attention to every detail of their surroundings, its effective goal is that they will not react to any of these events. In authentic Buddhist thinking, involvement with real life is a trap that destroys a true sense of being beyond the material. What world do we inhabit if we are beyond the material? It is the world of a different consciousness. Thus altered states of consciousness, as in pagan spirituality generally, become the desired result. Mind*fulness* becomes a pagan kind of mind*lessness*.

Eastern meditation techniques all involve silencing the mind—in contrast to Christian meditation, which fully involves and stimulates the mind.[12] "Silence the mind" is a term also found in ancient Gnosticism, for which meditation was an essential element. In Hinduism the same is true. Swami Vivekananda, a disciple of Ramakrishna, states that through yoga "we get beyond the senses, our minds become superconscious, we get beyond the intellect ... where reasoning cannot reach."[13] In *Bliss Divine*, Swami Sivananda states, "We must consciously destroy the mind ... Keep your intellect at a respectable distance when you study mythology. ... That which separates you from God [Brahma] is mind."[14] Intellect is a hindrance. A modern New Age teacher has put it this way: "The enemy of meditation is the mind."[15]

"Mantra" is a Sanskrit term, made up of two words, *man*, "think," and *tra*, "liberated from." If the great goal of yoga and meditation is "the joining of the opposites," then the mind must necessarily be silenced; the human mind can only truly function with the notion of opposites—this, not that; "A," not "non-A." The mantra helps you escape the reality of the world to discover the mystical state of bodilessness or mindlessness. When in that state, you experience liberation, stress reduction, and inner peace.[16] The goal of this spirituality is to destroy binary oppositions by self-induced altered states of consciousness, which is the domain of the paranormal—but, according to Thomas Berry, the ultimate goal is to become a shaman through transpersonal Jungian psychology.[17]

Modern "Shamans"

Shamanic practices that take us into ancient or obscure religious experiences no doubt seem remote to you. But the French have a saying, *reculer pour mieux sauter* (back up to get a better leap forward)—and this is exactly what our spiritual leaders are doing. The shaman of the past is now proposed as the perfect model of spirituality for 21st-century world citizens.

Carl Jung

Readers will recall that Jung was deeply involved in the paranormal and had a spirit-guide, Philemon. Jung saw the shaman as the model of spiritual maturity, and he himself performed the functions of a primitive shaman for his followers, fusing psychological science and religion—or, in other words, fusing the rational and the irrational in a psychological/religious synthesis that has captured the imagination of intellectuals, caregivers, and pastoral counselors throughout the Western world for the past two or three generations.

LSD researcher and mystic Timothy Leary noted many similarities between Jung's description of the psyche and shamanic beliefs about the soul.[18] Leary was not alone. Michael Smith, in his revealing book *Jung and Shamanism in Dialogue*,[19] explores the striking similarities between Jungian psychology and shamanism, noting that Jung saw in the classic shaman the embodiment of true psychological maturity.[20] In his personal bio, in addition to his PhD in Christian Theology, Smith presents himself as a "shamanic facilitator." He thinks that "both Jung and shamanism offer considerable possibilities for helping the modern Western health care professional to understand how to draw upon the sacred for healing purposes."[21]

Jung was convinced that the only way to heal neuroses was through what he delicately called experiences of the *numinosum*,[22] behind which term, as the *Red Book* clearly shows, are the occult experiences of the shaman, being in the presence of a divinity or spiritual being.[23]

Modern Jungians who have developed depth or transpersonal psychology have followed their shamanic master in opening the deep spiritual mysteries of the subconscious as the way forward for human spirituality in the new world. For them, the concept of the shaman is not just a symbol of effective leadership. It is disturbingly real—as the work of Stanislav Grof illustrates.

Stansislav Grof

At the death of a reigning king or queen, British tradition requires the following declaration to be spoken to the surviving successor: "The King is dead. Long live the King." As an impressionable 11-year-old lad, I heard this solemn phrase when King George VI died in his sleep, and his frail young daughter Elizabeth was told, "The King is dead. Long live the Queen." In the field of psychology, one might fairly say, "Jung is dead, long live Grof."[24]

Here we enter the deep spiritual heart and final arrival point of the pagan cosmology I have been describing in the previous chapters. Remember my thesis—if Jung was one of the powerful creators of the modern world, then his thinking and Grof's are the engines that will power the pagan bullet train into our global future. In describing the "new psychology" for the postsecular age, Mike King (a different type of king!) recognized Grof as both the leading continuator of Jungian methodology and the quintessential postsecularist. Stanislav Grof, born in 1931 in Prague, Czechoslovakia, was a disciple of Jung and a leading founder of the field of transpersonal psychology. His pioneering research in the use of altered states of consciousness for human healing and wise living represents the core of this transformed cosmology. Tarnas describes Grof's work as "the most epistemologically significant development in the recent history of depth psychology."[25] Grof's approach is developed in his well-documented, academic book *Psychology of the Future*.[26] For the new psychology, verbal counseling and analysis (talking) are out. Freud is old hat. Behind the new approach are Jung and the transforming power of virtually unutterable higher states of consciousness. Woody Allen could never have been more prophetic when he said in one of his often-repeated jokes: "I've been in [Freudian] analysis for thirteen years. I'm giving it one more year, and if it still doesn't work I'm going to Lourdes."[27]

Grof is the pagan equivalent of Lourdes. His work carries into the 21st century Jung's vision of magical transformation. He believes that the wave of the future will be deep paranormal experiences in the transpersonal realm (what Jung would have called the collective unconscious) through states of altered consciousness.[28] Consider the methods he proposes as "technologies of the sacred."[29]

- Work with breath, called "holotropic" breathwork (*holos* + *trepein* = moving towards wholeness)
- Sound technologies (drumming, rattling, use of sticks, bells and gongs, music, chanting, mantras)
- Dancing (whirling dervishes, Bushman trance dancing)
- Social isolation and sensory deprivation (American Indian vision quests, desert or cave isolation)
- Sensory overload (superphysical stimuli, extreme pain)
- Physiological means (sleep or food deprivation, purgatives, laxatives, bloodletting)
- Meditation, prayer (various yoga schools, such as Hatha, Kundalini, Tantra; Christian mysticism, exercises of Ignatius of Loyola)
- Psychedelic stimulation (hashish, peyote, LSD)

In faithful accord with his mentor, Jung, Grof insists that these sacred technologies are all techniques from ancient and worldwide paganism, essential to shamanism.[30] Ancient pagan magic becomes the hope of our future world. Grof sees shamanistic spirituality as the only hope for "confronting and transforming ... the psycho-spiritual roots of malignant aggression and insatiable greed."[31] Did you get that? From Grof's perspective, the basic human problems of aggression and greed can be solved only by becoming a shaman, a human being in direct touch with pagan deities. For Grof, these fundamental human problems are not moral problems, as the Bible teaches, but the result of a failure to be in touch with one's higher or true, shamanistic self. In the place of divine forgiveness of sin, Grof advocates "radical inner transformation of humanity" and its "rise to a higher level of consciousness" as "our only real hope for the future."[32] Essentially, only occult shamanistic spirituality will save the planet.[33]

And there's little new in Grof's prescription. Jungian and Western neopagan techniques are comparable to ancient practices known throughout the world. Michael York, in a wide-ranging overview of pagan cults, reveals that

> ...despite the great geographic range of shamanic practice, the initiatory experience exhibits a surprising uniformity. ... the use of ritual, sleep deprivation, [and] various austerities, including fasting and psychotropic substances, help induce the desired alternative state of consciousness within which the shaman operates.[34]

My understanding of what modern Jungians are proposing widened significantly when I visited Africa in the spring of 2006. In a conference in Johannesburg, I heard a fascinating lecture by a native Kenyan Christian scholar, Dr. Yusufu Turaki, dealing with African ancestor worship.[35] He had not read York, Grof, or Jung, but knew firsthand the spirituality of his tribe. He spoke of "direct communication from the spirit beings" made possible "through dreams, visions, vision quests and divination."[36] He spoke of the means of inducing spirit possession which included "meditative and contemplative exercises, self-inflicted tortures (including jumping from heights, walking on burning coals, thrusting skewers into cheeks and tongue), using drugs, dancing, drumming, chanting [and] singing oneself into a frenzy."[37] It became crystal clear to me that the spiritual techniques proposed by the sophisticated theories of transpersonal psychology differ little in essence from those used since time immemorial in the African bush.

The same might be said of a completely different source, Hinduism, in which the approach to altered states of consciousness, though less spectacular, can be very similar. Guru Paramahansa Yogananda, founder of the Self-Realization Fellowship in Los Angeles in the 1920s, taught the acquisition of bliss through meditation. His system of meditation included breath control,[38] one of the elements on Grof's list, and was intended to produce the same paranormal states.

Some readers may think that this occult spirituality and practice will always remain on the margins of normal life. I've come to believe that it cannot be so easily dismissed. It's cloaked in attractive ideological garb, claiming to resolve the present crises of faith, social justice, psychological health, ultimate meaning, and planetary survival.

Two other disciples of Jung—Thomas Berry and Jean Houston, who have already appeared in the pages of this book—make a stunning conclusion for Western intellectuals who are deeply influential at the United Nations. They believe that in order to go forward to a better world, we must step back in time to an era before the advent of Christianity, to the animism and polytheism of ancient times.

Thomas Berry

Thomas Berry specifically compares the coming spirituality to that of "shamanic times."[39] He believes our contemporary calling is to carry on "the Great Work of the first Peoples ... [who] established an intimate rapport with the powers that brought this continent [America] into existence"[40] long before Christianity arrived. We need to go back to the time "when Earth was the Great Mother, to the Age of the Gods." "Despite all the changes," admits Berry, "this age still holds many of our normative values."[41]

Thus, such reference to the past is not a mistake. Berry considers the animistic conjuring of spirits to be an indispensable present resource of spiritual power. When modern pagans profess that "the universe is the primary sacred reality,"[42] they are echoing what the ancients also believed and seek their wisdom. From these modern scholars we learn that the ancients' "profound intimacy with the natural world" was not simply the "local knowledge" of hunters and gatherers. For them, "the rivers and the mountains ... were spirit powers to be reckoned with."[43] Their intimacy with nature included the knowledge that "animals and humans were relatives,"[44] a truth expressed "in their totemic carvings."[45]

At the beginning of this book, we observed that pagan myths were essentially unknown in the West at the beginning of the 20th century and that the goal of Jung was to introduce such mythology into Western culture for psychological healing and spiritual fulfillment. That theoretical project has clearly become a reality in our day: Thomas Berry was a popular speaker at UN-sponsored events until his death in 2009 at the age of 94.[46] He also was the mentor of Mary Evelyn Tucker, who once bragged, in my hearing, of having incorporated elements of pagan spirituality into the United Nations' Earth Charter.

Jean Houston

Jean Houston is widely considered one of the top 10 New Age speakers in North America. Houston founded her Mystery School for teaching mysticism and psychophysical states of ecstasy and spiritual awakening through the practice of walking the labyrinth, which she adopted as the symbol of her work.[47] As Richard Noll perceptively has noted, "Jung was also a strong promoter of the occultic mandala, a circular picture with a sun or star usually at the center. Sun worship, as personified in the mandala, is perhaps the key to fully understanding Jung."[48] Jung-inspired Houston works for the United Nations both as Advisor to UNICEF and as part of the UN Development Program, training young leaders "in human and cultural development as well as in Social Artistry."[49] She clarifies what that entails: teaching young leaders in undeveloped countries how to reconnect with their old pagan myths. She intends to coach others to direct "both individual and social capital toward the creation of better societies and peoples ... providing strategies that can work in an interconnected world."[50]

Houston is a shaman—a medium and a channeler—who has practiced her arts around the globe and even, at one point, in the White House. Houston served as medium to then-First Lady Hillary Clinton, who wanted to make spiritual contact with Eleanor Roosevelt.[51] Houston helped write Clinton's book *It Takes a Village.* She also influenced Dr. Lauren Artress of the Episcopal Grace Cathedral of San Francisco, who, after learning of the labyrinth at Jean Houston's Mystery School, brought the practice to Grace Cathedral and became the leading promoter of labyrinth spirituality in many churches, including evangelical churches of North America.[52]

Houston believes that our broken society can only be saved by myth.[53] She clearly states: "Never has this mythic knowing been more needed than today."[54] Just what kind of saving myth does Houston envision for the global culture of the third millennium? Her book *The Passion of Isis and Osiris: A Gateway to Transcendent Love,* which came out during her time at the White House, proposes personal and cultural regeneration via Isis, the Egyptian goddess of magic and the underworld—ironically, the same goddess whose worship Julian the Apostate failed to reintroduce into newly Christian Rome.

Houston also shows how the sexual revolution is tied organically to this spirituality. As a student of history, Houston knows that homosexuals have historically had a spiritual role as shamans.[55] Such teachings aren't frivolous parlor games, fairy tales, or mere myths. As Grof notes, they involve "transpersonal experiences" that include "encounters with various blissful and wrathful archetypal deities."[56] He warns that these experiences also include "visions of divine light ... communication with spirit guides and superhuman entities, contact with shamanic power animals,[57] direct apprehension of universal symbols, and episodes of religious and creative inspiration."[58] These beings are "ontologically real ... not products of metaphysical speculation or pathological processes in the brain."[59] They are out there, awaiting human communication via states of mystical trance.

Shamans for a Planetary Utopia

This arrival in the West of ancient shamanism is doubtless part of what Berry meant when he spoke of the need of the future human to be transformed "at the species level."[60] He presupposed a radical spiritual conversion to a different conception of the human self as divine; only this will bring and maintain a kind of heaven on earth. But Jungian transpersonal techniques are not simply the sophisticated healing techniques of modern psychologists. Rather, they are identical to the methods of spiritual stimulation employed in modern-day neopagan cults, with the same goal—producing life-changing "paranormal experiences."[61] A contemporary sociological study of Western neopagans and witches notes that

> Neo-Pagans seek mystical experiences through rituals— drumming, dancing, chanting, and meditating—and in sweat lodges or through other techniques. By using these techniques, neo-Pagans hope to have a direct experience of the Divine or of infinity. Some speak of being in the presence of the goddess or a particular goddess or

god, while others speak of a powerful presence or sense
of the infinite when in altered states of consciousness.[62]

You may think this inconceivable in our sophisticated world of space
travel, the Internet, and quantum physics. It is most certainly con-
ceivable, since it is already happening. For instance, thousands of
professionals from Silicon Valley annually camp for a week in the
Nevada desert for the Burning Man gathering. Between orgies and art
shows, they build, then destroy, a temporary city built around an 80-
foot totemic statue of a man. The Burning Man website asks:

> Do we, as conscious beings, exist outside of nature's
> sway, or does its force impel us and inform the central
> root of who and what we are? ... Only from immediate
> experience, not *ideologies that stand outside of the created
> world* [that is, Twoism] may we regenerate a sense of na-
> ture as it moves within us and flows through us.[63]

This is the message that techies like those from Google and Amazon
take back from the desert to the regular scientific, high-finance world
of Silicon Valley.

There is only one conclusion. In new dress and terminology, primitive shamanism, replete with its totem poles, will drive the program
of global transformation. Modern theorist of pagan spirituality Ken
Wilber argues that "the experience of timeless unity with Spirit is not
an idea or a wish; it is a *direct* apprehension. ... Genuine mysticism,
as opposed to dogmatic religion ... relies on direct experiential evidence. ... The mystics ask you to take nothing on mere belief."[64] "Direct
apprehension" describes the deeply convincing, life-changing experience reserved for the shaman, who has been initiated into out-of-body
mysteries of monistic oneness. The difference is that to ensure the survival of humanity on the planet, neo-Jungians insist that everyone in
the future society be a mature, spirit-possessed shaman.

Gnostic Union for Global Unity

The eulogies of John Lennon, as contemporary culture's great shamanistic liberator, describe "Imagine" as the "quintessential song of the

shaman," removing all barriers—no countries, no religion, no heaven or hell.[65] This is the deep gnostic experience of liberation from the opposites. One is no longer hemmed in by the limiting notion that things were originally created separate. One knows oneself as both male and female and knows reality as including both right and wrong, true and false, good and evil. In primitive cultures this would be called the power beyond white and black magic. Gnostic spirituality is sometimes identified with the Egyptian goddess Isis. In a gnostic manuscript, *Thunder: Perfect Mind*, she describes herself as "the whore and the holy one ... the wife and the virgin ... the one whose wisdom is great in Egypt (Isis) ... sinless and the root of sin derives from me ... I am the one who is called Truth and iniquity."[66] She is joining the opposites for the realization of a "non-dual" spiritual state. The gnostic *Gospel of Truth* describes this knowledge as being swallowed up into the unity of all things.[67] The joining of the opposites means that we rise above all distinctions, which are dismissed as "maya," mere illusion.[68]

Remember that for Jung, all archetypes or mythical powers are finally united, pointing to "the sphere of the *unus mundus*, the unitary world ... the ultimate ground of the universe."[69] Experiencing this unity is the key to mental health. His analytic psychology saw the task of the self to unify all polarities into a psychic whole. The self is the total complex of unconscious archetypes (that is, our instincts) whose conscious integration brings wholeness. For wholeness to occur, good must be integrated with evil, male balanced with female, darkness with light. Of particular significance was what Jung called the shadow, the rejected or negative aspects of the self. If these are ignored, if they are not integrated into wholeness, they erupt in distortions, projections, and violence.[70]

Victory over Guilt

This joining of the opposites means that there is more to a spiritual high than mere trancelike ecstasy. Going beyond the limitations of the mind also goes beyond rational definitions of right and wrong. Everything about you is okay. All your instincts are valid. In pantheism, good and evil are part of the whole. When we go within, notions like right and wrong, guilt and bad conscience disappear. Jung speaks of drawing strength from the dark or shadow side of the self, accepting evil as the partner of good, assuming both to achieve self-reliance or individuation.[71] In alchemy and in psychotherapy, says June Singer, "we face our shames and guilts and evil aspects of our own natures, and we acknowledge ownership of them.[72] Bruce Davis of the Manson family, now a born-again Christian, says about LSD that it "enlarged my sense of what was permissible ... the unthinkable became the thinkable and the thinkable became the doable."[73] Richard Noll says, tongue-in-cheek, that Jung with his notion of individuation "redeemed generations of his followers from the burden of original sin."[74]

Noll understood perfectly where this view takes us—into the lap of Nietzsche, who famously declared that God was dead. Nietzsche characterized the consciousness of the Übermensch (the superman) as untrammeled by theistic morals:

> He who has to be a creator in good and evil [the superman], truly, has first to be a destroyer and break values. Thus the greatest evil belongs to the greatest good. For evil is man's best strength. Man must grow better and more evil ... the most evil is necessary for the superman's best.[75]

Over the corpse of God rose the liberated man, the "superman." Noll comments, "Jung conceived of the individuated [psychologically mature] person as one who was reborn as a genius [superman], as one who could directly perceive the universal in the particulars of life ... possessed by the divine genius within."[76]

The subtitle to Nietzsche's book *Beyond Good and Evil* has a prophetic ring: *Prelude to a Future Philosophy*.[77] In Jung's philosophy, which joins good and evil, we see one fulfillment of Nietzsche's vision. Under Jung's continuing influence, people are discovering their divine, guilt-free identity. Thus the individuated (mature) person is the one who realizes the experience of wholeness, holding together the "power of deity and devil alike."[78]

Al Mohler, in an essay on the denial of guilt associated with the therapeutic revolution, states:

Our post-Christian society has been working hard for well over a century to bury guilt in the cultural backyard and deny that guilt can be morally significant. In the wake of Sigmund Freud and the therapeutic revolution, the modern secular worldview demands that guilt be understood as the lingering residue of the Christian conscience, an experience merely forced upon us by a society that imposes oppressive moral judgments. It is to be overcome and denied, never heard.[79]

Jung has already taken our Western culture into a chilling lack of guilt on the basis of belief in inner divinity. One young woman had her abortion procedure filmed for publication on Facebook (the occasion for Al Mohler's article). This self-confident young lady shows that these ideas are not pure theory. She ends her video by saying: "I feel in awe of the fact that I can make a baby. I can make a life. I knew that what I was going to do [in killing it] was right, 'cause it was right for me and no one else."[80]

That thinking is the sign of "an absolutely godless worldview," as Mohler observes. His comment is profound; "[This young woman] grants to herself the power to give life; to 'make a life.' What she gives, she can destroy. Emily giveth, and Emily taketh away."[81] There is no guilt.

Such is what Thomas Berry also affirms, with different terminology. "We are ourselves a mystical quality of the Earth, a unifying principle, an integration of the various polarities ... If the human is *microcosmos*, the cosmos is *macroanthropos*. We are each the cosmic person ... the Great Person of Hindu India."[82] He goes on to say, "We probably have not had such a participation in the dream of the earth since earlier shamanic times."[83] Now such participation is readily available—online. A shaman describes what ecstasy awaits the seeker:

Shamanic ecstasy is the *real* "Old Time Religion," of which modern churches are but pallid evocations. Shamanic, visionary ecstasy, the *mysterium tremendum*, the *unio mystica*, the eternally delightful experience of the universe as energy, is a *sine qua non* of religion, it is what religion is for! There is no need for faith, it is the ecstatic experience itself that *gives* one faith in the intrinsic unity and integrity of the universe, in ourselves as integral parts of the whole; that reveals to us the sublime majesty of our universe, and the fluctuant, scintillant, alchemical miracle that is quotidian consciousness. Any religion that requires faith and gives none ... that heals not the gaping wound between Body and Soul, but would tear them asunder ... is no religion at all![84]

Is this the final curse from Jung's disciples on the modern West? Jung sensed the significance of what he was doing. He observed

...a mood of universal destruction and renewal ... what the Greeks called the *kairos*—the right moment—for a "metamorphosis of the gods." ... It is the unconscious man within us who is changing. Coming generations will have to take account of this momentous transformation.[85]

Berry does not avoid calling a spade a spade, telling us who this unconscious man is: "It is the role of the shamanic personality ... who journeys into the far regions of the cosmic mystery and brings back the vision and the power needed by the human community at the most elementary level."[86] Only this kind of person can speak wisdom in the future age.[87]

This is the vision of Richard Tarnas, who like Berry, consciously rejects his Roman Catholic past. The arrival of the shaman corresponds with a time of spiritual apocalyptic elation appearing in a "powerful crescendo"[88] as, in the seductive vision of Richard Tarnas, "many *gather now on the intellectual stage as if for some kind of climactic synthesis.*"[89] Tarnas's basis for synthesis is the recovery of ancient Babylonian astrology, and he defends it in his *Cosmos and Psyche: Intimations of a New World,*[90] a work that follows the astrological speculations of Jung.[91] We are back to ancient Babylon, Greece, and Rome. John Oswalt, a specialist in the ancient religions observes:

Once a person or a culture adopts the idea that this world is all there is, as is typical of pagan myth, certain things follow regardless of the primitiveness or the modernity of the person or culture. Among these are the devaluing of individual persons, the loss of an interest in history, fascination with magic and the occult and the denial of individual responsibility. The opposites of these, among which are what we have taken to be the glories of modern Western culture, are by-products of the biblical worldview. As that worldview is progressively lost among us, we are losing the by-products as well. Not realizing that they are by-products, we are surprised to see them go, but we have no real explanation for their departure.[92]

Having lost the biblical worldview, our culture no longer has the mental mechanisms to resist the outlandish expressions of radicals committed to pushing the envelope. As the Apostle Paul said, "Though they know God's righteous decree that those who practice such things deserve to die, they not only do them but give approval to those who practice them" (Rom 1:32).

When the light of the world is systematically removed, the world is plunged into moral and spiritual darkness. And how many Christians will fall for this subterfuge?

Certainly we have reached a tipping point. As Jude 7 clearly demonstrates, Sodom is an example of a city divinely judged for its godlessness and sexual perversion. Another example is the ancient nation of Israel, who, even as God's people, defiantly asserted, "We have made a covenant with death, and with Sheol we have an agreement, when the overwhelming whip passes through, it will not come to us, for we have made lies our refuge, and in falsehood we have taken shelter" (Isa 28:15). At the beginning of the church, Paul spoke of "the mystery of lawlessness ... already at work" (2 Thess 2:7) but then prophesied that things would get worse with the coming of "the lawless one" (2:8), empowered by "the activity of Satan" (2:9) and his "wicked deception" on those who "refused to love the truth and so be saved" (2:10). Mysteriously, God is also involved, for he "sends them a strong delusion, so that they may believe what is false" (2 Thess 2:11). There is an inevitable cultural implosion when human beings thoroughly reject God and his revealed wisdom.

PART 3

NOT GIVING UP

Our world may think it's on board the right train—but we've refused to follow the map. Faced with the stunning collapse of the centuries-old Christian culture and with the seductive power of this new pagan view of the "new humanity," based on Oneism, Christians need great wisdom—we can't afford to make mistakes; we can't just change directions later without any harm done. In this final part we'll examine what the wise and inspired Apostle Paul proposed to the woefully outnumbered Christians living in the heart of the ancient Graeco-Roman pagan culture, directions that are surely also appropriate for Christians today.

In Romans, Paul declares about rebellious peoples and nations—heading in the opposite direction from God—that God "gave them over (Greek—*paredoken*)" (Rom 1:24, 26, 28 NIV) to "shameful lusts" (1:26 NIV) and to a "depraved mind" (1:28 NIV). Using this same term, "given over," Paul repeats the same warning in Ephesians, that the Gentiles (pagans) are driven by "the futility of their minds. They are darkened in their understanding, alienated from the life of God because of the ignorance that is in them, due to their hardness of heart. They have become callous and have given themselves [over] (*paredoken*) to sensuality, greedy to practice every kind of impurity" (Eph 4:17-19). This is the stage where theory and practice complement one another, where the holistic justification of pagan discourse incites sinful, mind-numbing practice, so that mind and body, with no shame, become slaves to evil. 20th-century Scottish theologian John Murray gives an amazingly accurate, prescient description of our present culture in his explanation of what Paul was describing in first-century pagan Rome. Commenting on Paul's final statement in Romans 1 ("Though they know God's righteous decree that those who practice such things deserve to die, they not only do them but give approval to those who practice them," Rom 1:32), Murray observes:

> The most damning condition is not the practice of iniquity, however much that may evidence our abandonment of God and abandonment to sin; it is that together with the practice there is also the support and encouragement of others in the practice of the same ... iniquity is most aggravated when it meets with no inhibition from the disapproval of others and when there is collective, undissenting approbation.[93]

After what we've observed in part 2 of this book, we must ask: Have we reached this point in our formerly Christian Western culture, where "collective, undissenting approbation" has led to the creation of a totalizing cosmology of rebellion? Reilly, in his own terms, sees our situation similarly. He speaks about "the power of rationalization" that appears when people who instinctively know the moral law and deliberately suppress it must then justify their stance. This inevitable sense of "moral failure" is "hard to live with" and can only be "tolerated ... by creating a rationalization to justify it."[94] He goes on, "We convince ourselves that heretofore forbidden desires are permissible ... by obliterating conscience through a more permanent rationalization, an enduring inversion of morality."[95] This becomes a whole cultural phenomenon: "Entrenched moral aberrations [by certain cultural leaders] then impel people to rationalize vice not only to themselves but to others as well ... to become an engine of revolutionary change that will affect the society as a whole."[96] It is now being taught in schools, sacralized in marriage, legalized in law and public policy, and normalized by the highest-placed public officials. Since it is the Lie, it cannot stand any statements of the Truth and so must demonize as hateful even peaceful and rational opposition, demand silence, and ostracize all who speak against it. In the present dominance of this ideology of Oneism, we are witnessing the determined construction of a society that rejects God and his laws and is based on personal erotic fantasy, the god within, which is already tellingly expressed in the title of neo-Marxist Herbert Marcuse's book from a generation ago, *Eros and Civilization.*[97]

In response to the similar circumstances in his own times, Paul offers a warning and two responses. First, he warns of the great temptation for Christians to conform to the fallen world's manner of thinking and living: "Do not be conformed to this world" (Rom 12:2). And he proposes that the two fundamentally Christian responses must be Christian *living* (Rom 12:1) and Christian *thinking* (Rom 12:2).

As we face this brave new world, we cannot say we don't know what to do. And yet the cultural train seems destined to run off the tracks. Has the deceptive activity of Satan so overtaken us, been so systematized and normalized as a social, moral, and spiritual theory, that God must give us over to the disastrous implications of our diabolical, shaman-led embrace of the Lie? We must pray that perhaps God's "kindness and forbearance and patience ... will lead [some] to repentance" (Rom 2:4), but we must also realistically gear up for a struggle with a culture under the powerful sway of Satan. In such an apostate society, people are no longer confronted with the notion of the image of God reflected in the reality of "natural law," the awareness of a Creator and in the human being as responsible for the creational mandate, in sexual distinctions of male and female, and in the functioning of moral conscience. The conscience is seared; everything is rationalized. If this is true, we must conclude parts one and two by granting that Jung indeed has succeeded where the pagan apostate emperor Julian failed.

The Oneist train is headed to destruction—but we also can't just jump off the train of culture; we need to keep moving toward *some* future. Paul has given us his guidelines. So: What is the Christian response?

CHAPTER 10

CHRISTIAN COMPROMISE WITH CULTURE

"Be not conformed to this world" (Rom 12:2).

You may wonder why so much of this book is devoted to the present state of the West (and of America in particular). In part, it's due to my own surprise when, in 1991, I returned to the United States after 18 years in France. Before the French chapter of my story, I had studied in the United States for nine years, during the Beatles period. As I discovered, I would return to a very different, far less Christian-seeming America.

Blithely unaware of the enormity of the cultural tsunami that has overrun the United States since the Sixties, many Christians are ill-equipped to face the opposition that the new cosmology presents. Certainly, most Christians have a sense that things are not right. I often speak to Christian audiences and hear them say that things are "awful," but such a vague sense is not much help. How do we engage "awful"? We need to return to the basics of worldview in order to respond to the new situation. Without such an analysis, believers may even embrace significant elements of what they do not realize is a very unbiblical cosmology. And the trouble is, once you take one piece of the pagan pie, the rest is—as they say in England—very "more-ish."

An Old Problem

In Psalm 11, King David grieves over the calamity of religious and cultural implosion, passionately expressing himself in a question that has often been quoted in the history of the church: "If the foundations are destroyed, what can the righteous do?" (Psa 11:3). When, like David, Christians see that "the wicked bend the bow; they have fitted their arrow to the string to shoot in the dark at the upright in heart" (Psa 11:2), they are likely to follow the faulty advice offered by David's enemies: "Flee like a bird to your mountain" (Psa 11:1). Some Christians have acted on this temptation, creating closed communities stockpiled with supplies. And those who don't go that far are still tempted to disengage.

However, we must not give up. Though the spiritual and moral foundations of Western civilization are shaken, though so many have been given over to the new worldview, we have enduring hope—for there is one foundation that lasts. It is not Christian America, Western Christendom, or a coming utopian planet. There is one sure place of refuge:

> The Lord is in his holy temple;
>> the Lord's throne is in heaven;
>> his eyes see, his eyelids test the children of man.
> The Lord tests the righteous,
>> but his soul hates the wicked and the one who loves violence. ...
> For the Lord is righteous;
> he loves righteous deeds;
>> the upright shall behold his face (Psa 11:4–5, 7).

God, our refuge, made the mountains and will one day remake his creation into a truly *new* and *renewed* cosmos where righteousness dwells. We know, with the eye of faith, that clothed with his righteousness we shall "behold his face" (Psa 11:7). In the meantime, what must the righteous do? Knowing that our Father is refining and testing us and that he loves "righteous deeds," even when the foundations are crumbling, we seek to display righteousness to the watching world. Clearly we can't give up or give in. But that's the constant temptation when things get tough.

Faced with unprecedented opposition to the Christian faith—a faith which was once the dominant source of social and moral definitions in Western culture—the response of believers is crucial for the very survival of the gospel in our day. This is a time unparalleled since the beginning of the history of the church, when religious paganism ruled the culture. Will the present church see the true nature of this situation and react in a way that honors Christ and his gospel—as the early church did?

Conformity with the kind of world we have described above is the worst possible response—conformity throws a spirit of immobilizing confusion over one and all. As the Apostle Peter said in an ancient warning to Christians living in Asia Minor, within the pagan Roman Empire, "To the elect who are sojourners of the Dispersion in Pontus, Galatia, Cappadocia, Asia, and Bithynia ... not fashioning yourselves according to your former lusts in the time of your ignorance" (1 Pet 1:1, 14 ASV). Paul repeats this warning to Christians living in the heart of Nero's capital city: "Do not be conformed to this world" (Rom 12:2).

Christians in the first century lived under a regime that continually tempted them to modify their beliefs and adapt their behavior to a culture that didn't share their essential faith. Christians throughout history have been in similar social settings, in cultures and under governments that had no regard for Christian principles. Christians, not just in the United States but everywhere, are called by God in his Word to know the particular ideas that constitute the world's pattern of thinking and belief; in this way, we can both resist the Lie and make a statement of the Truth that understands and exposes the Lie and offers the only true hope in the gospel. Ignorance of this will produce faith-destroying conformity and compromise.

Fearing our Culture

Christians today often conform or compromise out of fear. We may fear verbal attacks, accusations of hate speech, or loss of friends, jobs, or respect. Sometimes Christians even receive threats of physical violence. Students on the campus of the University of Regina in Saskatchewan in 2014 cheered the arrest of my friend, Peter LaBarbera, head of *Americans for Truth about Homosexuality*. His crime? He and a friend were distributing literature proposing the biblical view of sexuality and marriage.[1]

Fear of reprisals either from students or from a university administration is affecting evangelical campus ministries as the 21st century gets underway. Once known for unapologetic gospel preaching and open evangelism, many student groups are forced to take a low profile and describe themselves more in terms of a "spiritual hospital" or a "home away from home." It is increasingly difficult for Christian groups to sponsor events such as public debates, let alone campus-wide public lectures. How can Christians be an outpost for speaking gospel truth to the university when they increasingly are not allowed to speak at all? Low-profile presence seems the only alternative. The temptation is for Christians either to pull up the drawbridges, bar the windows, and disappear from view, or contribute positively to the life of the community only through culturally approved acts of service. Service is a great thing, of course, but notice that in each of these scenarios, the Word of Truth is silenced.

Obviously, the new situation calls for tact, wisdom, and grace for college ministries as well as for all Christians. We must pray for one another, especially for Christian millennials and those who will come after them. I include myself in those who need to remember the prayer request of the Apostle Paul as he sat in a Roman prison, chained to a well-armed soldier:

> [Pray] also for me, that words may be given to me in opening my mouth boldly to proclaim the mystery of the gospel, for which I am an ambassador in chains, that I may declare it boldly, as I ought to speak (Eph 6:19–20).

Seeking Approval from our Culture

Some modern Christians believe that the church's difficulties getting along with the culture are largely self-imposed and avoidable. The culture dislikes us because Christians are socially obnoxious and go about Christian witness all wrong. Some believe that cultural opposition will disappear if the church tweaks its witness techniques, updates its message, and participates more heartily in compassionate care for the earth and its inhabitants. The goal for the church almost becomes the promotion of this-worldly "human flourishing"—as defined by the surrounding culture.

In *UnChristian*,[2] Gabe Lyons and David Kinnaman discovered that young Americans hold overwhelmingly negative views of Christianity.[3] The authors tend to agree with that negative view of the church. While we can always find weaknesses in the church and in the faith and practice of individual Christian believers, the methodology of Lyons and Kinnaman seems suspect. Though they grant that "[t]his generation's world, *like none other*, is coming 'unglued' "[4] and that young Americans "perceive the world in very different terms than people ever have before,"[5] the authors seem to treat these perceptions as inherently true. From this assumption, Kinnaman and Lyons conclude that Christianity today is indeed something of an embarrassment and a failure. Rather than seeking a coherent map of the true Christian faith and worldview, however, they try to figure out which aspects of Christian values the world might like—environmental care, social justice, forms of mysticism, tolerance for differing views of truth—and then serve up these things as the heart of the gospel. But why is it obvious that Christianity needs to change just because the current generation does not find it immediately palatable?

In a situation like ours, Christians must not first and foremost seek to be liked but to be lovingly faithful to the gospel. Otherwise, compromise can seem like a virtue rather than a serious danger. For example, Lyons' Q, a series of high-powered conferences where cultural leaders of many different religious persuasions are invited to lecture, appears to be an answer to the church's main problem—that Christianity is culturally unpopular. However, Q lacks a clear biblical cosmology undergirding its convictions and commitments. So they have invited non-Christian cultural leaders like Soledad O'Brien, a prominent American broadcast journalist, and Eboo Patel, a Muslim member of the Advisory Council on Faith-Based Neighborhood Partnerships, to speak. They also invited Rachel Held Evans, a popular progressive evangelical blogger and author with highly controversial views on the Bible, gender, and sexuality. Theirs is an attempt to propose a cool, intelligent, sophisticated, open-minded evangelical pluralism. Who doesn't want to be cool, intelligent, sophisticated, and open-minded? But can this particular path remain *evangelical*?

Pleasing the culture by conforming to its ideas has become a recasting of all things Christian for some progressive evangelicals. The first goal of the CANA Initiative, featuring "Emergent, Progressive, Missional Christians" like Brian McLaren, Stephanie Spellers, Doug Pagitt, Tony Jones, and Diana Butler Bass, is to "create a more attractive public opinion of Christianity."[6] The most radical, perhaps, is the Wild Goose Festival, which in 2014 featured an "Old Time Gospel Hour" led by a drag queen reverend and a sign at the entrance welcoming attendees that read:

> You do not have to be good.
> You do not have to walk on your knees
> for a hundred miles through the desert repenting.
> You only have to let the soft animal of your body
> love what it loves.[7]

A similar, though far less wild, temptation befalls other millennial-focused evangelical groups. Catalyst is a mainline evangelical conference organized by a team of millennial Christians. In their 2013 conference, in addition to addresses by plenary speakers like pastor John Piper, Catalyst emphasized issues of social justice such as poverty and sex trafficking. Yet it also featured a plenary speaker, Cory Booker, a politician who supports no-restriction, taxpayer-funded abortions. As at Lyons' Q, the message was confusing, but the event was certainly cool.[8]

Many churches will doubtless adopt a similar culture-embracing stance—particularly on the issue of gay marriage. Cultural influences abound, from President Obama, in his 2015 State of the Union address, calling on the Supreme Court to legalize gay marriage to well-funded, supposedly Christian groups systematically seeking to influence evangelical churches with their teaching of inclusive acceptance.[9]

This is a future warning of a tsunami that will doubtless hit the church in the days ahead. A good example is EastLake Community Church, a six-campus evangelical megachurch in the greater Seattle area that has "[come] out as one of the first openly LGBT-affirming evangelical churches in the U.S."[10] Another, New Heart Community outside Los Angeles, was recently part of the Southern Baptist Convention but is now calling itself a "third-way church, where leaders acknowledge a range of views about sexuality."[11] One of EastLake's pastors, Ryan Meeks, 36, justifies his church's decision on emotional and subjective ground: "I refuse to go to a church where my friends who are gay are excluded from Communion or a marriage covenant or the beauty of Christian community. ... It is a move of integrity for me—the message of Jesus was a message of wide inclusivity." He sees the response of his fellow evangelical Christians as being expressed in "D-Day terms. ... So many other pastors are afraid. ... Perhaps [EastLake's] contribution is to die on the beach."[12] But this isn't heroism—it's unwittingly compromising his gospel witness with Oneist "binary-busting," which brings down any belief in God the Creator as separate from the creation. Thus, he fails to affirm the cosmological significance of Twoism—both for theology (the nature of God) and sexuality (the nature of humanity, made in God's image, as Twoism shows).

In the name of walking more closely with Jesus and seeking to love those around them, are evangelicals running unwittingly into the embrace of a rising Oneist worldview and its integral views on spirituality and sexuality? Thorough, biblical cosmology puts these elements into a consistent worldview that is able to take on the culture. Piecemeal discourse inevitably skews the gospel. We need a full-orbed understanding of where our world is headed and how the gospel speaks to all human concerns.

Progressive Evangelicalism

Let's return to progressive evangelicalism, starting with Rachel Held Evans. In a recent op-ed for CNN, "Why Millennials Are Leaving the Church," Evans, like Kinnaman and Lyons, claims that young Christians are leaving the church because Christianity has become "too political, too exclusive, old-fashioned, unconcerned with social justice and hostile to lesbian, gay, bisexual and transgender people." In the process, she pleads for the church to become less concerned with sex (abortion and contraception) and more consumed with eradicating poverty and embracing same-sex marriage.[13] Brian McLaren sees his CANA Initiative, noted above, as developing a "more attractive public opinion of Christianity, spirituality and faith"[14] by creating "new ways of being Christian ... *new ways of doing theology.*"[15]

The model for this is Diana Butler Bass, a historian of Christianity and another leading voice in progressive Christianity.[16] She is the author of *Christianity After Religion: The End of Church and the Birth of a New Spiritual Awakening.*[17] Her brand of progressivism is entering the evangelical church. Bass's book is endorsed by mainline liberals such as Marcus Borg—a fellow of the Jesus Seminar—but also by evangelicals like Shane Claiborne, who hails her analysis as "new life budding from the compost of Christendom."[18] For Brian McLaren, Bass's work is "provocative, inspiring ... a sage guidance for the future."[19]

In *Christianity After Religion*, Bass announces the Fourth Great Awakening.[20] But this awakening has little to do with historic Christianity and even less to do with historic evangelicalism.[21] Bass is actually celebrating a "religionless Christianity," really more of a Christianless religion, shorn of creeds, dogmas, authority structures, unchanging moral codes, and an authoritatively revealed Bible.

Bass notes that "Catholics, Jews, Muslims, Hindus, and Buddhists have been undergoing similar revitalizations"[22] and concludes that "the next great awakening will have to be an interfaith awakening."[23] She argues that the 1970s were "the first stirrings of a new spiritual awakening," consisting of "a vast, interreligious movement"[24] that incorporates practices of other faiths. She adopts the truth of the interspiritual age, and the pagan cosmology behind it. Her remarks about the beginnings of the Fourth Great Awakening[25] in the 1960s fit the line of development I have set forth; it is the organic connection between Jungian pagan spirituality, Sixties East/West enlightenment and present interfaith mysticism. Bass says God is now "defined in less dualistic terms"[26]—in other words, less Twoist. The idea of "submitting to a transcendent— and often distant—God" is ditched in favor of "finding one's self in God and find[ing] God in one's self." This involves praying to God as "our Mother," and seeing God "less in terms of an absolutist, sin-hating, death-dealing 'almighty Father in Heaven' and more in terms of ... the nourishing spirit of mother earth."[27]

New Gnosticism

Such a union with nature in the lap of the "mother goddess" leaves little need for a divine savior (except perhaps as an example or guru), so Bass' Christology, like that of Jung, is gnostic. In this regard, Bass is a great admirer of the 14th-century mystic Meister Eckhart[28] (as was Jung).[29] In the biblical Gospels, Jesus' question "Who do you say that I am?" gives rise to the heavenly revelation of Christ's divine nature. In Bass' account, the question "plunges Jesus' friends into the corresponding self-query, 'And who am I?'" But where does Bass find this question? Not in the canonical Gospels, but in the gnostic gospels. In the gnostic *Gospel of Thomas*, Jesus tells Thomas not to call him Lord because both he and Thomas are of equal status.[30] Bass cites another gnostic gospel, the *Book of Thomas the Contender*, to prove her point that self-knowledge is true salvation: "He who has known himself has already understood the depth of all things."[31] This gives meaning to Bass's general Oneist position about spirituality—found in statements such as, "Finding one's self in God is also to find God in oneself,"[32] which is what the Gnostics meant by "gnosis," an experience of the divine within.[33] To develop this sense, she recommends "practices of faith" like "prayer, yoga or meditation."[34]

Bass, in turn, recommends the work of Phyllis Tickle, a leader in the evangelical Emergent movement, and sees that work as directly in line with her own research on the religious changes in the Western world since the Sixties.[35] In *The Great Emergence: How Christianity Is Changing and Why,*[36] Tickle recognizes the importance of Jung's legacy, especially in his questioning "the old standing definitions of 'self.' "[37] Tickle likewise recognizes the importance of Joseph Campbell:

> Jung ... was a motivating force behind Joseph Campbell. ... It would be very difficult, in speaking of the coming of the Great Emergence, to overestimate the power of Campbell in the disestablishment of what is called "the Christian doctrine of particularity" and "Christian exclusivity."[38]

Tickle calls the Great Emergence and widespread resurgence of spirituality a "new reformation," this time based on *solo spiritu* (according to the spirit alone), as opposed to *sola scriptura* (according to Scripture alone)—though the original Reformers never opposed Scripture in order to affirm the Holy Spirit who inspired the Scriptures. As far as Tickle is concerned, Emergent leader Brian McLaren can be seen as the Martin Luther of this new reformation.[39]

McLaren, in turn, sees his "transforming framing story" benefiting "other religions and ideologies."[40] Indeed, when McLaren looks at the movement of modern culture and the process of history and various religions and spiritualities, he sees

> the beautiful whole that is as big as the cosmos, and bigger still, in which every particle is known, named, and loved. Can we even say something absurd? Can we say that this beautiful whole is even bigger than God, because it begins with God in all God's infinite fullness, and then adds creation? Isn't that the most beautiful whole imaginable?[41]

This openness to other faiths on one hand is met with a decided dissatisfaction with historic orthodoxy on the other. In a 2006 radio interview, McLaren flatly stated: "The cross is almost a distraction and false advertising for God."[42]

One final example: Franciscan priest Richard Rohr has spoken to evangelical pastors about "Third Eye, non-dual thinking" and spirituality.[43] Elsewhere, Rohr has said, "The incarnation actually happened 13.7

billion years ago with a moment that we now call 'The Big Bang.' That is when God actually decided to materialize and to self-expose ... as the cosmic Christ."[44] For Rohr, the world is the "body of God."[45]

Evangelical Acceptance

We might have expected liberal theologians to seek a home in the integral spirituality and sexuality of neopaganism, now known as progressive or evolutionary spirituality. A mystical, suprarational state promises sinners liberation from the claims of the mythological Sky God of supposedly outmoded biblical theism while satisfying a need for something more than rationalist, nonsupernatural forms of Christianity are able to offer. We might have expected such thinking from esoteric "unity" spiritualists, who claim a form of Christianity such as that expressed in *Can Christians Be Saved? A Mystical Path to Oneness* by Virginia T. Stephenson and Buck Rhodes. They suggest "a new reformation of Christianity ... turning away from the dualism that creates separation ... toward the principle of Oneness or non-dualism."[46] But we wouldn't have expected such thinking to be, essentially, endorsed by evangelicals.

Certainly, the church has been guilty of all sorts of sins. But these deep critiques of the contemporary church's faith and practice come not from within its grand tradition of prophetic calls for repentance and return to the "old paths," but from without, from the perspective of a biblically hostile worldview that Christians simply cannot hope to appease while remaining faithful.

Well-meaning Christians have often made the mistake of thinking that their surrounding culture is, at worst, neutral and, at best, a redemptive work of the Spirit that shares authority with the Scriptures. Emergent church leader Kester Brewin, for example, believes we must admit "our dependence on [our] host culture"[47] and "open ourselves to ... and adapt to it,"[48] recognizing its "essential goodness."[49] If we accept Brewin's analysis, conformity to culture will seem natural and faithful.

But the basis of the church and that of the culture are not the same. Biblical teaching is quite clear:

Do not be unequally yoked with unbelievers. For what partnership has righteousness with lawlessness? Or what fellowship has light with darkness? What accord has Christ with Belial? Or what portion does a believer share with an unbeliever? What agreement has the temple of God with idols? For we are the temple of the living God; as God said,

"I will make my dwelling among them and walk among them,
      and I will be their God,
      and they shall be my people.
Therefore go out from their midst,
      and be separate from them, says the Lord,
and touch no unclean thing;
      then I will welcome you,
and I will be a father to you,
      and you shall be sons and daughters to me,
says the Lord Almighty" (2 Cor 6:14–18).

Paul goes on to exhort all Christians, "Since we have these promises, beloved, let us cleanse ourselves from every defilement of body and spirit, bringing holiness to completion in the fear of God" (2 Cor 7:1). Here's both a healthy mistrust of the culture and a love for sinners.

Let's not be fooled. The culture has a mind of its own, a worldview, the "wisdom of this world," which is the cosmology of the Lie that causes people to worship the creation rather than the Creator. The stakes are enormous, since contemporary Christian expressions of conformity with the culture—insofar as they compromise with the culture's religious convictions and depart from the biblical witness—are in various ways beholden to the Lie. The world does not need more conformity; it needs *transformity*. The world needs to hear the Word from God, from outside of itself. It needs to hear and see the Truth.

CHAPTER 11

A WHOLE OR HOLY COSMOS?

"...present your bodies as a living sacrifice, holy and acceptable to God" (Rom 12:1).

Twoism isn't just descriptive of the structure of biblical cosmology; it's a worldview that flows out of a way of life, the way of holiness. As we've seen, believers today—tempted to conform to the Oneist world all around them—fail to see that holiness is a way to speak of the cosmological binary of twoness, which maintains natural, created distinctions in order to bear witness to the Twoist Creator God. And in failing to see this, they inevitably assist the present pagan invasion of our culture with the Oneist-conceived order of existence in order to undermine the place of the Creator.

In this chapter, we will examine the profoundly biblical principle of separation as key to understanding the nature of reality. Holiness isn't an ancient doctrine, only interesting for the modern prudes of today's world. Rather, it's the very essence of the present religious conflict between Oneism and Twoism.

I've studied the Bible my whole life, but my study of the word "holy" in the Greek and Hebrew texts still revealed amazing things. It took me two full days because the term appears in one form or another 1097 times![1] Holiness is one of the most frequently described and most important concepts in both the Old and the New Testaments. It is treated most often in the New Testament by the Apostle Paul. After describing the nature of pagan thinking in Romans 1, then developing the character of the gospel in Romans 2–11, Paul begins Romans 12 with one of his favorite words: "therefore," which, in this case, introduces four chapters of gospel application. In the light of the pagan nature of the world and of God's saving action in Jesus, Paul calls believers to respond in two ways:

1. "[P]resent your bodies as a living sacrifice, holy and acceptable to God, which is your spiritual worship" (Rom 12:1); that is, self-sacrificially offering their bodies as holy to God.

2. "Do not be conformed to this world, but be transformed by the renewal of your mind" (12:2); that is, by understanding the cosmology of the Bible (which we will treat in the next chapter), seeking to think God's thoughts after him.

Christians are not only called to refuse conformity with the cosmology of the world, they are also called to embrace a cosmology of *holiness*. The exhortation to holiness is everywhere in Paul's writings. Here are just a few examples:

- Romans 6:19: "For just as you once presented your members as slaves to impurity ... so now present your members as slaves to righteousness leading to sanctification [holiness]."

- Romans 6:22: "But now that you have been set free from sin and have become slaves of God, the fruit you get leads to sanctification [holiness] and its end, eternal life."

- 1 Thessalonians 4:3–4: "For this is the will of God, your sanctification: that you abstain from sexual immorality; that each one of you know how to control his own body in holiness and honor..."

- 1 Thessalonians 4:7: "For God has not called us for impurity, but in holiness."

- 2 Corinthians 7:1: "[L]et us cleanse ourselves from every defilement of body and spirit, bringing holiness to completion in the fear of God."

- 1 Corinthians 3:17: "For God's temple is holy, and you are that temple."

We'll examine just what holiness is and why it is so important in a world given over to the Lie. The term holiness might seem old-fashioned and moralistic to some; but in the present situation it couldn't be better attuned to what is required of Christians in response to the times in which we live. Just as the cosmologies of Oneism and Twoism are finally irreconcilable, so the biblical understanding of right living in relation to God and others—*holiness*—is the polar opposite of what today's spirituality proposes—*wholeness*.

Defining Our Terms

Ironically, because "wholeness" and "holiness" sound and seem similar, they are sometimes mistaken for the same idea. David Tacey, a contemporary Jungian, confuses them, suggesting that "holistic and holy have the same etymology."[2] Huston Smith does the same thing, claiming that "holiness" comes from "whole," meaning complete.[3] Evangelical Mark Foreman—who is biblically faithful in his actual conclusions—likewise states that "holy" and "whole" are "etymologically connected," and "holiness is the manifestation of wholeness."[4] Confusion in this crucial area can be hazardous to spiritual health. Jung criticized God himself for lacking "wholeness" in the form of a "dark side," as we have already seen.[5] So we must think and speak with clarity. Behind these two English words, "holiness" and "wholeness," are two Greek words that are *not* related—*hagios* and *holos*.

In classical Greek, the adjective *hagios* (holy) stems from the noun *hagos*, meaning an "object of awe." *Hagios* is used of sanctuaries, or of the gods—that is, of "things not accessible to the public," things set apart for a special purpose, or which are distinctive and unique.[6] This Greek term translates the Hebrew term, *qodesh* from the verb, *qod*, "to divide."[7] Things that are holy, like "holy ground" (Exod 3:5) or the Sabbath day, are separate, set apart and divided from things that are common. God "blessed the seventh day and made it holy" (Gen 2:3) as a special day. (And so, in English we have holidays—that is "holy days," special days that are set apart.) To "sanctify" something is to dedicate that thing to God's possession "as something exclusively belonging to him."[8]

On the other hand, the Greek, *holos* is often translated "whole" or "universal," from which we get terms like "holistic." In a sense, *hagios and holos* are opposite in meaning. The term *holos* means that nothing is distinctively other, or specially set apart, as it would be in "holiness." *Everything* is included. Behind the sense of these two words is a world of difference—indeed, in one sense they might be said to represent two antithetical worldviews, Oneism and Twoism. By describing something as holistic, modern spirituality roughly means the same thing that Jung taught about the joining of the opposites on the path toward self-realization. Jeffrey Satinover, an ex-Jungian, suggests that this kind of holism implies an underlying rejection of the moral order:

> For Jung good and evil evolved into two equal, balanced, cosmic principles that belong together in one over-arching synthesis. This relativization of good and evil by their reconciliation is the heart of the ancient doctrines of Gnosticism, which also located spirituality, hence morality, within man himself. Hence "the union of opposites."[9]

We must realize that this search for a holistic "relativization of good and evil" leads to their ultimate extinction. This is at the very heart of the pagan cosmology. And there are no *inherent* moral or logical barriers as to where that relativization should stop.

An example comes from one of the philosophical champions of this modern cosmology, French philosopher Michel Foucault. Foucault promoted the idea that he was a modern-day Friedrich Nietzsche, overturning all moral absolutes, especially sexual ones. A recent biographer describes with disorientating frankness how this search took Foucault into sadomasochism:

> Foucault [participated] in the orgies of torture, trem-
> bling with "the most exquisite agonies," voluntarily ef-
> facing himself, exploding the limits of consciousness,
> letting real, corporeal pain insensibly melt into pleasure
> through the alchemy of eroticism. ... Through intoxica-
> tion, reverie, the Dionysian abandon of the artist, the
> most punishing of ascetic practices, and an uninhibited
> exploration of sadomasochistic eroticism, it seemed
> possible to breach, however briefly, the boundaries
> separating the conscious and unconscious, reason and
> unreason, pleasure and pain—and, at the ultimate limit,
> life and death—thus starkly revealing how distinctions
> central to the play of true and false are pliable, uncer-
> tain, contingent.[10]

Although rarely as extremely pursued, this joining of the opposites is
what Jung and many other spiritualists have referred to by "wholeness."
Yet is not such a shattered and broken self the total opposite of integrity,
health, and vitality? What kind of wholeness is that?

Such thinking is not an option for Christians. As our world becomes
more like the ancient Roman Empire, we must hear again the text of
Romans 12:1–2, able, perhaps, to understand it more like the original
hearers than have many of our Western forebears:

> I appeal to you therefore, brothers, by the mercies of
> God, to present your bodies as a living sacrifice, holy
> and acceptable to God, which is your spiritual worship.
> Do not be conformed to this world, but be transformed
> by the renewal of your mind, that by testing you may
> discern what is the will of God, what is good and accept-
> able and perfect.

This is not simply a text about personal piety or what we do in Sunday-
morning worship. What can we propose to this new, powerful, unholy,
pagan empire other than the coming of an infinitely greater empire—
the kingdom of God in the form of a sanctified cosmos? This grand
vision lies behind Paul's seemingly innocuous exhortation to the Roman
Christians to give to God their bodies in self-sacrificial, *holy* living. Paul

knows they are called to bear witness before the "kingdoms of this world" (both by word and by personal, embodied deeds) to the coming transformed cosmos of absolute holiness over which Jesus, not Caesar, is Lord.

How does an entire cosmos get sanctified? Obviously, if Jesus is now reigning over all things in heaven and earth, our necessary and good attempts at social justice and acts of mercy are only a small part of the vast picture. In his earthly ministry, Jesus announced the coming kingdom of God, which included the destruction of sin and evil and the subjection of demons and idolaters, a kingdom which promises the only *true* utopia—when all will be two (God and humanity, united in love), not one (an impersonal cosmos, forever alone).

How interesting that via these different terms of "holy" and "holism," we come back to our starting point, the fact of only two religions, Oneism and Twoism. Oneism is a form of spiritual holism where everything is considered good because it is an aspect of the whole—including God and Satan, virtue and vice. Twoism in its very essence contains holiness, where things are not confused but have their special, God-ordained places.

As we look for a meaningful response to a pagan worldview that explains everything from a Oneist perspective—folding right and wrong, beauty and ugliness together—we have a compelling cosmology of holiness in the biblical vision of an ordered, God-created cosmos. We affirm things in their rightful, complementary places for fitting, life-promoting functions. Because a person's cosmology invariably develops from the nature of God, or from whatever that person identifies as the origin and ultimate meaning of everything, then from a Twoist perspective, the Bible's revelation of a "holy cosmos" makes beautiful sense.

A Beautifully Holy God

This term is supremely applied to God as uniquely distinguished from his creation, both in terms of his self-existent being and (in light of humanity's rebellion) in terms of his moral purity from all darkness and sin. Thus, in the presence of God, the seraphim cry out, "Holy, holy, holy," and Isaiah trembles, sensing his own contrasting mortality and, especially, uncleanness (Isa 6:3–5). This holy distinction between God and creatures is maintained throughout eternity; though God's people will always be with him and holy through him, God will always be the only Holy One—to his glory and for our enjoyment. In the vision John sees of heaven, "the four living creatures, each of them with six wings, are full of eyes all around and within, and day and night they never cease to say, 'Holy, holy, holy, is the Lord God Almighty, who was and is and is to come' " (Rev 4:8)![11]

The West has conceived of holiness in primarily moral terms—which in my generation sometimes led to treating the church as a "holy huddle" or acting as if an authentically Christian mindset is an ethically superior, holier-than-thou attitude. But when we say God is holy, we are not only saying he is morally pure (though he is). We are primarily speaking cosmologically. We are saying he is utterly unique and primary in his being, and that, relative to everything else, he is Other. Nowhere does Scripture define God's essential being as found within or defined by the cosmos. In his creating and saving work, by his Spirit, God upholds all things and even dwells *within* believers. But without fail, the God of Scripture is Other—with us, but beyond us and before us. God is holy, independent from the creation and separate from the mythical, pagan gods, which are mere human projections, without life in themselves. A popular Christian song says it simply but well:

> God of wonders beyond our galaxy, You are holy, holy!
> The universe declares your Majesty![12]

Israel emerged from captivity in the land of Egypt where the worship of Isis, the Earth Mother and goddess of the underworld, held sway. Moses himself had been raised in this traditional spirituality, but something changed him from top to bottom. He met the transcendent Lord of the universe in a bush, which burned but was not consumed, and was commanded: "Do not come near; take your sandals off your feet, for the place on which you are standing is holy ground" (Exod 3:5). Wherever God appears in this world in glory the place is frighteningly holy. For Moses it was Yahweh the Creator or Isis, the goddess of the underworld. Talk about polar opposites!

Later Moses declares, "Who is like You, O Lord, among the gods? Who is like You, glorious in holiness, fearful in praises, doing wonders?" (Exod 15:11 NKJV). This is why God will reveal himself five chapters later in the Ten Commandments as the only Creator and Redeemer, declaring, "You shall not make for yourself an idol, or any likeness of what is in heaven above or on the earth beneath or in the water under the earth. You shall not worship them or serve them" (Exod 20:4–5 NASB). Later, Israel is judged for forgetting this when God speaks through Ezekiel: "[M]y holy name you shall no more profane with your gifts and your idols" (Ezek 20:39). The God of Israel is not to be confused with anything created, and certainly not with what is falsehood and sin.

The psalmist, centuries after Moses, declares the same otherness of God and the lowliness of creation in comparison: "Worship the Lord in the splendor of holiness; tremble before him, all the earth" (Psa 96:9). Jesus himself teaches us how we should pray to God, saying, "Our Father in heaven, hallowed [holy] be your name" (Matt 6:9).

God is not only holy in his relation to the world. Not only does he look down "from his holy height ... at the earth" (Psa 102:19), but he is holy in himself, even if there were no earth on which to look down.[13] Though the words "Holy Trinity" are not found in the Bible, the concept is. God's divine being consists of three distinct persons, Father, Son, and Holy Spirit, who are never confused, and so always retain their individual distinctiveness or holiness from one another. Thus God comprehends both distinction and complementarity within his Trinitarian being, and as an independent Creator, without a beginning, is necessarily separate or holy relative to the dependent creation he makes, sustains, and redeems.

A Beautifully Holy Cosmos

In a comparable way, the created order is fashioned according to the model or principle of God's holiness. As we noted, God blesses the seventh day and makes it holy "because on it God rested from all his work that he had done in creation" (Gen 2:3). Thus the seventh day of the human week carries the sign of holiness in recalling forever both the God who is distinct from the creation and the manner in which he made it, with work and rest. But the principle of holy separation is at work

as the Lord turns unformed matter into an ordered, beautifully functioning cosmos, where things have their distinguishing, rightful place
in relation to one another. God separates day from night, the seas from
dry land. He creates different kinds and gives them specific, individual
names. Everything is "very good."¹⁴ To create is to separate and to separate is to make holy. They are synonymous terms.¹⁵ Thus, created things,
in their separateness, reflect in a creaturely way the holiness of God.

The psalmist catches the full-orbed nature of this cosmological truth
when he says about the cosmos, "You [God] have put all things under his
feet" (Psa 8:6)—one more expression of God's sanctifying activity, setting all things in their appropriate places. My Old Testament professor
at Princeton captured well the force of Genesis 1: "All things are created
in their order to perform their special functions. The universe and all its
'host' (2:1) are ready to offer their praise and worship to their Creator on
the [first] Sabbath day."¹⁶

When our second daughter (a brilliant, successful woman) was two
years old, we discovered that she had been born profoundly deaf. We sud-
denly had to learn a lot about the ear, especially the amazing "organ of
Corti." This structure, part of the cochlea, is made up of 15,000–20,000
microscopic hairs, each of which sends vibrations to the brain that en-
able hearing. The complexity still defies medical science. In the next
generation of our family, we learned that one of our grandchildren may
have problems in the macula of his eyes. The macula is the size of a pin-
head but processes vast amounts of complicated optical data which it
sends to the brain, enabling sight. Both in hearing and in seeing, we depend upon created differences in sound, shapes, and colors. And these
are mere microscopic parts of God's creation!

The high point of God's creational activity is his creation of humanity, on whom he places the image of the Twoist Trinitarian God as the
source of both distinction and unity. Marked by this sign of ultimate
dignity, human beings alone receive the high calling to witness throughout time to the personal God as their Father and Creator. Needless to
say, this must constitute a fundamental element of evangelism, since
all human beings are marked as unique by the image of God they carry.
Last Christmas, my oldest daughter, a missionary in Germany, sent me
a YouTube video, "Gloria! - Flashmob der Berliner Stadtmission zum

Advent." This was an event in a huge, high-class department store in downtown, "godless" Berlin, where some "shoppers"—actually a mass choir of German Christians—were strategically situated on the five floors overlooking the escalators. They broke out in praise to God the Creator, singing *Gloria in excelsis Deo*. People applauded vigorously and some shed tears at hearing something that comes from deep within the cosmos and goes deep into the human soul—the praise of our Creator!

Even when aspects of our cosmos have gone wrong, like deafness or difficulties seeing, because of the fall, we should be excited about this cosmos—reflecting its Creator by a glorious blend of difference in unity. God's creative intelligence and care is written all over the physical world. God's qualities, says Paul, "have been clearly seen ... from what has been made" (Rom 1:20 NIV). And what do we see? A cosmos of brilliantly functioning elements, distinct from one another yet all working together. The Prophet Isaiah quotes the seraphim, saying, "[T]he whole earth is full of his glory" (Isa 6:3). To this same Isaiah, God, "the Holy One" declares:

> Lift up your eyes on high and see:
>> who created these?
> He who brings out their host by number,
>> calling them all by name,
> by the greatness of his might,
>> and because he is strong in power
>> not one is missing" (Isa 40:25-26).

Ah, the "music of the spheres." People in the Middle Ages used this expression to describe their sense of the harmonic and mathematical complexity of the created universe. This symphony of sight and sound reflects the biblical notion of a world created by the Holy One. He is of infinite thought and imagination, according to the fundamental principle of holy distinctions and eye-catching complementarity. The summit of the glory of God's handiwork is captured in the Bible's view of humanity as a glorious and wonderful creation, as the psalmist exclaims: "When I look at your heavens, the work of your fingers, the moon and the stars, which you have set in place, what is man that you are mindful of him...?" (Psa 8:3-4). That glory is bound up with the sign of holiness, the image of God, which humanity carries as distinctly male and female (Gen 1:27), a complementarity declared by God to be "very good" (Gen 1:31; or, as Gerhard von Rad translated the phrase, "completely perfect").[17] This essential cosmic splendor was reflected in the garments of the high priest, a sanctified, set apart representative of the Lord on earth. His robes were holy, tailored "for glory and for beauty" (Exod 28:2).

Twoism is beautiful—and trustworthy. God "swears by his holiness."[18] It is a worldview that can be trusted, because it reflects the character of the God who can be trusted.[19]

A Beautifully Holy People

Both God's holy nature and the holy, created cosmos constitute the basis of the particular holiness of God's people, who reflect their Lord in a now-unholy world, whether in the Old or New Testament. The Apostle Peter exhorts his new-covenant flock to be holy but cites the command already given to old-covenant Israel: "[A]s he who called you is holy, you also be holy in all your conduct; since it is written, 'You shall be holy, for I am holy'" (1 Pet 1:15–16; see also Lev 11:45). There are many Old Testament examples of this call.[20] The New Testament is equally well-furnished with such exhortations.[21] The believers are called "saints";[22] they are collectively and individually "a holy temple" (Eph 2:21; see also 1 Cor 3:17) and "a holy nation" (1 Pet 2:9); they are exhorted to bring "holiness to completion" (2 Cor 7:1); and to be "holy and blameless" (Col 1:22). In a word, they are called to holiness (1 Thess 4:7; 2 Pet 3:11).

The command to give God "holy bodies" and not to be conformed to the world, as we have heard from Paul in Romans 12, is repeated by Peter in similar terms:

> As obedient children, do not be conformed to the former lusts which were yours in your ignorance, but like the Holy One who called you, be holy yourselves also in all your behavior; because it is written, "You shall be holy, for I am holy" (1 Pet 1:14–16 NASB).

How do we not conform to "the former lusts"? By putting into practice the principles of holiness, as a response of gratitude to the one who did this for us, as Paul shows in his Letter to the Ephesians. Using the same Old Testament sacrificial image as that of Romans 12:1, Paul applies this imagery to Jesus. Thus he exhorts Christians to "walk in love, as Christ loved us and gave himself up [Greek, *paredoken*—see below] for us, a fragrant offering and sacrifice to God" (Eph 5:2). We offer our bodies as a sacrifice out of love for Jesus who sacrificed his body for us, to proclaim in embodied form the gospel we preach in word. As Paul and Peter testify, an important part of what this further means is adopting a biblical cosmology of holiness as the basis for witness in word and deed in an unholy world now profaned by the very humans created to enjoy and watch over it. Alas, the unholy is all around us (and in us!).

The creation is marred, and people are inclined to evil. The world needs hope and help. That hope and help is Jesus himself, before whom the demons shrieked in fear when confronted with "the Holy One of God" (Mark 1:24). The crowds were amazed and blurted out: "What is this? A new teaching with authority!" (Mark 1:27). Just as these people saw, recognized, and honored Jesus the Messiah, so *our* world needs, by the work of the Spirit, to see the holiness of Jesus lived out in the transformed lives of believers.

A Beautifully Holy Life

The biblical notion of holiness, therefore, isn't just a theory that leads to holier-than-thou self-satisfaction. The "thou" is the "other" who needs our self-giving care. Sartre famously said, "Hell is other people";[23] well, in the Bible, *heaven* is other people. This is why the exhortation to holiness in Romans 12:1 is immediately followed by instructions for selfless living for others. The apostle urges believers, "Love one another with brotherly affection. Outdo one another in showing honor" (Rom 12:10). Notice that in the term "one another" is the term "other." "Let no one seek his own good, but the good of his neighbor" (1 Cor 10:24; in the Greek, "neighbor" is actually "the other," *heteros*). "Owe no one anything, except to love each other, for the one who loves another (*heteros*) has fulfilled the law" (Rom 13:8).[24] The whole law is hetero-focused. See the next verse—"For the commandments ... are summed up in this word: 'You shall love your neighbor as yourself' " (Rom 13:9).

The exhortations continue: "Contribute to the needs of the saints and seek to show hospitality. Bless those who persecute you; bless and do not curse them. Rejoice with those who rejoice, weep with those who weep. Live in harmony with one another. Do not be haughty, but associate with the lowly. Never be wise in your own sight. Repay no one evil for evil, but give thought to do what is honorable in the sight of all" (Rom 12:13-17). Thus, Twoism doesn't turn inward—to feed one's fantasies, to realize the self—but outward, toward the other—to feed the poor, care for the broken, love the unlovely.

The secret to powerful, Spirit-filled living under the cosmology of holiness is submission.[25] This term for some may evoke images of a battered and crushed wife or a fearful, wailing child under the authority of a vicious, violent parent. We may alternatively connect it with Islam, which means "submission" in Arabic. This conjures up images of jihadists doing atrocious things. What changes everything, of course, is the definition of the God to whom submission is due. In Islam, Allah is a singular, solitary, arbitrary being; in Christianity, submission is given to a personal, merciful, Triune God who is our loving Father.

Submission is an unavoidable biblical category. Let's look at the Greek again. The Greek translation of the Old Testament (the Septuagint) uses the verb *hupotasso*, meaning to "set under" or "to submit," 27 times, while the New Testament uses it 76 times. "Submit" is used as an exhortation to Christians in their present lives to be salt and light (Matt 5:13-14), to take control by actively submitting ourselves to the structures God has created in the world, witnessing to the fact that God is still in control and that everything God created is good (1 Tim 4:4). As redeemed saints living in God's new family, we are, in a sense, reliving the experience of Adam and Eve, who failed in their task. In the power of the resurrection and the Spirit of Christ, we reclaim the cosmos, honor the Creator, and exercise our godly role of filling and subduing the earth by honoring the goodness of creation's structures and submitting to them.

In the Bible, submission is everyone's calling. No group or category of person is excused. This is the force of Ephesians 5:21: "[Submit] to one another out of reverence for Christ." Even Jesus submitted himself to the Father's will every moment of his earthly life and continually gives glory to his Father, even as he is glorified (1 Cor 15:28). All areas of life are included:

- *Personal holiness:* "The mind that is set on the flesh is hostile to God, for it does not submit to God's law; indeed, it cannot" (Rom 8:7; see 1 Tim 1:8). The clear implication of this text is that the believer does submit to God's law, walking in the freedom of his love. "You shall be holy to me, for I the LORD am holy and have separated you from the peoples, that you should be mine" (Lev 20:26).

- *Sexual purity:* Christian believers are required to "flee from sexual immorality (*porneia*). Every other sin a person commits is outside the body, but the sexually immoral person sins against his own body" (1 Cor 6:18). The reason is submission to holiness, for "your body is a temple of the Holy Spirit within you, whom you have from God ... You are not your own, for you were bought with a price. So glorify God in your body" (1 Cor 6:19–20). Robert Reilly clarifies this issue:

  > If the definition of morality is based on [mere] desire, eventually described as love, no moral distinctions can be made between hetero, homo, adultery, pederasty, even incest. Sexuality has to have meaning outside of the mere act, serving 'unitive and procreative ends' for the sake of the larger community.[26]

  For Reilly, the determining factor is natural law, but behind natural law, a larger canvas must be in view, namely the otherness and holiness of God and how the cosmos reflects his character.

- *Marriage:* Human sexuality is intended for submission to the one-flesh structure of heterosexual, lifelong holy matrimony, which is the complementary relation of a man and a woman who contribute different but equally important identities and roles to the marriage. This is part of what makes matrimony holy. Though all Christians are called to submit to one another, in marriage the wife in particular is called to submit to her husband (Eph 5:22), while the husband must submit to love his wife more than himself. Gay marriage, in this light, is unholy because it attempts to create sameness, suppressing or merging difference, and thus departs from the biblical holiness of complementary difference. From a cosmological perspective, these two stances are opposed and cannot be reconciled, however much even some Christians attempt to do so.[27]

- *The family*: Just as Jesus submitted himself to the law concerning obeying parents (Luke 2:51; 1 Tim 3:4), so children should submit themselves to their parents in the Lord (Eph 6:1-3).

- *The church:* The entire church, members and leaders, "submits" to Christ (Eph 5:24), and all God's children are "subject" to their heavenly Father (Heb 12:9; see also Jas 4:7). All Christian believers are called to submit to church leaders (1 Pet 5:5), which is why the church must reflect in its organization the structure of complementary family distinctions. Male leadership in the historic church hasn't been—or at least, shouldn't be—a patriarchal power trip but an integral part of the church's understanding of the place of distinctions and order in the biblical cosmology of Twoist holiness.

- *Civic life:* Both men and women are "subject" to the civil magistrate (Rom 13:1; 1 Pet 2:13; see also Titus 3:1; 1 Tim 2:3) and to employers (Titus 2:9; 1 Pet 2:18; cf. Eph 6:5-8; 1 Tim 3:4-7); all arenas of human experience are places where witness to a holy God must be seen.

Such submission is never onerous or humiliating. It is an alignment of the individual in joyful faith before God to the cosmic structures God has created and ordained for the common good. Sarah Ruden—a classics scholar with deep knowledge of ancient Roman life, particularly the military—has a fascinating take on the language Paul uses. She interprets Paul's notion of submission in terms of the Graeco-Roman Empire and its concepts of privilege, by which military service was understood and which the verb "to submit" presupposes. Ruden understands submission not as grudging obligation but as honorable "self-deployment":

> When Paul wrote about "subjection" ... the images his
> readers had were not of shoveling manure or being
> beaten into submission. They were of respected, re-
> warded functions. He was in effect urging his followers
> to become stakeholders, leaders themselves through
> their cooperation.[28]

Being stakeholders in a holy cosmos—or "vice-regents," as Psalm 8 puts
it—is the privilege to which human beings are divinely called. This is
what Paul is presupposing when he states that God is a "God not of disorder but of peace" (1 Cor 14:33 NIV) or when congratulating the Colossians
on their "good order" (Col 2:5). With such terms Paul is presupposing
that behind everything there is an ordained structure, a coherent cosmology. So from this perspective, sin is the rejection of God's creative,
well-structured oeuvre, as in "chef d'oeuvre." "[The sinful mind] does
not submit to God's law" (Rom 8:7) and "does not submit to" what God
has ordained. On the other hand, Christians submit both from respect-
ful admiration and "for the sake of conscience" (Rom 13:5).

Further, it is from a biblical understanding of holiness—things in
their rightful, God-ordained places—that the civic principles of justice
and rights derive. According to Robert Reilly, justice is "giving to things
what is their due according to what they are," as enshrined in the "Laws
of Nature and Nature's God."[29] From justice flow human rights that
make possible successful communal living. Rights are not the freedom
to do anything one pleases, but to be the recipient of justice. Reilly adds:
"If Nature is denied, then justice will necessarily be reduced to what is
willed, which, in turn, becomes right as the rule of the stronger."[30]

For all kinds of reasons, Christians must engage in the privilege
of holy living in the present culture—to glorify God as Creator, to be
a source of justice for the common good, and to produce strong marriages and loving families that function as outposts of hope in a Oneist
world that eventually will produce "enlightened"—yet desperately
lonely—individuals. Such holy living also serves as a sign of the coming
resanctified heavens and earth. Hope, not destruction, is the final word.
Therefore Christians must "[s]trive ... for the holiness without which no
one will see the Lord" (Heb 12:14).[31]

At the death and resurrection of Jesus, in his defeat of sin and his power over death and corruption, the future sanctification of the cosmos was objectively achieved. Thus, holiness is now a gift to God's people, who are already called "saints." So God is now known and praised not only as the holy Creator but also as the holy Redeemer and future Consummator, now preparing a mind-blowing renewed cosmos of unimaginable holiness.

David Horowitz—a brilliant Jewish ex-Marxist Sixties revolutionary who became a social conservative later in life—changed his tune after witnessing the fallenness of human nature in himself and in the idealistic revolutionary friends from his youth, some of them still active. In the Sixties, he saw past the optimistic visions of a this-worldly utopia to people's inability to change themselves and, finally, past the rhetoric, the ugliness of living for nothing but themselves. This has produced in Horowitz, who remains an agnostic, a sad but honest realism: "To be a conservative is to understand that there is no solution to the dilemmas of the human condition. ... We have no permanent abode in this world ... If there is a home for us that is truly permanent, it is not of this time or of this place."[32]

Perhaps someday a simple Christian believer will show him that there is a permanent abode, that there is a home that Christ is preparing for those who love him.

A Beautifully Holy Future

If the first creation was holy, so will be the second one—and "how much more" (Rom 5:12–21 NIV)! God's continuing work consists in "[vindicating] the holiness of my great name, which has been profaned among the nations ... And the nations will know that I am the Lord ... when through you I vindicate my holiness before their eyes" (Ezek 36:23). Actually, Christians have a calling to show "the whole earth," the watching world, through our intentional holy living that creation is not simply an evolving meaningless mass of anything we want it to be, due to mere chance or the instinct of survival in which we live autonomous but ultimately purposeless lives. Creation is, rather, the intentional, gloriously finely-tuned product of a personal holy God who has his own holy place and has given us ours, and through it all receives the glory due to his name.

There is a permanent home which we have seen from afar in the face of Jesus, the Holy One of God, that the Lord will bring to earth, the Holy City, the new Jerusalem, which is the fulfillment of the Old Testament "holy mountain" (Psa 99:9), where righteousness will dwell forever (Rev 21:2). In other words, the holy future is God-centered. Christians get to attend that great moment of vindication and, by grace, we get to "share in his holiness" (Heb 12:10). Everything will be made new, everything will be holy. You can count on it—these words are "trustworthy ... for: If we died with him, we will also live with him" (2 Tim 2:11). At the fall, God subjected the creation to "futility" (Rom 8:20), but the hope remains of a renewed creation, now restored not to vanity but to glorious subjection to the will of God, where he is everywhere recognized Lord of all.

Christ is the firstfruits of the new humanity, the "new Adam," whom Jung longed for but could never see because he was looking in the wrong place, looking within. Christ's objective, historical, redemptive work on the cross and in the resurrection by the power of "the Spirit of holiness" (Rom 1:4) in history places him as head or authority over all things (Eph 1:22; Col 2:10). As head, he resubjects all things, resets all things in their rightful, reconciled places, beneath his rightful rule. In other words, as head over all things, he sanctifies—or rather resanctifies—the cosmos into its rightful place of submission to the will and design of God, and everything will be "very good" (Gen 1:31). This is our great hope, as it was the hope of God's people in the past, in the words of the Prophet Isaiah, who prophesies a new way of holiness:

> Say to those who have an anxious heart,
>   "Be strong; fear not! ...
>   He will come and save you."
>
> Then the eyes of the blind shall be opened,
>   and the ears of the deaf unstopped;
> then shall the lame man leap like a deer,
>   and the tongue of the mute sing for joy.

> For waters break forth in the wilderness,
>   and streams in the desert;
> the burning sand shall become a pool,
>   and the thirsty ground springs of water;
> in the haunt of jackals, where they lie down,
>   the grass shall become reeds and rushes.
>
> And a highway shall be there,
>   and it shall be called the Way of Holiness;
> the unclean shall not pass over it. ...
> And the ransomed of the Lord shall return
>   and come to Zion with singing;
> everlasting joy shall be upon their heads;
>   they shall obtain gladness and joy,
>   and sorrow and sighing shall flee away (Isaiah 35:4–10).

This holy living based on a Twoist understanding of God's person and will also transforms our sin-stained minds, making possible clear Twoist thinking. This will be the subject of the next chapter, for, as the proverb says, "knowledge of the Holy One is understanding" (Prov 9:10 NIV).

CHAPTER 12

BLOWING THE MIND

"...be transformed by the renewing of your mind" (Rom 12:2 NIV).

The Need for Distinctions

As a little Jewish rabbi, Paul, was taken in chains to the "eternal city," the very center of the glorious "civilized" world of the Roman Empire, few could have understood the enormity of the event. Everyone knew that there was only one state and only one lord, Caesar. In league with the gods of nature, Caesar ruled over all, and all was spiritually one. Before arriving in Rome, Paul had written to the Christians in that capital city, calling for a complete transformation of the mind, a thorough overturning of all the classic categories of pagan thinking. Paul's message turned out to be world shattering. All is not one. All is two.

Two Views of God: Creator or Created

As we have learned, our cosmology flows from our view of the divine. According to the Bible, only two gods are possible: creation or the Creator (Rom 1:25).[1] Both starting points are in essence religious, describing the character of the divine as either ontologically transcendent and separate from nature or ontologically immanent within nature. These two options are mutually exclusive; there is no hope of bringing them together in some kind of hybrid system. The struggle will go on until the end of history, when the Truth will be finally and fully revealed.

The reader will recall that for Jung, the gnostic god within was the only one worth worshiping: "Abraxas, half man, half beast, as a God higher than both the Christian God and the Devil, which combines all opposites."[2] Jung dismissed the biblical God, the transcendent Creator "outside of man," viscerally describing such belief as "systematic blindness."[3]

For the Apostle Paul, blindness goes in the opposite direction of Jung's claim; seeing creation as God is blindness. People see evidence of the true God in creation, but then choose to become blind. "[W]hat can be known about God is plain to them, because God has shown it to them ... they became futile in their thinking, and their foolish hearts were darkened" (Rom 1:19, 21).

Two Possible Conclusions: Truth or Lie

The human mind, even in its fallen state, is capable of amazing intellectual constructions but also of irrational conclusions that dehumanize culture. When pro-choice people speak of the activities of an abortionist as his "abortion ministry" or of abortion as "a gift from God" yet refuse to show any graphic pictures of the violence done to the child, they exhibit a serious lack of logic. Should they not be holding up the glorious results of God's great gift of dismembered babies for all to see? This is not simply irrational and inconsistent; it is dishonest.

The Lie will always contradict itself. Heinrich Himmler—rational, intelligent, jovial, and friendly—was raised in a pious, Roman Catholic, middle-class family. He was also head of the brutal SS corps under Hitler in the 1940s. Himmler admitted to being physically sick at the sight of the mass extermination of other human beings, even though he himself had organized the slaughter. But then with pride he stated, "To remain decent has made us tough ... This is a page of glory in our history which has never been written before."[4] How can you feel sick looking at "decency" and "glory"? Moreover, at the end of the war, Himmler secretly met with Jewish leaders, without Hitler's knowledge, and sent messages to Churchill proposing an end to the Holocaust as part of the peace negotiations, presumably to save his skin and apparently contradicting his previous notions of "glory" and "decency."[5]

Pontius Pilate declared Jesus innocent three times before having him flogged and crucified. The fallen world, with its godless view of truth, is forever teetering on the brink of irrationality, for the Lie finally abhors the Truth.

Two Possible Minds: Undiscerning or Discerning

Now is a time for clear speech, not for the conformist confusion we've noted previously. What human beings need is a transformed mind, able to discern the will of God the Creator who is blessed forever (Rom 12:2; 1:25). Genuine human discernment and ultimate human flourishing depends on this. Talk about mind-blowing—compared to the god within, the true God is unfathomable and goes beyond anything we can imagine. This kind of thinking is our spiritual worship as opposed to the false worship of the creation.

Paul contends that there are only two kinds of minds:

1. The undiscerning, debased mind (Rom 1:28) that elevates the creature (or all of nature) into god by worshiping and serving the creation as God. It builds a worldview on the Lie.

2. The transformed, discerning mind (Rom 12:2), freed from the blindness of sin, which understands God as separate from the creation, and worships and serves him alone as the only object worthy of reverence. It builds a worldview on the Truth.

The "discerning" mind of Romans 12:2 and the "undiscerning" mind of Romans 1:28 are expressed in words that share the same root.[6] Here we find not only a clear antithesis between two ways of using the mind, but a moral element as well. One way of using the mind is true (discerning);

the other is false (undiscerning). The created world ultimately faces us with the moral choice for or against a personal Creator.

As we saw in chapter 1, this is the most essential question for the mind: Does the world create itself, or is there a Creator, different from the world? Is reality One or Two? Your answer will affect the way you think about theology, spirituality, and sexuality, as Paul shows in Romans 1.[7]

Jung succeeded where Julian failed. Jung's great objection to Christian orthodoxy in the modern West was its belief in divine transcendence (Twoism). His was truly an undiscerning mind. According to Jung, it is the Bible's teaching that grace comes from outside[8] which should be considered "spiritual blindness" and an insult to the human soul. The transcendent Other God, Jung argued, denied to humanity its "access to the divinity of its own soul."[9] The modern person needs to be healed from this blindness, he said.

Though I have used Jung as a powerful example of Oneist thinking, he is far from the only one affected by an undiscerning mind. Oneism is espoused by globalist politicians, United Nations documents defining the planet's future, Hollywood spiritualists, leaders from all the world's religions, and self-proclaimed progressive liberals (both "Christian" and non-Christian). These have no place for God the Creator and celebrate the Oneism of universal justice, pansexuality, and interfaith religion. Modern Oneism claims we can create a paradise of human flourishing where all people will get along. The vision seems good and beautiful, but it is based on the delusional fantasy of the Lie and will become a world-wide nightmare.

Though this stark choice between Oneism and Twoism has existed from the beginning, Jung and his disciples have placed it before us again in different dress. Interestingly, Jesus already said long ago that there are only two ways, the broad and the narrow. In light of the powerful ideological agenda that I have been calling pagan cosmology, which stresses a false Oneist unity, how do Christians heed the warning to avoid conformity? As we've said, our minds need transformity, not conformity.

Transformation of the Mind

Paul has in mind a massive transformation. The only other time he uses the verb "transform" is in 2 Corinthians 3:18, where he writes, "We all, with unveiled face" (recalling the experience of Moses on Mount Sinai), "beholding the glory of the Lord, are being transformed" (2 Cor 3:18). This reference also recalls the glory of God revealed on another mountain, the Mount of Transfiguration, when Jesus was transformed (same verb) or "transfigured" before them, and "his face shone like the sun" (Matt 17:2). The word carries the meaning of a worldview transformation, brought about by the glory of God, revealed in a sinful world, changing people from top to bottom, and preparing them for the coming transformed physical cosmos.

Speaking of this eyewitness experience, the Apostle Peter contrasts it with mythical stories of the pagan gods:

> For we did not follow cleverly devised myths ... but we were eyewitnesses of his majesty. For when he received honor and glory from God the Father, and the voice was borne to him by the Majestic Glory, "This is my beloved Son, with whom I am well pleased," we ourselves heard this very voice borne from heaven, for we were with him on the holy mountain (2 Pet 1:16–18).

In hearing the gospel, we meet Jesus, the most incredible person who ever existed. Jesus was a unique human being, both because he was perfect and because he was God in human form. Thus, what he did was of vast, eternal value for those who trust in him. He is God, bearing the sins of the world. "If anyone is in Christ, he is a new creation" (2 Cor 5:17). Hearing and receiving the gospel transforms one's thinking about God and about oneself—understanding the depth of one's rebellion and the enormity of God's restorative love.

We find wisdom for a sound mind not by heeding the world's "cleverly devised myths" (2 Pet 1:16) based on the god within, but by listening to the teaching of eyewitnesses confronted by the objective act of God the Creator, the God who acted in history to save us. This is where wisdom is to be found—understanding who God is as Creator and Redeemer and who we are as creatures.

The transformation of the mind is the work of the Holy Spirit and includes one's entire being, both spiritual and rational, but it is neither mystical (self-referential) or irrational (a denial of the faculty of intelligence, one of the greatest of God's creative acts). By the Spirit and through the written Word he inspired, we begin to understand the nature of God's world. From a text 3,000 years old we read:

> By wisdom the Lord laid the earth's foundations,
>> by understanding he set the heavens in place;
> by his knowledge the watery depths *were divided,*
>> and the clouds let drop the dew.
>
> My son, do not let wisdom and understanding out of your sight,
>> preserve sound judgment and discretion;
> *they will be life for you,*
>> an ornament to grace your neck (Prov 3:19-22 NIV,
>> emphasis mine).

This ancient text shows that the wisdom God employed to create the world as a distinct entity over against the Creator and to *divide* elements within it for their best functioning is reflected in the wisdom given to creatures to maintain distinctions within the created order—*for the sake of life.* Clear thinking—a discerning mind—understands that the ultimate reality is not matter that creates itself and then miraculously creates thinking human beings, as paganism foolishly claims. The ultimate reality is that of the personal Creator of matter, from whom comes an intelligent, personal Word from outside of nature to call it into existence in a supreme act of creation *ex nihilo.* This unique Word, God's mind, unknown in any other world religion, ancient or modern, from which derives this incredibly intelligible cosmos, became at one point a human person in the flesh, "the Word ... full of grace and truth" (John 1:14).

The context of *undiscerning mind* in Romans 1:28 is defined by the previous affirmations about sinful human knowing (Rom 1:18). When people "by their unrighteousness suppress the truth" (Rom 1:18), knowing God as Creator but not honoring him as God, they "[become] futile in their thinking, and their foolish hearts [are] darkened" (Rom 1:21). It is in this state of a darkened heart that they worship creation as divine. But in such a system, there is no true Other, the only possible object of genuine worship. Rejecting the Creator has fearful results. "God [gives] them up to an undiscerning mind" (Rom 1:28), which has implications for their theology (Rom 1:20-21), their spirituality (Rom 1:24) and their sexuality (Rom 1:26-28). The renewed mind, on the other hand, sees true, healthy differences between the Creator and creation and between the distinct roles of created things in God's meaningful world. It sees in the fallen world the antithesis between truth and falsehood, the holy and the unholy.

Making Distinctions with a Transformed Mind

The transformed mind has learned how to think clearly about the world in light of God's revealed truth of Twoism. Its views of God, spirituality, and sexuality are diametrically opposed to "the wisdom of this world." God is not nature. God is the good Creator of nature (Rom 1:18-20); spirituality consists not in the worship of elements within nature, but the worship of the Creator outside of nature; sexuality is correctly defined not as "anything goes" homo- and pansexuality, but as the celebration of difference: sexual Twoness in monogamous, health- and life-producing heterosexuality, what Paul calls "the natural" (Rom 1:26 NASB) or "according to creation" (Rom 1:26).

Do you want to discern God's good will for your life? Then put the world together based on the fundamental principle of the Creator as separate from the creation. This is how you make sense of a world in the grip of Satan's lies in order to bring your thoughts into conformity to the mind of Christ.

This major choice is perhaps clarified by the following terminology. We either embrace:

- Homocosmology or heterocosmology
  - Essential nature is either a homocosmology of union and synthesis (i.e., Oneism; *homo* implies singularity), or

- Essential nature is a heterocosmology, whose key is difference (i.e., Twoism; *hetero* means "different").

- Homotheology or heterotheology
  - Any existent god is the same as us, so that all things are divine, or
  - God is the divine Other and we are created.

- Homospirituality or heterospirituality
  - We worship nature and ourselves, or
  - We worship and serve the Creator and celebrate God's otherness.

- Homosexuality or heterosexuality
  - We embody the Oneist spiritual notion of sameness, or
  - We embody the God-inspired notion of a union that includes difference.

We are up against the final wall in our defense of Truth, with only a definition of God on which to base our arguments for human life. But what better basis, since everyone knows God and is without excuse? It is a comfort to know that the Bible was written as an apologetic cosmology to the pagan world. The stark choice between Oneism and Twoism has been presented throughout biblical history:

1. Moses proposed the beauty of Twoism to the Egyptian and Canaanite Oneist cultures of pantheism and pansexuality.

2. Shadrach, Meshach, and Abednego in the sixth century bc gave their witness to the God of Twoism before Nebuchadnezzar, who finally understood and publicly declared, "Blessed be the God ... who has sent his angel and delivered his servants, who trusted in him, and set aside the king's command, and yielded up their bodies rather than serve and worship any god except their own God" (Dan 3:28).

3. Paul announced this same truth to the pagan Graeco-Roman culture, that people who worship and serve nature should be worshiping and serving the Creator.

Twoist Cosmology

Now it's our turn. This message needs to be heard again in our time, in our global "Roman Empire," where, after centuries of the dominance of Christian truth, the pagan cosmology is being adopted as the only truth by which we can save the planet. Let's examine how biblical thinking works in various areas of thought that are related via the principle of Twoism.[10]

Theology: The Nature of God

If God is "other," or distinct or from us, then his qualities of lordship, sovereignty, transcendence, and hierarchy make sense, though these are offensive to the modern mind, raised as it was on egalitarianism and brainwashed into the "god within." Katy Perry caricatures the God of her evangelical upbringing as an "old man in the sky." We may never know if this misperception is due to her inability to hear the gospel or to the message she was given. But she must consider the impenetrable mystery of the great Other, the eternal God without beginning, who gives "beginning" or existence to everything else. Such a God boggles the mind. Such a God is uniquely revealed in the Bible. Before a God of these dimensions we can only bow in humble adoration.

The mystery deepens. Though an unfathomable mystery, this God is personal. The gods of the false Twoisms, such as rabbinic Judaism and Islam, are not personal. In Islam, God is a lone, impersonal singularity. In Judaism, God is not Trinity and thus has no face-to-face divine Other. This means that in order to be "personal," he is dependent upon a relationship with his creation. Only the biblical God of Scripture revealed by Jesus through the Holy Spirit is truly personal in his very being, since he is the Trinity. When apostate bishop John Shelby Spong states that "there is not much value in the doctrine of the Trinity,"[11] he reveals the superficiality of his own "Christian" system since he fails to see that the Triune God enables God to be both transcendent and personal without being dependent on the creation. This combination of God's characteristics distinguishes Christianity from every other religious system.

Anthropology: The Nature of Humanity

Twoism reveals an enormously high view of the human person. Each person is unique and distinct from all others. That individual identity will never be lost in some impersonal nirvana, which on earth quickly becomes a collectivist tyranny in which "the less equal" serve "the more equal." The Twoist understanding explains the essence of human dignity. The most significant Divine Other gives to humans the gift of having a nature stamped in his own image, which distinguishes human creatures from all other created things (Gen 1:27). That unique image also liberates human beings from the false totalitarian claims of other fallen human beings. This human dignity in God's image also includes the privilege of vice-stewardship of the earth's environment and the noble calling of service for those who are suffering.

In a book dealing with the dangers of dehumanizing pornographic obsession, William Struthers observes, "We are made as God's agents in this world for his pleasure and for our own. We are made for each other, to be present and relational with each other."[12] Only Twoism explains this dynamic, creative need we have for "the other."

This similarity between creature and Creator does not mean that human beings are little gods (who would inevitably turn out to be "divine" demons). Humans are *always* created, always submitted to God's ordained structures. Twoism makes sense of gender. From this image of God reflecting his being as Trinity (unity and difference) come the natural distinctions of heterosexuality for the cultural, biological mandate of filling the earth (Gen 1:28; Rom 1:26–27) and genuine love for the other in lifelong monogamy. This binary vision of the ultimate significance of heterosexual gender is redemptively fulfilled in Christ the bridegroom's love of his bride, the Church. The heterosexual mandate is not hate-filled, old-fashioned bigotry. It is cosmological and eschatological truth.[13]

Logic: The Nature of Rationality

Twoism makes sense of the world. The mind is a distinction-producing, sense-making factory. This is why classic Oneist gurus call their followers to "flee the mind." For them, the mind tells us too much about who we are and who God is. The obvious problem with "fleeing the mind," however, is that you would not board an airplane flown by a mind-fleeing pilot nor allow a "mindless" cardiologist to begin a 12-hour surgery on your heart.

The mind and rationality are gifts from God, part of the image of God in man, and thus an integral part of created reality, a system behind which stands a personal, meaning-producing God. To affirm that A = not-A would be nonsense—the sound of one hand clapping, as Buddhist Oneists say. Roman Catholic philosopher Robert Sokolowski, arguing from the Twoist starting point of the Creator/creature distinction, notes that reason is "the power of affirming and denying,"[14] that is, making distinctions, which is ultimately not possible in a Oneist world. Without presupposing the truth of distinctions, logical thought is impossible.

From the complex life of a bee to the teeming logical signals in the eye to our ability to communicate using music, art, or language—everything in the cosmos depends upon order and distinction. We can observe all this with our rational capacities, but we cannot stand outside the system to give a global, objective explanation of it. This is why secular humanism came apart; it seemed to claim ultimate authority for human reason, but it failed miserably at justifying such a position, as postmodernism has shown. All these logical processes, all the subject and object distinctions we are constantly making—all find their satisfactory explanation not in self-referential human reason but in the mind of God. His mind is the objective reference point, assuring us that what we know intuitively and practically is true—that we inhabit a rational universe, not a human, inevitably finite, circular construct that will always fail us, nor mystical fallible myths from the "god within." This intuitive sense of the rationality of God's universe has enabled the scientific discoveries of the laws of nature and accounts for the incredible complexities of the technological world. Faith in words has produced the immense literary civilization of the West, made up of logical statements, propositions, theses and dissertations, creeds and doctrines, and scientific laws and mathematical constructions.

Revelation: Knowledge of God

Though rationality and distinction permeate the universe, we cannot get perspective on creation without a sure word of divine revelation from *outside* human experience. The unrighteous, dishonest human tendency is to suppress the truth implicit within nature (Rom 1:18–21), which speaks of the God beyond it, so as to draw the conclusion that there is no Creator. The personal, Trinitarian God who created nature is a God of verbal communication; after all, "[i]n the beginning was the Word" (John 1:1). Because the Word is at the beginning, the universe is a rational place, and true meaning comes from beyond the human scene. Since God is transcendent and all-knowing, his wisdom far surpasses that of human beings. This revelation, finally revealed in Scripture, brings true (though not exhaustive) knowledge from God to man, without which history would be an unrelieved and frustrating conundrum.

Story: Knowledge of History

The "story" of eternal Oneist matter can never be told! While we have been created to desire the elements of a true story—a believable beginning and a satisfying end—these elements cannot exist for the Oneist story, which affirms the eternity of matter. It is humanly impossible, working within the changing events of our lives, from our limited perspectives, to bring a satisfactory explanation of the whole. We are like miniscule ants trying to write the history of the Roman Empire from the hold of an ocean-going first century grain ship, transporting food supplies to Rome from Egypt: That is a picture of our place in the cosmos.

Moreover, Oneism has a cyclical view of time that precludes the notion of progress. There can only be repetition or eternal recurrence. If there is no divinely-ordered beginning with God creating "the heavens and the earth" (Gen 1:1) and no posthistoric ending which only God can produce, then no final meaning to things can possibly emerge. The resolution of history cannot come from within history, so waiting for one will always be frustrating. The resolution will come from beyond.

The God of Twoism provides a genuine beginning as Creator (protology) and a just ending as the righteous Judge and Re-creator (eschatology). A Twoist linear time line has a beginning, a middle, and an end and sees God at work in history so that there are distinct, meaningful events. The future is different from the past, and humans have significant, historical roles to play. Oneist paganism has no interest in or access to past origins or future hopes and can only provide a continually turning wheel of self-creating, insignificant repetition and reincarnation, all of which comes from nowhere and goes nowhere.

Morality: The Nature of Right and Wrong

We can say the same about morality as what we said about rationality. Twoism explains the sense of right and wrong that everyone knows. Jung's solution is not the answer. He recommended joining good and evil in a world beyond morality to give free reign to one's fantasies. But human beings are just as incapable of fusing right and wrong and remaining moral as they are of affirming both A and non-A while remaining logical.

Twoist Morality

People are inconsistent, wanting all the benefits of a personal moral universe without paying the price. Someone who claims to reject the moral universe, living only for himself, will still take you all the way to the Supreme Court if you steal his property or murder his child.

The beauty of the law is that it is both written on our hearts (Rom 2:15) and in stone. God first wrote his commandments with his own finger for Moses to use in teaching and instructing the Israelites. We get the law from the "inside" and from the "outside." From the inside we are given the image of God to intuitively long for justice. But God's law is also given from outside, because it is from the God who is Other—and he is not a human relative invention.

As Sokolowski observes, cosmic goodness flows from the nature of God as transcendent Creator: "Because God is so independent of the world we can say that he created the world out of sheer generosity, not out of any sort of need ... In doing so he has shown the charity that is at the heart of things."[15] Goodness and rightness are essential elements of the created moral universe.

As created moral beings, we cannot silence the voice within, the voice of conscience and guilt. In spite of our noble aspirations, something within us is desperately wrong, as an honest look within reveals. One particular verse from the Bible rings true: "The heart is deceitful above all things and beyond cure. Who can understand it?" (Jer 17:9 NIV).

Oneist Morality

A Oneist view of the heart is very different. There is a current attempt by a missionary-minded Indian Hindu foundation to introduce yoga into US state schools. The program is now accompanied by a children's song book, *The Heart is Smart*.[16] The song is upbeat about "the heart" and openly encourages 10-year-olds to "calm your mind, promote clarity and peace, and connect to your heart." It affirms that when you are paying attention to your heart and let it be completely in charge, "your thoughts and beliefs will then follow,"[17] assuming that the heart is inherently good. But this represents the great weakness of Oneism. If all is one, then all the atrocities of human history must be embraced as eventually good. So it is said that Hitler is in heaven—his deeds weren't evil, they were mistakes. He didn't really mean it!

Antithetical Moralities

The antithesis between the Oneist and the Twoist views of the self underlines the unbridgeable difference between the two religious approaches to life. Clearly, if Hinduism (or Buddhism) succeeds in becoming part of Western education, the Oneist falsehood will have succeed in brainwashing numerous generations of future Westerners, and Twoism will be driven underground. The good news of the gospel will no longer make any sense.

If, as Oneism teaches, there is no otherness or difference, then all is the same and all is well. The only sin is ignorance of our innate goodness. However, if the universe is indeed two, and human beings perversely refuse to recognize the God who stands outside of creation, then this rejection is the very root of sin and an offense against the personal Triune God. As we noted above, holiness is not as much a moral category as an affirmation of the created order of things; the rejection of this holy cosmos indicates that things are seriously out of order—demonstrated by our sad record of cruelty and egotism throughout history, on both personal and national levels. The problem is bigger than we think. A solution of cosmic proportions is needed. Humans "going within" to find their inner divinity will not produce the desired results! We need a savior from the outside.

Divine Redemption: The Only Solution

If Twoism is true in describing two kinds of existence, then the disruption that separates God and creation is not a minor dysfunction but a fundamental dislocation of reality. Nothing more catastrophic could be envisioned. The reconciliation of God and creation requires an unimaginable, divinely conceived solution that goes beyond anything human beings could devise. God's solution is the only answer to our constant human problems.

The Twoist notion of redemption answers our deep need of a genuinely efficacious Savior—who, as both God and man, a unique mediator, and an effective go-between, joins these two types of personal reality in a lasting state of covenantal reconciliation. This is accomplished through the miracle of the incarnation, where the human and divine coexist without confusion. Redemption cannot be self-salvation but depends entirely on the gracious act of the Creator. It produces freedom from genuine guilt, not through our subjective and ineffective relativizing of good and evil but through God's sin-defeating work on the cross.

In Scripture much is made of God's love for his creatures, even in their sin. The Lord passed before Moses and proclaimed himself "The Lord, the Lord, a God merciful and gracious, slow to anger, and abounding in steadfast love and faithfulness" (Exod 34:6 NIV). In the New Testament, Paul describes the gospel as "God's love ... poured into our hearts through the Holy Spirit" (Rom 5:5). Only in Twoism is there the possibility of love because real love needs a genuine other, and God is genuinely other.

As noted above, cosmic goodness flows from God as transcendent Creator. God created "out of sheer generosity, not out of any sort of need ... In doing so he has shown the charity that is at the heart of things."[18] God's separateness holds the key to cosmic goodness! The *something* that exists is a *someone*, and he is good!

The essence of redemption is the miracle of the bodily resurrection of Jesus. Liberal theologians are happy to speak of a "spiritual resurrection" of a Jesus whose physical body remains in the grave but whose memory lives on in the faith of his disciples. Jung argues that the true Christian message has nothing to do with Jesus "rising from the dead in AD 33" but with a gnostic discovery that the psyche is the place where we meet the divine.[19]

But the New Testament unmistakably affirms a bodily event. The tomb is empty. A missing body is the major problem. The physical, mortal body of Jesus is missing because it had been transformed by the power of God into a spiritual, heavenly, yet still physical, body (1 Cor 15:44) of the kind we are promised (1 Cor 15:49). We are reminded that Jesus' resurrection body was seen by hundreds of his followers and touched by many of them, who also spoke and ate with him. God's act of resurrection is an act of God from the outside that respects the bodily reality of the original physical creation. The body does not become divine, so that even in resurrection, our Twoist nature as creatures under the Creator is maintained.

True Spirituality

Much attention is given to "spirituality" in our time, especially to the practice of meditation. Meditation is often and sometimes deliberately confused with prayer. First, there are two kinds of meditation. Eastern meditation involves focusing on one's inner divinity to develop ecstatic trances or out-of-body experiences. The psalmist understood a different kind of meditation, conscious thinking about the person and works of God, the Twoist Creator and Savior. He says: "I will ponder all your work, and meditate on your mighty deeds" (Psa 77:12). Again, "I will meditate on your precepts and fix my eyes on your ways. I will delight in your statutes; I will not forget your word" (Psa 119:15–16). This is not meditation on one's divine self, but communion with the transcendent Creator in the immense beauty of his person, the justice of his laws and the kindness of his deeds.

The other element of spirituality is praise, and the Bible is overflowing with tributes to God's glory. This, says the book of Hebrews, is what Jesus our example did. The author cites Psalm 22:22, saying: "I will tell of your name to my brothers; in the midst of the congregation I will sing your praise" (Heb 2:12).

Praise was an element clearly lacking in the Parliament of the World's Religions in Chicago in 1993, which I attended. Nor was there a hint of thanksgiving—whom does a Oneist thank? Indeed, the Apostle Paul says the mark of Oneists is that "they neither glorified him as God nor gave thanks to him" (Rom 1:21 NIV). By turning people to praise nature as divine, Oneism eventually makes them self-worshipers, since they are a part of creation. The Bible is bursting with exhortations to praise God, because he is the ultimate, genuine object worthy of worship. Self-worship and self-praise naturally disgust us all. True worship and true praise are only genuine if turned toward another. Pagans will never write Handel's *Messiah*, Robert Bridges' words to Bach's *Jesu, Joy of Man's Desiring*, nor Bach's music to which the words were affixed.

In expression of love, self-sacrifice, moral courage and praise, these elements, so fundamentally uplifting to and defining of the human spirit, we see the discrete yet stunning beauty of Twoism, because behind the worldview system is the reality of the personal God who seeks fellowship with human persons made in his image.

Conclusions

The transformed mind that Scripture describes and offers enables us to know the essence of God's revelation of the truth of existence. We are called to think and to worship God with all our mind, our heart, our soul, and our strength. I have tried to simplify this by calling God's truth "Twoism." Here are the far-reaching elements of this truth, which enables us to know and do the will of God:

- **Ontology:** We glorify the person of God by recognizing his holiness as a radically distinct being, expressed as the essence of Twoist truth.

- **Theology:** We recognize in God's self-disclosure the personhood of God in the Twoist character of the Trinity—three distinct persons joined in the perfect unity of the godhead.

- **Cosmology:** Because of the being of God as Creator and everything else as creature, the nature of existence is two.

- **Anthropology:** We know who we are as intended created beings, not the results of chance, made for God's glory.

- **Morality:** Because God creates everything in its place, creation is holy, and from this we derive notions of right and wrong.

- **Soteriology:** Because God is Trinity, and thus upholds a Twoist cosmology, he can be the effective Redeemer.

- **Eschatology:** This salvation has a final, cosmos-transforming moment.

The final goal of Twoism is not to know an intellectual system, but to know the personal God behind it and be saved. Twoism reveals the most incredible compliments that humanity can ever be given: First, the human creature, both man and woman, and only the human creature, is made in God's image. Second, God becomes man. God the eternal Son takes on human flesh, the Creator becomes a creature to atone for the sins of the world. This is the Christian gospel. There is nothing in Jungian theory that compares with this transforming, saving truth.

But herein lies a serious problem. Does the gospel, in bringing together Creator and creature, undermine Twoism? For that, you'll need to read the last chapter.

CHAPTER 13

GOSPEL POWER: A GIVEN-OVER SAVIOR

After reading the previous pages one might be tempted to believe that the Twoist worldview is merely an intellectual proposition intended for out-of-touch theorists, not for ordinary human beings. But just like the cosmology of paganism—at its heart a meeting with occult powers for individual "enlightenment"—so at the heart of biblical cosmology, extended to all, is a transformational meeting with the power of God.

The Gospel for a Relationship with a Holy God

Twoism presents us with a problem. If God, in his mysterious eternal being, is so distinct from us, how can we hope to have any relationship with him?[1] Jung called Christianity a no-win situation—to be asked to believe in a God we cannot understand produces psychological neurosis.[2] This was Jung's problem. His solution was to find the god within, eminently discoverable within the human psyche in an experience of the *numinosum*. But for many, it is Jung's solution that creates a no-win situation, for who really believes that we can save ourselves? Who can honestly say that he or she is worthy of divine worship?

As you will recall from chapter 3, Jung's fundamental view of Christianity had much to do with his childhood background. He judged Christianity as mere formalism. Caught between the pagan spirits of his family on one side and the empty Christian faith of his father on the other, Jung was unable to see that the gospel is power, and so he finally turned to the spirits. As John Calvin said, "the greatest geniuses are blinder than moles ... who never ever sensed the assurance of God's benevolence towards us ... to understand who the true God is, or what sort of God He wishes to be towards us."[3]

Jung, blind mole that he was, interpreted the vicarious atonement of Christ at a particular time in past history as myth, an event that merely described the inner painful struggle of all human beings in search of psychological maturity.[4] For Jung, getting in touch with one's true harmonious self, joining the opposites of good and evil and eliminating guilt, was the world's only hope. This solution illustrates a major problem of paganism and emergent liberalism—no real recognition of evil and thus the inability to genuinely deal with it. Everything is finally excused and relativized away—but how do you deal with the vicious beheadings of hundreds of 20-something Syrian soldiers by the jihadists of the Islamic State? How do we explain away the two million Cambodians who lost their lives through the genocidal vision of Pol Pot and his willing goons? Only the gospel offers an effective answer for the problem of cosmic evil.

Our Source of Power

We're all fascinated by power. In politics, power often comes out of the end of a gun; for Islam, it comes from the edge of the sword;[5] for progressive spiritualists, as we noted above, it comes from occult experiences. Jordan Paper, a Western polytheist, says he meets the gods face to face.[6] Stanislav Grof, like Paper, speaks of "transpersonal experiences" that include "encounters with various blissful and wrathful archetypal deities."[7] Richard Tarnas locates power in the recovery of ancient pagan astrology.[8]

The Christian faith, however, affirms that power comes from outside the self and outside of the created world—flowing through the Spirit-inspired Word of God, bringing to the world the good news of Jesus' triumphant victory over sin and death, achieved once for all at the cross of Golgotha. This powerful event took place in real time, at a real place. At the time, Tiberius was emperor, and just a few years earlier, "Quirinius was governor of Syria" (Luke 2:1-2). Something from the outside came to change the course of human history by answering the insolvable problem of human evil. This is the news the world must hear. There is no other answer—if Twoism is true, we can't abandon the struggle to hold up this truth, because the only genuine help available must be a radical solution from God the Creator. Only he who is outside of creation can do anything about the sin problem. Ultimate good news cannot come from mere creatures, however united and Oneist they might be. As the psalmist says: "From where does my help come? My help comes from the Lord, who made heaven and earth" (Psa 121:1-2).

Our Source of Acceptance

As we have seen, Paul assigns to Christians, faced with the powerful Oneist influence of Rome, the task of giving to God their holy bodies and transformed minds. But believers know that in their selves of human frailty and sinfulness, they can't do it. That is the whole point of Jesus' earthly ministry—to show us that we can't fulfill God's requirement: "[B]e holy, for I am holy" (1 Pet 1:16). I have a dear friend who understood the power of the gospel because she read that command and realized that there was no possible way she could be accepted by God—for who can be holy as God is holy? The task is impossible. We cannot take on the tasks Paul lays before us without the power of God.

Oneism refuses the notions of sin and guilt and believes that we are the answer to the world's problems. If Charles Murray is right, we are actually coming apart. Twoists come at the world's problems from a completely different set of assumptions. Christian believers come realistically and honestly to God's demands for bodily holiness and right thinking, painfully aware of their sin-stained bodies and messed-up minds. We long for purity and yearn for wisdom, but when we look inside we see not high, pure selves, but the filthy rags and mental folly of a desperately wicked heart (Jer 17:9). This is realism, not negativism, for it fits with what the biblical Twoist revelation of reality affirmed in both the Old and the New Testaments. In assessing the human situation, Paul cites a number of Old Testament texts:

> ...all, both Jews and Greeks, are under sin, as it is written:
>
> "None is righteous, no, not one;
>   no one understands;
>   no one seeks for God.
> All have turned aside; together they have become worthless;
>   no one does good,
>   not even one."
> "Their throat is an open grave;
>   they use their tongues to deceive."
> "The venom of asps is under their lips."
> "Their mouth is full of curses and bitterness."
> "Their feet are swift to shed blood;
>   in their paths are ruin and misery,
>   and the way of peace they have not known."
> "There is no fear of God before their eyes" (Rom 3:9–18).

Even the most positive read of this text means that we're so far gone that we certainly can't save ourselves. For bodily holiness and transformed thinking, so unpopular in our present pagan culture yet so clearly what we need, we depend entirely on one amazing thing: the incredibly powerful message of the gospel, which is the ultimate expression and goal of Twoism. The only hope is in Christ alone.

Twoism is not just a satisfying cosmology but the description of the Creator's powerful act of salvation. Indeed, the Christian gospel is not called the gospel of Paul or the gospel of the Church but "the gospel of God."[9] It is *God's* solution, not a human theory. This is good news from the outside about an act of God, who intervenes within the creation for our salvation. The Greek term "gospel" in the ancient world referred not to a piece of stirring human poetry or to a carefully defined system of philosophy, but to news of important historical events, such as a critical military victory or the birth of an emperor. It is a news item like those you see on TV, a formal announcement of an event that took place in history for our redemption. There has been no comparable statement in any other religion in the entire history of the world. For 2,000 years, the Christian church has confessed this mind-blowing mystery, that "in Christ God was reconciling the world to himself" (2 Cor 5:19). The Nicene Creed expresses well what the Church has always believed:

> I believe in one God, the Father Almighty, Maker of heaven and earth, and of all things, visible and invisible.
>
> And in one Lord Jesus Christ, the only-begotten Son of God, begotten of the Father before all worlds; God of God, Light of Light, very God of very God; begotten, not made, being of one substance with the Father, by whom all things were made.
>
> Who, for us men and for our salvation, came down from heaven, and was incarnate by the Holy Spirit of the Virgin Mary, and was made man; and was crucified also for us under Pontius Pilate; he suffered and was buried; and the third day he rose again, according to the Scriptures; and ascended into heaven, and sits on the right hand of the Father; and he shall come again, with glory, to judge the quick and the dead; whose kingdom shall have no end.
>
> And I believe in the Holy Ghost, the Lord, the Giver of Life, who proceeds from the Father and the Son; who, with the Father and the Son together, is worshiped and glorified; who spoke by the prophets.
>
> And I believe one holy catholic and apostolic Church. I acknowledge one baptism for the remission of sins; and I look for the resurrection of the dead, and the life of the world to come. Amen.

The Reconciliation of Creator and Creation:
The Twoist Problem

The Nicene Creed is named after Nicaea (modern-day Iznik, Turkey), the city where it was adopted as the belief of the whole church in AD 325. Why did it take the church so long to formalize its beliefs? One reason was that for three centuries, Christians had been under persecution throughout the Roman Empire, and international gatherings were impossible. All changed when the emperor Constantine converted to Christianity in AD 312, and this international council was able to meet. However, the council was not inventing new material. It only confirmed what the church had believed since its beginning. This creed faces the serious problem mentioned at the end of chapter 12. Two bold phrases in the creed express an unparalleled mystery of the Church's message, which seem, at first blush, to undermine the very notion of Twoism, with its clear separation of the Creator and the creature. The "only-begotten Son of God," the second member of the Trinity, is described as "very God of very God, of one substance with the Father." Yet he was "made man." The Creator became a creature!

Among the early Christians were brilliant thinkers, theologians, and philosophers who realized the problem of God becoming man. They were familiar with their culture's version of Oneism. Indeed, the Council of Chalcedon in AD 451 recognized the growing problem of Oneism, then expressed by a dubious kind of Christian thinking called "monophysitism," or "One Nature-ism," from *monos* (single) and *physis* (nature). This view joined Christ's humanity and deity into a single entity—a position that ultimately denied the Twoist view of reality. In addressing this heresy, the council in Chalcedon spoke of the incarnation as Christ's "two natures"—human and divine—but added an explanatory phrase: "without confusion, without change, undivided, inseparable." These early church fathers understood the absolute importance of keeping separate the notions of Creator and creature (the essence of Twoism) while affirming the indescribable mystery of their reconciliation in the incarnation of the Son for our salvation. The formulations of Chalcedon carefully stated that the Son is:

...co-essential with the Father according to the
Godhead ... co-essential with us according to the
Manhood ... before the ages begotten of the Father as to
the Godhead, but in the last days ... for us and for our
salvation [born] of Mary the Virgin.

These formulations are only unpacking what the Apostle Paul says
about the mystery of Christ, that "in him the whole fullness of deity
dwells bodily" (Col 2:9).

Why was this theological precision necessary in the early centuries
of the church? It was (and is) necessary to do justice to the astonishing
assertions of the gospel message in the pages of Scripture. We cannot cross *all* the t's and dot all the i's that constitute the mystery of
God's being:

- how his sovereign power and our sinful, willful actions can
  be reconciled

- how eternal separation of unbelievers from his smile of forgiveness is just[10]

- why at various times in history so few seem to respond to the
  call of God's elective power

- how God can never have a beginning, though we do

The reason we cannot fathom these seemingly contradictory aspects
of God's revelation to us is that we cannot stand outside created reality
to look over God's shoulder and explain him to our satisfaction. As fallible human creatures, we cannot see the whole picture, like the ants I
mentioned in the deep hold of the grain ship, with no idea of their final
destination. The Bible is well aware of this problem—it is not embarrassing, but speaks to the truth of the God revealed in Scripture, who
declares: "[M]y thoughts are not your thoughts, neither are your ways
my ways, declares the Lord" (Isa 55:8).

By definition, the God of Twoism is indescribably larger than created
life, bigger than anything we can imagine, but because in Jesus he made
himself visible and accessible to us, sharing our human body with its
pains and trials, this God can be known and trusted. That is the kind

of God I can worship, not the "god" that shows up every morning in my bathroom mirror with a scruffy beard that needs shaving! I know *that* person, and he is not worthy of worship—just ask my wife! Neither can rabbinic Jews or Muslims, who deny the Trinity, know the love of God in the Son without destroying God's transcendence.

The Power of the Gospel

In seeking to be liked by the culture, or even to do good in the culture, we modern Christians often forget or soft-sell the gospel, the power behind everything we do. As we noted above, this gospel only works as power if God is truly both transcendent *and* personal, and he can only be that if he is the Trinity. The good news of God's love depends on this mysterious but majestic doctrine. And only love will powerfully move our sinful souls as we understand both God's genuine personhood and his condescension or self-abasement. "See what kind of love the Father has given to us," says the Apostle John, "that we should be called children of God; and so we are" (1 John 3:1). This is the message of the whole Bible, God's condescension to reach sinful creatures. "For thus says the One who is high and lifted up, who inhabits eternity, whose name is Holy: 'I dwell in the high and holy place, and also with him who is of a contrite and lowly spirit, to revive the spirit of the lowly, and to revive the heart of the contrite'" (Isa 57:15). It is God by his Spirit who empowers the preaching of the gospel to bring rebellious human hearts to conviction of sin and to show them the need of a loving Savior.

The gospel is good news because there is bad news. Part of the mystery of God's person is his necessary function as moral source and final judge. In introducing the gospel, Paul reminds us that "the wrath of God is revealed from heaven against all ungodliness and unrighteousness of men, who by their unrighteousness suppress the truth" (Rom 1:18). You might have shuddered a bit when I mentioned wrath. The notion of wrath in human beings suggests out-of-control anger. However, God's wrath is never out of control, and its function is to assure us that we live in a moral universe with moral accountability. The gospel depends on this. It is part of the gospel Jesus teaches; he states, "I came to cast fire on the earth, and would that it were already kindled! I have a baptism to be baptized with [death on the cross], and how great is my distress until it is accomplished! Do you think that I have come to give peace on earth? No, I tell you, but rather division" (Luke 12:49–51).

There must be bad news for there to be good news. Human beings are by nature sinners and need to be made aware of this, as Jesus says. The level of sin can get worse. At certain points, God as judge must act as judge within history. You remember that in Romans 1 the inspired text declares three times that God gave over sinners to the effects of their sin: "God gave them over to the lusts of their hearts" (Rom 1:24), to "dishonorable passions" and to "a debased mind" (Rom 1:26, 28). God "gives over" sinners, who, at a deep level, exchange the Truth for the Lie. This act of God, the righteous Judge, in giving them over means "his abandonment of the persons concerned to more intensified and aggravated cultivation of the lusts of their own hearts with the result that they reap for themselves [in this life] a correspondingly greater toll of retributive judgment."[11]

In other words, this action of God within history is an anticipation of God's final judgment, when it will be too late for mercy (Rom 2:6–10). But it is also an occasion for hope, for seeing our sin can bring us to Christ. For this we pray, even though now we see our culture's blatant disregard for God's truth—as shown clearly in nature, his Word, and his Son—which may indeed lead to God "giving over" those who resist him in unbelief. In such a case, the development and increase of lust, ungodly passion, and debased minds is hardly hopeful for moving a culture toward utopia!

The Message We Must Proclaim

Such a state may make you want to give up. You may ask, "What's the point? I'll just stay home with my kids and try not to get involved! If the world is given over, then I'm giving up!" But believers should never give up. "If God is for us," says Paul, "who can be against us?" (Rom 8:31). Certainly we can never give up the hope that God's patient kindness in postponing the final judgment and in showing people their sin will lead to repentance (Rom 2:6). But God does not stop there. He takes action— there is a remedy for sin.

God Is For Us!

We spoke earlier about power. This is power: God for us. Here is Twoist confidence in the God who is other and who is in sovereign control of all things, working them out for our good (Rom 8:28). For believers, this promise guarantees certain victory. The Creator of the cosmos is *for us.* This little phrase, "for us," is full of meaning. It expresses in very short form the objective fact of the gospel as the event in history of God's saving intervention, as we discussed above. How is God for us? Almost all—14 of 15—times when this two-word phrase, "for us," is used in the New Testament, it has to do with God's act of redemption and related actions. Some examples:[12]

- For us God made Christ to be sin who knew no sin, so that in him we might become the righteousness of God (2 Cor 5:21).

- For us Christ became a curse to redeem us from the curse of the law (Gal 3:13).

- For us Christ died, so that whether we are awake or asleep we might live with him. God has not destined us for wrath, but to obtain salvation through our Lord Jesus Christ (1 Thess 5:9-10).

- For us Christ gave himself to redeem us from all lawlessness and to purify for himself a people for his own possession who are zealous for good works, [while we are] waiting for our blessed hope, the appearing of the glory of our great God and Savior Jesus Christ (Titus 2:13-14).

In three examples, the work of redemption is specifically associated with "love," which is only possible if God is truly personal in his Trinitarian being:

- God shows his love for us in that while we were still sinners, Christ died for us (Rom 5:8).

- Walk in love, as Christ loved us and gave himself up for us, a fragrant offering and sacrifice to God (Eph 5:2).

- By this we know love, that he laid down his life for us, and we ought to lay down our lives for the brothers (1 John 3:16).

In two examples, the "for us" is associated with Christ's intercession on our behalf before the Father:

- Who is to condemn? Christ Jesus is the one who died—more than that, who was raised—who is at the right hand of God, who indeed is interceding for us (Rom 8:34).

- For Christ has entered, not into holy places made with hands, which are copies of the true things, but into heaven itself, now to appear in the presence of God on our behalf (literally, "for us") (Heb 9:24).

In some of these cases, God is the subject of the act, giving his Son for us; in others, Christ is sacrificially giving himself for us. This ambiguity is explained by the doctrine of the Trinity, because God the Father and God the Son are acting together. This Trinitarian reality is especially clear in Titus 2:14, where the expression "our great God and Savior" is applied directly to Jesus Christ, affirming clearly that Christ is both the divine and human Savior.[13]

Jesus Was Given Over for Us

What these texts affirm, like so many others in Scripture, is that God has acted objectively for us in our sinful state by taking on the problem of our evil and dealing with it, in one place at one time, in the vicarious work of the Son. Scripture says it clearly: "for all have sinned and fall short of the glory of God, [but they] are justified by his grace as a gift, through the redemption that is in Christ Jesus, whom God put forward as a propitiation by his blood, to be received by faith" (Rom 3:23–25). Christ's substitutionary death meets God's righteous demand, stated all the way back in Eden, when he warned Adam about the tree of testing: "[T]he day that you eat of it you shall surely die" (Gen 2:17). At the cross justice is done. God is both "just and the justifier of the one who has faith in Jesus" (Rom 3:26). He punishes sin as it is borne by Jesus. He justifies the believer by granting Christ's righteousness to us.

How God is specifically for us is beautifully and surprising stated in Romans 8.[14] There is one more exchange and one more giving over. "He who did not spare his own Son but gave him [over] (*paredoken*) for us all, how will he not also with him graciously give us all things?" (Rom 8:32). Behind this text is a scene in the Old Testament that de- scribes God testing Abraham to see if he loved God more than Isaac, the son of God's promise. Genesis records what God said to Abraham: "[B]ecause you have done this and have not withheld your son, your only son, I will surely bless you, and I will surely multiply your off- spring as the stars of heaven and as the sand that is on the seashore" (Gen 22:16–17). Abraham was willing to sacrifice his son on whom God's promise of future blessing depended. In other words, he was willing to risk everything, in order to be in obedient communion with God, having faith that God would provide a sacrifice (Gen 22:14). And God provided a sacrifice in place of Isaac, in the form of a ram caught in a bush. Fast forward to the cross: This time, God provides a greater sacrifice than the ram. Unlike Abraham, the Father does not spare his only Son, but gives him over (*paredoken*) for us. But we need to fill in the real implica- tions of the phrase. Paul says that Christ, taking on death, became "a curse" (Gal 3:13) and "sin" for us (2 Cor 5:21). God the Father gave his Son to destruction in order to release repentant sinners from the chains of the curse of Satanic power. Just as Jesus was released from that power by the resurrection, so he gives to repentant sinners "all things pertaining to life"—the Abrahamic blessing.

Without doubt there is a major play on words here. While sinners "exchange the truth of God for the lie" (Rom 1:25), exchange true worship for idolatry (Rom 1:23) and exchange the natural use of sexuality for the unnatural (Rom 1:26), and are then given over (*paredoken*; Rom 1:24, 26, 28) to a totally sinful way of thinking and living, so God exchanges his Son for sinners. He is given over (*paredoken*) as their substitute. In this exchanged place, the realm of death, the Son triumphs over Satan by his obedience, bearing our sins, not his own. The exchange we get is righteousness and eternal life. The given-over Jesus takes the place of given-over sinners and gives them his life. All this is the ultimate ex- pression of God's patience and kindness (Rom 2:4).

Paul knew what he was saying. In Isaiah 53:6, we read: "All we like sheep have gone astray ... and the Lord has laid [literally, "given over," *paredoken*] on him the iniquity of us all" (Isa 53:6). Six verses later, the text makes things abundantly clear: "[H]e poured out his soul to death [literally, he "gave over his soul unto death"] and was numbered with the transgressors; yet he bore the sin of many, and makes intercession for the transgressors" (Isa 53:12). This is certainly the way Jesus saw his own death. Before his crucifixion, Jesus declared, "For I tell you that this Scripture [Isa 53:12] must be fulfilled in me: 'And he was numbered with the transgressors'" (Luke 22:37).

Jesus is for Us by Dying for Us

The death of Christ for us is the demonstration that God is for us because Jesus is the divine Son. He's God in the flesh. The term in Romans 8, "his own Son" (8:32), is only used of Jesus. Identifying Jesus as God's Son explains how Paul, in Titus 2, can call him "our great God and Savior" (2:13). As the confessions say, he is both man and God. At his birth, Jesus is called Immanuel, which means "God with us" (Matt 1:23). At his baptism, the divine voice from heaven declares, "This is my beloved Son, with whom I am well pleased" (Matt 3:17). The Devil himself recognizes who Jesus is when he says, "If you are the Son of God, command these stones to become loaves of bread" (Matt 4:3). This is also true of Satan's minions, who "cried out, 'What have you to do with us, O Son of God? Have you come here to torment us before the time?'" (Matt 8:29).

Given Over but Not Giving Up

This is the essence of the Twoist gospel, the message that must be spoken by transformed minds to a culture lost in Oneism, whose only hope is in the sinful self. This is the essence of the power of truth. Paul affirms, as he goes to Oneist Rome: "I am not ashamed of the gospel, for it is the power of God for salvation to everyone who believes, to the Jew first and also to the Greek" (Rom 1:16). Again, do not miss the original text's play on words here: The God who is utterly other and of impeccable justice, who rightly gives us over (*paredoken*) to our sin, is also the God of stunning and surprising grace, who places the whole weight of our sins on his Son, who gives him over (*paredoken*) as a sin offering in our place[15] and blesses us by setting us free and giving us life. What God—and only God—could do, he has done. It is the power of that divine act, powerfully communicated in the gospel, that "transforms" our minds, sanctifies our bodies, and causes the Holy Spirit to dwell within us. Then, and only then, can we respond in acts of holy living and God-honoring thinking.

Our culture is beginning to put pressure on Christian pastors to avoid preaching the full extent of Romans 1. But covering up sin and denying the fall by failing to reflect the Bible's position on homosexuality and other sins will only conceal and silence the liberating, glorious power of the gospel. Not preaching the gospel means we will never hear testimonies like this from a former lesbian:

> In October 2008 ... I was convicted of my sin in a way that made me consider everything I loved, and its consequences ... My eyes were opened, and I began to believe everything God says in his word. I began to believe that what he says about sin, death, and hell were completely true.
>
> And amazingly, at the same time that the penalty of my sin became true to me, so did the preciousness of the cross. A vision of God's Son crucified, bearing the wrath I deserved, and an empty tomb displaying his power over death—all things I had heard before without any interest had become the most glorious revelation of love imaginable.[16]

To hear the good news we must hear the bad. How can we deny to our world the best news it could ever hear—"God did not spare his own Son but gave him over for us all"? How can we deny those we love the best news in the world? We must preach the gospel, even if doing so gives us over to persecution or even death. We cannot give up. We will not give up.

Do you long for true power? You can have the justifying, liberating power from guilt and sin and the free conscience found when we discover and receive faith in Jesus Christ. In consenting to being given over, Jesus did not give up—and three days later God raised him from the dead. So the gospel is all about God's work: the forgiveness of our sins and a future life resurrected with him.

The same message that the early church preached is the one we now carry forward by the Spirit of God. The culture cannot renew the planet, forgive sins, or create eternal life. All is God's doing.

Our Calling: A Different Giving Over

In presenting holy bodies to be the salt of the earth and transformed minds to be the clarifying light of the world, we follow Jesus, our Savior and model. The gospel is both a fact of history and the basis for a life on track with the Twoist worldview, seeking for the good of the "other."[17] It is a "given over" lifestyle of self-sacrifice, following the example of Jesus. Paul exhorts the Christians in Philippi, "Do nothing from selfish ambition or conceit, but in humility count others more significant than yourselves. Let each of you look not only to his own interests, but also to the interests of others" (Phil 2:3–4). (Notice the Twoist emphasis on "the other.") But the real motivation comes from the power of the gospel, from the self-sacrifice of Jesus for the "other"—so the text continues:

> Have this mind among yourselves, which is yours in Christ Jesus, who, though he was in the form of God, did not count equality with God a thing to be grasped, but emptied himself, by taking the form of a servant, being born in the likeness of men. And being found in human form, he humbled himself by becoming obedient to the point of death, even death on a cross (Phil 2:5–8).

This he did for us, to save sinners.

There is a deep relationship between what Jesus did and what believers must do. Thus Jesus predicts that his disciples would be "given over (*paredoken*)" (Matt 10:19) and "hated ... for my name's sake" (Matt 24:9). Paul agrees: "For we who live are always being given over (*paredoken*) to death for Jesus' sake, so that the life of Jesus also may be manifested in our mortal flesh" (2 Cor 4:11). The given-over Christ is our constant model, "who loved me and gave himself over (*paredoken*) for me" (Gal 2:20).[18] This is the lifestyle of husbands who must love their wives "as Christ loved the Church and gave himself over (*paredoken*) for her" (Eph 5:25). It is living, as Paul says "given over (*paredoken*)[19] to death for Jesus' sake" for others (2 Cor 4:11), that people might hear the Truth of the gospel, see our good works, and turn to our Father in heaven.

The Blessing of the Gospel

So we live given over but not giving up, because we're assured that God "will surely bless [us], and ... will surely multiply [our] offspring" (Gen 22:16–17). We have confidence that he will "freely give us all things," as Paul says (Rom 8:32 NASB). We do not give up, even in the face of persecution, because "if God is for us, who can be against us?" (Rom 8:31). For God's glory, we now respond to divine mercy by doing the good works he has prepared for us. We celebrate God's good work of creation by our acts of sacrificial kindness and mercy, by taking social responsibility and contributing to cultural excellence. We await the final great work of creation, namely its miraculous re-creation, when God will transform this wonderful but fallen cursed creation by his incredible resurrecting, life-giving power, into the new heaven and earth "in which righteousness dwells" (2 Pet 3:13). Both the original creation and the creation of a new heavens and earth are utterly miraculous, produced by the Twoist God who controls all things. He who originally creates matter in its fabulous, utterly complex forms also reverses the effects of sin and death and raises Jesus in a glorified, re-created body far beyond the glorious capabilities of the human body before the fall.

In this day of small things, we need to be big thinkers about a big God. The big picture is not pie-in-the-sky, but it includes the sky as the only vision that makes final sense. We tend to think in terms of our own short life span, but that's too shortsighted. Jesus is our greatest example of human flourishing, and he was nailed to a cross at age 33! In this fallen world, great obedience and gutsy self-sacrifice are the order of the day. And one day, having been faithful, we will reign with Jesus, our example and leader, over a new heavens and earth.

We do not give up, knowing that God will have the last—good—word.

Our Challenge

What then is the challenge before us? In this fallen world, we must embrace two realities:

First, the challenge of witnessing before the world to the Twoist, Trinitarian character of God and how it looks in everyday living. The task isn't to bury our heads in the sand and deny the growing seduction of the pagan cosmology of Oneism. It's not to conform our thinking to that of the world, as some believers are doing (whether intentionally or unwittingly). Rather, we are called to understand the Lie in order better to articulate the Truth. Perhaps in your witness to Christ and the gospel, you will find the simple notions of Oneism and Twoism a useful paradigm.

Second, we must ask God to show us how to speak his truth faithfully and courageously in the difficult days ahead. Do not be surprised: Jesus said he "came not to be served but to serve, and to give his life as a ransom for many" (Mark 10:45). He calls us to take up that same cross and follow him. Indeed, the time is coming when "all who desire to live a godly life in Christ Jesus will be persecuted" (2 Tim 3:12). Without the transformative power of the gospel, we will lack courage, and our efforts will be in vain. But we must remember that the difficult days are the most revealing. A southern Californian pastor says it well: "Brokenness is somehow key to transformation in this broken world. Grace is often more evident on the heels of disgrace and truth is often more evidence on the heels of falsehood."[20]

We do not know if our future will be a period of blessing or of persecution. King David, in a cave, in dire circumstances, in the midst of "lions and fiery beasts," with enormous faith declared: "[B]e exalted, O God, above the heavens! Let your glory be over all the earth!" (Psa 57:4-5). The faith of David must be ours, because God's promise to Israel before the threat of Babylon is also ours.

> The nations shall see your righteousness,
>   and all the kings your glory ...
> You shall be a crown of beauty in the hand of the Lord,
>   and a royal diadem in the hand of your God ...
> for the Lord delights in you ...
> as the bridegroom rejoices over the bride,
>   so shall your God rejoice over you (Isa 62:2-5).

Our Goal

We go forward with one eye on the coming marriage supper of the Lamb (Rev 19:9). In the meantime, we need the other eye on our calling to "cover the earth [this earth] with the knowledge of the truth," with the "glory of the Lord as the waters cover the sea" (Hab 2:14). We do this in the power of the gospel, with transformed thinking, with the clear message of Romans 1, with the simple arithmetic of Oneism and Twoism as the only options, one the Lie, the other the Truth. This is the only hope for a planet drowning in pagan fantasy and a Church wandering in deep confusion, seriously conformed to this world.

May the Lord grant us the strength and faith to witness to the Truth. And why? What Paul says at the very end of Romans as he wraps up the letter, from which we have taken so much, reveals the only genuine purpose of life: God's glory.

> Now to him who is able to strengthen you according to my gospel and the preaching of Jesus Christ, according to the revelation of the mystery that was kept secret for long ages but has now been disclosed and through the prophetic writings has been made known to all nations, according to the command of the eternal God, to bring about the obedience of faith—to the only wise God be glory forevermore through Jesus Christ! Amen (Rom 16:25–27).

ENDNOTES

Preface

1. David P. Goldman, "How Tolkien Ennobled Popular Culture (While *Star Wars* Degraded It)," *PJMedia* (December 1st, 2014), http://pjmedia.com/spengler/2014/12/01/how-tolkien-ennobled-popular-culture-while-star-wars-degraded-it/?singlepage=true.
2. Nirpal Dhaliwal, "How movies embraced Hinduism (without you even noticing)," *The Guardian* (25 December 2014), www.theguardian.com/film/2014/dec/25/movies-embraced-hinduism. This article shows how vaguely Hindu-inspired movies like *Star Wars, The Matrix,* and *Interstellar,* as some of the greatest recent box office hits, have deeply affected Western notions of spirituality.

Chapter 1: A Ticket to Ride—But to Where?

1. Carl Jung, *The Red Book: Liber Novus,* ed. Sonu Shamdasani (New York: Norton, 2009), 217.
2. Herman Kahn and Anthony J. Wiener, *The Year 2000: A Framework for Speculation on the Next Thirty-three Years* (New York: Macmillan, 1967), cited without page number in Peter L. Berger, *A Rumor of Angels: Modern Society and the Rediscovery of the Supernatural* (Garden City, NY: Doubleday, 1969), 16.

3. Elizabeth Fox-Genovese, *Women and the Future of the Family* (Grand Rapids: Baker, 2000), 17.

4. I recently discovered another Sixties feminist leader who eventually converted to Christianity, Gabriele Kuby. Her work on the nature of the Sixties revolution has never been translated into English, though its importance was publicly recognized by Pope Benedict XVI. I recommend Kuby's latest book, *Die globale sexuelle Revolution: Zerstörung der Freiheit im Namen der Freiheit* [*The Global Sexual Revolution: Destruction of Freedom in the Name of Freedom*] (Kißlegg, Germany: Fe-Medienverlag, 2012).

5. I take this up in chapter 10.

6. Peter Occhiogrosso, *The Joy of Sects: A Spirited Guide to the World's Religious Traditions* (New York: Doubleday, 1996), xxi.

7. Occhiogrosso, *Joy of Sects*, xvii.

8. Andrew Cohen, "The Significance of Non Duality: There is Only One, Not Two" (lecture, EnlightenNext winter retreat, Tucson, AZ, Dec 27–Jan 6).

9. See e.g., Colin Campbell, *The Easternization of the West: A Thematic Account of Cultural Change in the Modern Era* (Boulder, CO: Paradigm, 2007).

10. Philip Goldberg, *American Veda: From Emerson and the Beatles to Yoga and Meditation, How Indian Spirituality Changed the West* (New York: Harmony, 2013).

11. Plato's system, though it has a creator, is based on oneness. The creation is not outside and separate from the divine, but something in which the deity participates. Since his god is not triune, the divine is a singularity, finally dependent on everything else in a derivatory chain of being. See A. H. Armstrong. *An Introduction to Ancient Philosophy* (Ottawa: Rowman and Allanheld, 1983), 49.

12. Jean Benedict Raffa, *Healing the Sacred Divide: Making Peace with Ourselves, Each Other, and the World* (New York: Larson, 2012), 72, 74.

13. http://dotsub.com/view/d7e69b19-300f-4efc-b951-385da53f08f6/viewTranscript/eng. See also Thomas Keating, *Open Mind, Open Heart* (New York: Continuum, 1986).

14. http://integrallife.ontraport.net/c/s/6zW/6QcyW/U/yX/JE6/626uLH/6BdUL8RLJi.

15. Kurt Johnson and David Robert Ord, *The Coming Interspiritual Age* (Vancouver: Namaste, 2012), 371. See also Ernest Steed, *Two Be One: The Revealed Secrets of Long Hidden Mysticism and Religion* (Plainfield, NJ: Logos International, 1978) and Mircea Eliade, *The Two and the One* (London: Harville, 1962). My humble contribution is *One or Two: Seeing a World of Difference* (Escondido, CA: Main Entry, 2010).

16. Colin E. Gunton, *The Triune Creator: A Historical and Systematic Study* (Grand Rapids: Eerdmans, 1998), 3–4.

17. Camille Paglia, *Sexual Personae: Art and Decadence from Nefertiti to Emily Dickinson* (New Haven, CT: Yale University Press, 1990), 1.

18. Robert Sokolowski, *The God of Faith and Reason: Foundations of Christian Theology* (Washington, DC: Catholic University of America Press, 1995), 23.

19. So again Sokolowski, *God of Faith and Reason*, x: "Because God is so independent of the world, we can say that he created the world out of sheer generosity, not out of any sort of need. ... In doing so he has shown the charity that is at the heart of things."

20. Colin E. Gunton, *The Triune Creator: A Historical and Systematic Study* (Grand Rapids: Eerdmans, 1998), 7-9.

21. Claus Westermann, *Genesis 1-11: A Commentary*, trans. J. J. Scullion (Minneapolis: Augsburg, 1984), 127.

22. G. Ernest Wright, *The Old Testament against its Environment* (London: SCM, 1950), cited in John N. Oswalt, *The Bible among the Myths* (Grand Rapids: Zondervan, 2009), 11.

23. Oswalt, *The Bible among the Myths*, 28.

24. Readers who know a little Greek will note that Paul uses the definite article "the" before both "truth" (ἡ ἀλήθεια) and "lie" (τό ψεῦδος). In Greek, indefiniteness is typically expressed by the absence of the definite article. Most English translators leave out the definite article in this passage, though other languages like French and German have it. The parallelism is also clear: the truth and the lie, the creature and the Creator.

25. I am not inventing anything other than a simplified terminology. Other descriptions of the two options include biblical faith or paganism, monism or theism, or the Creator/creature distinction.

26. Sokolowski, *God of Faith and Reason*, xi: "The pagan religious and philosophical attitude is always with us and is not a point of view proper to a particular period of human development."

27. If this is the *biblical* worldview, how does one relate it to Rabbinic Judaism and Islam, whose followers also claim to respect the Bible (though in very different ways)? There is only one pure Oneist—Satan—and one pure Twoist—Jesus Christ. Judaism and Islam have a defective view of biblical Twoism. Their denial of the Trinity leaves them with a transcendent yet impersonal God (an attempt at Twoism), who ultimately depends upon his relationship with human beings in order to constitute his personhood (which ends up in Oneism by a circuitous route). Rabbinic scholar Abraham Heschel (1907-1972) rightly critiqued Islam for seeing God as "unqualified Omnipotence," who can never be "the Father of mankind," and thus is radically impersonal. See Heschel, *The Prophets* (New York: Harper, 1962), 292, 311. Yet postbiblical Judaism cannot escape Heschel's critique entirely. The medieval rabbi Maimonides, for example, also confessed an "absolutely transcendent God who is independent of humanity." See Reuven Kimelman, "The Theology of Abraham Joshua Heschel," *First Things* (Dec 2009). On the other hand, Kimelman notes that Heschel commits the opposite error to that of Maimonides (and Islam), namely that of making God dependent on man in a covenantal relationship that both God and man need in order to be who they are. Heschel adopts the rabbinical concept that it is human witness that in some sense makes God real (Kimelman, "The Theology of Abraham Joshua Heschel"). Once more, God is dependent upon

humanity. This is the classic dilemma of a monotheism without the Trinity. Because Heschel does not believe God to be triune, God depends on man to be personal and therefore cannot be "Wholly Other" in relation to creation.

28. Romans 8:32 and 4:25.

Chapter 2: The Rise and Fall of Secular Humanism

1. See John Frame, *A History of Western Philosophy and Theology* (Phillipsburg, NJ: P&R, 2015), 293.
2. Pierre-Simon Laplace, *Le Systeme du Monde* [The Politics of Science](Cambridge, MA: Harvard University Press, 2005), 172.
3. Ludwig Feuerbach, *The Essence of Christianity* (London, 1841), cited in Alister McGrath, *The Twilight of Atheism: The Rise and Fall of Disbelief in the Modern World* (New York: Doubleday, 2004), 57.
4. Peter Berger, *A Rumor of Angels* (New York: Anchor, 1970), 45.
5. The words of the Harvard paleontologist George Gaylord Simpson of the last generation, cited by John West, "Darwinian Evolution," in *The Coming Pagan Utopia: Christian Witness in Tough Times,* ed. Peter Jones (Escondido, CA: Main Entry Editions, 2013), 108. This volume is a collection of essays from the truthXchange 2013 Think Tank.
6. See Edward Norman, *Secularization* (London: Bloomsbury Academic, 2003), 52.
7. Karl Marx and Friedrich Engels, *On Religion* (Moscow: Foreign Languages Publishing House, 1957), 14, cited in Marcel Neusch, *The Sources of Modern Atheism: One Hundred Years of Debate over God* (New York: Paulist, 1982), 62.
8. Friedrich Nietzsche, *The Gay Science* (1882, 1887) §125; See also Peter Berkowitz, *Nietzsche: The Ethics of an Immoralist* (Cambridge, MA: Harvard University Press, 1995), especially 14–21. Berkowitz demonstrates that this statement is an essential part of Nietzsche's philosophy.
9. Cited in Mary Eberstadt, "How the West Really Lost God: A New Look at Secularization," *Policy Review* 143 (June/July 2007.).
10. Richard Dawkins, *The Selfish Gene* (Oxford: Oxford University Press, 2006), 330.
11. Evelyn Waugh, *A Little Learning* (New York: Little Brown, 1964), referring to a diary entry of June 18, 1921.
12. For this account, see Albert Mohler, "Commonplaces: Evelyn Waugh the Young Atheist," *AlbertMohler.com*, last modified 15 May 2014. http://www.albertmohler.com/2014/05/15/commonplaces-evelyn-waugh-the-young-atheist/.
13. See chapters 3–6 of James Herrick's *The Making of the New Spirituality: The Eclipse of the Western Religious Tradition* (Downers Grove, IL: InterVarsity Press, 2003) for a full-scale account of the effects of rationalism on Christianity from the Enlightenment to the Modern period.
14. Davis v. Beason, 133 US 333, 342, 1890, cited in Martha M. McCarthy, "Secular Humanism and Education," *Journal of Law and Education* 19, no. 4 (1990): 470.
15. Cited in Mike King, *Postsecularism: The Hidden Challenge to Extremism* (Cambridge: James Clark, 2009), 125.
16. Vishal Mangalwadi, *Missionary Conspiracy: Letters to a Postmodern Hindu* (India: Good Books, 1996), front cover.

17. *Nature of President Clinton's Relationship with Monica Lewinsky* (Washington, DC: U.S. Government Printing Office, May 19, 2004).

18. Michel Foucault, *Madness and Unreason: History of Madness in the Classical Age,* ed. and trans. J. Khalfa and J. Murphy (London: Routledge, 2006).

19. Alister McGrath, *The Twilight of Atheism: The Rise and Fall of Disbelief in the Modern World* (New York: Doubleday, 2006).

20. Modern day atheists include Sam Harris, *The End of Faith: Religion, Terror, and the Future of Reason* (New York: Norton, 2005) and *Letter to a Christian Nation* (New York: Knopf, 2006); Daniel C. Dennett, *Breaking the Spell: Religion as a Natural Phenomenon* (New York: Penguin, 2007); Richard Dawkins, *The God Delusion* (Boston: Houghton Mifflin, 2006); Christopher Hitchens, *God Is Not Great: How Religion Poisons Everything* (New York: Twelve, 2007); Michel Onfray, *Atheist Manifesto: The Case Against Christianity, Judaism, and Islam,* English ed. (New York: Arcade, 2005); Victor J. Stenger, *God: The Failed Hypothesis: How Science Shows that God Does Not Exist* (Amherst, NY: Prometheus, 2007).

21. Antony Flew with Roy Varghese, *There is a God: How the World's Most Notorious Atheist Changed His Mind* (New York: Harper Collins, 2007), 121, 132, cited by Melanie Phillips, *The World Turned Upside Down* (New York: Encounter, 2011), 336. See also Eric Kaufmann, "God Returns to Europe: The Slow Death of Secularism," *Prospect* (Nov 2006).

22. Sam Harris, *Waking Up: A Guide to Spirituality Without Religion* (New York: Simon and Schuster, 2014), 6.

23. Rationalistic and spiritual forms of Oneism have coexisted or alternated for much of philosophical history. A flashback to Gnosticism indicates that a similar process took place as what we have noted between the modern and the postmodern. Giovanni Filoramo, an expert in the study of ancient Gnosticism, in *The History of Gnosticism* (Oxford: Blackwell, 1990), 23, speaks of the gnostic "mythological revival." "There was a revival after a period of rationalism [the critique of *mythos* by Socrates, Plato and Aristotle, using *logos*], when *mythos* was rediscovered and given new meaning. At that point, the Roman historian, Plutarch, described the Greco-Roman empire of the first century Mediterranean world as 'a goblet seething with myths'" (*Def. or.* 421 A). See also Lit-Sen Chang's account of the Taoist critique of Confucianism in *Asia's Religions: Christianity's Momentous Encounter with Paganism* (Phillipsburg, NJ: P&R, 1999), 102–04.

24. Richard Tarnas, *The Passion of the Western Mind: Understanding the Ideas that Have Shaped Our World View* (New York: Ballantine, 1991), 402.

25. Negative theology attempts to describe God by negation, only speaking of what may not be said about perfect goodness (God).

26. Bible and Culture Collective, *The Postmodern Bible* (New Haven, CT: Yale University Press, 1997), 135.

27. Terrence W. Tilley, ed., *Postmodern Theologies: The Challenge of Religious Diversity* (Maryknoll, NY: Orbis, 1995), 160.

28. Tarnas, *Passion of the Western Mind,* 402.

29. See T. J. J. Altizer and William Hamilton, *Radical Theology and the Death of God* (Indianapolis: Bobbs-Merrill, 1966).

30. David L. Miller, *The New Polytheism: Rebirth of the Gods and Goddesses* (New York: Harper and Row, 1974).

31. In the words of Mary Eberstadt, research fellow at Stanford University's Hoover Institution: "As everybody also knows, much about the current scene would seem to clinch the point, at least in Western Europe. Elderly altar servers in childless churches attended by mere handfuls of pensioners; tourist throngs in Notre Dame and other cathedrals circling ever-emptier pews roped off for worshippers; former abbeys and convents and monasteries remade into luxury hotels and sybaritic spas; empty churches here and there shuttered for decades and then re-made into discos—even into a mosque or two. Hardly a day passes without details like these issuing from the Continent's post-Christian front. If God *were* to be dead in the Nietzschean sense, one suspects that the wake would look a lot like this." Mary Eberstadt, *How the West Really Lost God: A New Look at Secularization* (West Conshohocken, PA: Templeton, 2013), 2.

Chapter 3: Carl Jung's Dream for a "New Humanity"

1. A close colleague of Jung, history of religions scholar Mircea Eliade, used this term. See David Cave, *Mircea Eliade's Vision for a New Humanism* (Oxford: Oxford University Press, 1993).

2. Carl Jung, *The Red Book: Liber Novus,* ed. Sonu Shamdasani (New York: Norton, 2009), 211.

3. John Dourley, *The Illness That We Are: A Jungian Critique of Christianity* (Toronto: Inner City Books, 1984), 158.

4. Carl Jung, "The Difference between Eastern and Western Thinking," in *The Portable Jung,* ed. Joseph Campbell (New York: Penguin, 1976), 476.

5. Quoted without reference in Richard Noll, *The Aryan Christ: The Secret Life of Carl Jung* (New York: Random House, 1997), 65.

6. Noll, *Aryan Christ,* 54.

7. Huston Smith states: "The world has had enough of the meaninglessness that came with modernity. Modernity's mistake was to think that the empirical world that our physical senses report—together with science's extrapolations from them—is the only world there is. Carl Jung and transpersonal psychology have punctured that mistake and elaborated its alterative." Smith, "The Re-enchantment of the World," (lecture, Pacifica Graduate Institute, Santa Barbara, CA, May 20, 2005), http://www.pacifica.edu/public-programs/public-programs-previous-events/masters2005/masters-huston-smith.

8. Harry Oldmeadow, "C. G. Jung & Mircea Eliade: 'Priests without Surplices'? Reflections on the Place of Myth, Religion and Science in Their Work" (Bendigo Department of Humanities, La Trobe University, *Studies in Western Tradition, Occasional Papers Series* 1, 1995).

9. Noll, *Aryan Christ,* 158.

10. Richard Noll, *The Jung Cult: Origins of a Charismatic Movement* (Princeton, NJ: Princeton University Press, 1994).

11. Noll, *Aryan Christ*, xv.

12. Noll, *Aryan Christ*, 159.

13. David Cloud, *The New Age Tower of Babel* (Way of Life Literature, Amazon Digital Services eBook, 2011), n.p.

14. Norvene Vest, *Re-visioning Theology: A Mythic Approach to Religion* (New York: Paulist, 2011), 50.

15. Jung, *Analytical Psychology: Notes of the Seminar Given in 1925* (Princeton, NJ: Princeton University Press, 1989), 86, 98.

16. June Singer, *Androgyny: Toward a New Theory of Sexuality* (New York: Doubleday, 1976), 264, 255.

17. Singer, *Androgyny*, 255, 264.

18. Cited in Sean Kelly, *Individuation and the Absolute: Hegel, Jung, and the Path Toward Wholeness* (New York: Paulist, 1993), 3.

19. Jung, *Red Book*, 360.

20. Carl Jung, *The Undiscovered Self*, trans. R. F. C. Hull (New York: New American Library, 1958), 58. See J. Budziszewski, "C. G. Jung's War on the Christian Faith," *Christian Research Journal* 21, no. 3 (1998).

21. Cloud, *Tower of Babel*, n.p.

22. Carl Jung, *Memories, Dreams, Reflections*, ed. Aniela Jaffé (New York: Vintage Books, 1989), 18.

23. John Kerr, *A Most Dangerous Method: The Story of Jung, Freud, and Sabina Spielrein* (New York: Vintage Books, 2011), 50, 54.

24. Jung, *Memories, Dreams, Reflections*, 13.

25. Charles Darwin, *Beagle Diary*, 8 March 1836.

26. W. H. Auden, "The Public v. the Late William Butler Yeats," in *The Complete Works of W. H. Auden: Prose, vol. II: 1939-1948*, ed. Edward Mendelson (Princeton University Press, 1996), 2:5.

27. David L. Miller, *The New Polytheism: Rebirth of the Gods and Goddesses* (New York: Harper and Row, 1974).

28. Sonu Shamdasani, introduction to Jung, *Red Book*, 215.

29. Jung and Jaffé, *Memories, Dreams, Reflections*, quoted in Oldmeadow, "Priests without Surplices."

30. Gilles Quispel, "Gnosis and Psychology," in *The Allure of Gnosticism: The Gnostic Experience in Jungian Psychology and Contemporary Culture*, ed. Robert Segal (Chicago: Open Court, 1995), 13.

31. Richard Tarnas, *The Passion of the Western Mind: Understanding the Ideas that Have Shaped Our World View* (New York: Harmony, 1991), 424.

32. Tarnas, *Passion of the Western Mind*, 405.

33. John N. Oswalt, The Bible *among the Myths* (Grand Rapids: Zondervan, 2009), 52.

34. Mircea Eliade, *The Two and the One* (University of Chicago Press, 1979), 97. As a young man, Eliade voraciously read the writings of Freemason Manly P. Hall, including *The Secret Teaching of All Ages: An Encyclopedia of Masonic, Hermetic, Qabbalistic and Rosicrucian Symbolical Philosophy* (1928). See Mitch Horowitz,

Occult America: The Secret Mystic History of Our Nation (New York: Bantam, 2009), 163.

35. Eliade, *Two and the One*, 46.

36. Eliade, *Two and the One*, 81, quoted in Sean M. Kelly, *Individuation*, 4. Eliade defines individuation as "the emergence of the self as a complex whole or dialectically self-articulating totality."

37. Dourley, *The Illness That We Are*, 158.

38. Carl Jung, *Collected Works*, ed. and trans. Gerhard Adler and R. F. C. Hull, vol. 14, *Mysterium Coniunctionis* (Princeton, NJ: Princeton University Press, 2014).

39. Kelly, *Individuation*, 4, describes individuation as "the emergence of the Self as a complex whole or dialectically self-articulating totality."

40. Noll, *Aryan Christ*, 197.

41. The vital importance of the secret volume is seen by what the translator/editor said: "Once it's published, there will be a 'before' and 'after' in Jungian scholarship...it will wipe out all the biographies, just for starters." See Sarah Corbett, "The Holy Grail of the Unconscious," *The Wall Street Journal* (16 Sept 2009).

42. Jung, *Red Book*, 214.

43. Jung, *Red Book*, 200–01.

44. Jung, *Red Book*, 205.

45. Jung, *Collected Works*, vol. 9, *Aion*, 2:41. For Jung, it was regrettable that Christ in his goodness lacked a shadow side, and God the Father, who is the light, lacked darkness. See John Dourley, *The Psyche as Sacrament: A Comparative Study of C. G. Jung and Paul Tillich* (Toronto: Inner City Books, 1981), 63.

46. Jung, *Red Book*, 211.

47. The statement also is reprinted in one of the opening pages.

48. Jung, *Collected Works*, 10:852 and 11:295, cited by Kelly, *Individuation*, 18.

49. Noll, *Aryan Christ*, 157–58.

50. Noll, *Aryan Christ*, 158.

51. Clifford Williams, *Existential Reasons for Belief in God: A Defense of Desires and Emotions for Faith* (Downers Grove, IL: InterVarsity Press, 2011), 100–03.

52. Jeffrey Satinover, *Homosexuality and the Politics of Truth* (Grand Rapids: Baker, 1996), 47-848. See also C. Michael Smith, Jungian psychologist and adjunct professor in psychology and religion at the Chicago Theological Seminary, *Jung and Shamanism: Retrieving the Soul/Retrieving the Sacred* (New York: Paulist, 1997), who sees a positive integration of Jungian analysis and shamanism.

53. Satinover, *Politics of Truth*, 240. If one wonders why the Episcopal Church is now split over the issue of homosexual bishops, note Satinover's comment in *The Empty Self: Gnostic and Jungian Foundations of Modern Identity* (Cambridge: Grove Books, 1995): "In the United States, the Episcopal Church has more or less become a branch of Jungian psychology, theologically and liturgically." See Ed Hird, "Carl Jung, Neo-Gnosticism, and the Myers-Briggs Temperament Indicator (MBTI)" (unpublished manuscript, last modified 8 March 1998), Anglican Renewal Ministries of Canada, http://www3.telus.net/st_simons/armo3.htm.

54. Noll, *Aryan Christ*, 213.
55. Fr. Dariusz Oko, "With the Pope against the Homoheresy" [in French], *Le Courrier de Rome*, Année XLVIII 364, no. 554 (March–April 2013):10.
56. Satinover, *Politics of Truth*, 168–69.
57. Sheila Grimaldi-Craig, "Dirty Harry," *Spring* 94 (June 1993): 154.
58. Noll, *Aryan Christ*, 207.
59. Christopher Lasch, *The Culture of Narcissism: American Life in an Age of Diminishing Expectations* (New York: Norton, 1991).
60. Noll, *Aryan Christ*, xv.
61. Monsignor Robert Hugh Benson, *Lord of the World*, cited in Jim Tonkowich, "Your Faith is Now Intrinsically Offensive. Are You Ready for the Fallout?" *Aquila Report* (1 June 2014), http://theaquilareport.com/your-faith-is-now-intrinsically-offensive-are-you-ready-for-the-fallout/

Chapter 4: The Perennial Philosophy—The Origin of Contemporary Spirituality

1. Catherine L. Albanese, *A Republic of Mind and Spirit: A Cultural History of American Metaphysical Religion* (New Haven, CT: Yale University Press, 2007), 5.
2. Tony Schwartz, *What Really Matters: Searching for Wisdom in America* (New York: Bantam, 1995), 431. Interestingly, he sees the blend of Jungian psychology and the new spirituality.
3. George B. Shaw, preface to *Plays Pleasant and Unpleasant*, vol. 2 (1898).
4. Antoine Favre, "Renaissance Hermeticism and Western Esoterism," in *Gnosis and Hermeticism from Antiquity to Modern Times*, ed. Roelef van den Broek and Wouter J. Hanegraaff (Albany, NY: State University of New York Press, 1998), 110.
5. Peter Occhiogrosso, *The Joy of Sects: A Spirited Guide to the World's Religious Traditions* (New York: Doubleday, 1996), xvi. See also Favre, "Renaissance Hermeticism," 114, 120.
6. Aldous Huxley, *The Perennial Philosophy: An Interpretation of the Great Mystics, East and West* (New York: HarperPerennial, 1944, 1945), vii.
7. Occhiogrosso, *Joy of Sects*, xvi.
8. Occhiogrosso, *Joy of Sects*, xxi.
9. Stanislav Grof, *Psychology of the Future: Lessons from Modern Consciousness Research* (Albany, NY: State University of New York Press, 2000), x. See also James Olney, *The Rhizome and the Flower: The Perennial Philosophy—Yeats and Jung* (Berkeley: University of California Press, 1980).
10. Cited in James Herrick, *The Making of the New Spirituality: The Eclipse of the Western Religious Tradition* (Downers Grove, IL: InterVarsity Press, 2003), 241.
11. Phil Cousineau, ed., *The Way Things Are: Conversations with Huston Smith* (Berkeley: University of California Press, 2003), 80.
12. See Philip Goldberg, *American Veda: From Emerson and the Beatles to Yoga and Meditation, How Indian Spirituality Changed the West* (New York: Harmony, 2013), 104 (without reference).
13. "Tradition and Modernity," *Sacred Web Journal* (Sept 2006).
14. Foster Bailey, *The Spirit of Masonry* (New York: Lucis Trust, 1957), 83.

15. *Gospel of Philip* 67:31–35.
16. Rhonda Byrne, *The Secret* (New York: Atria Books, 2006), inside cover and page v.
17. Don Richard Riso and Russ Hudson, *The Wisdom of the Enneagram* (New York: Bantam Books, 1999), 9, 21. These principal scholars and innovative thinkers in the practice of Gurdjieff's Enneagram state: "The modern Enneagram of personality type has been synthesized from many different spiritual and religious traditions. Much of it is a condensation of universal wisdom, the perennial philosophy accumulated by Christians, Buddhists, Muslims (especially the Sufis), and Jews (in the Kabbalah) for thousands of years. The heart of the Enneagram is the universal insight that human beings are spiritual presences incarnated in the material world and yet mysteriously embodying the same life and Spirit as the Creator. Beneath surface differences and appearances, behind the veils of illusion, the light of Divinity shines in every individual." For further information on the use of the Enneagram, I highly recommend Pam Frost's chapter, "Pagan Contemplative Techniques," in *On Global Wizardry: Techniques of Pagan Spirituality and a Christian Response*, ed. Peter Jones (Escondido, CA: Main Entry Editions, 2010), 186–202.
18. Riso and Hudson, *Wisdom of the Enneagram*, 60.
19. Huston Smith, *Beyond the Postmodern: The Place of Meaning in a Global Civilization* (Wheaton, IL: Quest Books, 2003), 46.
20. Ronald Hutton, "Revisionism and Counter-Revisionism in Pagan History," *Pomegranate: The International Journal of Pagan Studies* 13, no. 2 (2011), www.equinoxpub.com/journals/index.php/POM/article/view/16291, p.1.
21. Jung, *Psychology and Alchemy* (Princeton, NJ: Princeton University Press, 1968), 306, 312, cited in Glenn Magee, *Hegel and the Hermetic Tradition* (Ithaca, NY: Cornell University Press 2001), 207–08.
22. Alice Bailey, *The Destiny of Nations* (New York: Lucis Trust, 1949), cited in Marianne Williamson, *Healing the Soul of America: Reclaiming Our Voices as Spiritual Citizens* (New York: Simon & Schuster, 2000), 195.
23. Hermetic adepts claim their tradition is part of the perennial philosophy.
24. Éliphas Lévi, *Transcendental Magic: Its Doctrine and Ritual*, trans. Arthur Edward Waite (London: Rider, 1968).
25. Aleister Crowley, *Magick Without Tears: "Letter C"* (Las Vegas: New Falcon, 1991).
26. Thomas Berry, *The Great Work: Our Way into The Future* (New York: Bell Tower, 1999).
27. Berry, *The Great Work*, 159.
28. Berry, *The Great Work*, 106.
29. Berry, *The Great Work*, 2.
30. Christopher Partridge, *The Re-Enchantment of the West: Alternative Spiritualities, Sacralization, Popular Culture, and Occulture* (London: T&T Clark, 2004), 1:68.
31. Joachim Köhler, *Zarathrustra's Secret: the Interior Life of Friedrich Nietzsche*, trans. Ronald Taylor (New Haven, CT: Yale University Press, 2002), 256.
32. Köhler, *Zarathrustra's Secret*, x.

33. Jessie Weston, *From Ritual to Romance* (1920), cited in Mark Gaffney, *Gnostic Secrets of the Naassenes: The Initiatory Teachings of the Last Supper* (Rochester, VT: Inner Traditions, 2004), 173.

34. James Garlow and Peter Jones, *Cracking Da Vinci's Code: You've Read the Fiction, Now Read the Facts* (Colorado Springs: Victor, 2004).

35. Foster Bailey, *The Spirit of Masonry* (New York: Lucis Trust, 1957), 120–21.

36. Carl Jung, "The Difference between Eastern and Western Thinking," in *The Portable Jung*, ed. Joseph Campbell (New York: Penguin, 1976), 476.

37. Carl Jung, *Letters*, 2:138, cited in Dourley, The Illness That We Are: *A Jungian Critique of Christianity* (Toronto: Inner City Books, 1984), 35.

Chapter 5: The Sixties Spiritual and Sexual Revolution

1. Richard Noll, *The Jung Cult: Origins of a Charismatic Movement* (Princeton, NJ: Princeton University Press, 1994).

2. Bob Dylan, "The Times They Are a-Changin,'" on *The Times They are a-Changin'*, Columbia 8786, 1964, 33⅓ rpm.

3. Colin Campbell, *The Easternization of the West: A Thematic Account of Cultural Change in the Modern Era* (Boulder, CO: Paradigm, 2007), 375.

4. Carl Jung, *Memories, Dreams, Reflections*, ed. Aniela Jaffé (New York: Vintage Books, 1989), 232.

5. Jung, "The Difference between Eastern and Western Thinking," 476.

6. Carl Jung, *Letters*, 2:138, quoted in Dourley, *The Illness That We Are: A Jungian Critique of Christianity* (Toronto: Inner City Books, 1984), 35.

7. Carl Jung to H. G. Baynes, 12 Aug 1940, in *Letters*, ed. Gerhard Adler, trans. R. F. C. Hull (Princeton University Press, 1973), 1:285.

8. The 5th Dimension, "Medley: Aquarius/Let the Sunshine In (The Flesh Failures)," on *The Age of Aquarius*. Soul City, 1967, 33⅓ rpm.

9. Don McLean, "American Pie," on *American Pie*, United Artists, 1971, 33⅓ rpm.

10. Don McLean, "Commentary: Buddy Holly, Rock Music Genius," CNN (1 Feb 2009), http://www.cnn.com/2009/SHOWBIZ/Music/02/01/mclean.buddy.holly/

11. Peter Collier and David Horowitz, *Destructive Generation: Second Thoughts about the Sixties* (Los Angeles: Second Thoughts Books, 1989).

12. "Episode 2: Joseph Campbell and the Power of Myth—'The Message of the Myth,'" March 8, 2013: http://billmoyers.com/content/ep-2-joseph-campbell-and-the-power-of-myth-the-message-and-the-myth-audio/

13. Mark Gaffney, *Gnostic Secrets of the Naassenes: The Initiatory Teachings of the Last Supper* (Rochester, VT: Inner Traditions, 2004), 5.

14. James Robinson, introduction to *The Nag Hammadi Library in English* (Leiden: Brill, 1977), 1.

15. In 1932 Jung gave a substantial seminar in yoga, which was later published in book form: Carl Jung, *The Psychology of Kundalini Yoga: Notes of the Seminar Given in 1932 by C. G. Jung*, ed. Sonu Shamdasani (Princeton, NJ: Princeton University Press, 1996).

16. Philip Goldberg, *American Veda: From Emerson and the Beatles to Yoga and Meditation, How Indian Spirituality Changed the West* (New York: Harmony, 2013).

17. Goldberg, *American Veda*, 5.
18. Colin Campbell, *The Easternization of the West: A Thematic Account of Cultural Change in the Modern Era* (Boulder, CO: Paradigm, 2007), 39–41.
19. Sachi Fujimori, "Health care profession is increasingly adopting meditation," *The Record* (September 3, 2013), http://www.northjersey.com/news/222032201_Health_care_profession_is_increasingly_adopting_meditation.html?page=all#sthash.gEbakD3d.dpuf.
20. See chapter 9.
21. Mary Eady, *Letter to a Friend: Yoga* (Escondido, CA: Main Entry Editions, 2013). See also Pam Frost, "Oneist Spirituality" (lecture, truthXchange, Escondido, CA, March 2011), MP3, 1:01:59, https://truthxchange.com/wp-content/uploads/2011/03/1-5-2011_Frost_One-ist%20Spirituality.mp3; Frost, "Eastern Spiritual Visions of Utopian Oneism" (lecture, truthXchange, Escondido, CA, February 2013), MP3, 52:09, https://truthxchange.com/wp-content/uploads/2013/02/Wednesday-Morning-lecture-Pam-Frost-64kbps.mp3
22. Dr. David Frawley, *How to Become a Hindu: A Guide for Seekers and Born Hindus* (Kapaa, HI: Himâlayan Academy, 1989).
23. Carl Jung, "'Unus Mundus' and Synchronicity," quoted without reference in Bernie Quigley, "John Lennon's Shamanic Journey," *Free Liberal* (August 19, 2005).
24. Heather Eaton, "Ecofeminism, Cosmology and Spiritual Renewal," *Eglise et Théologie* 29 (1998): 120.
25. Hippolytus (AD 170–236), in *Refutation of All Heresies* 5:9:10, documented that the gnostics of his day were interfaith practitioners who sought "the wisdom of the pagans." He noted that Christian gnostics attended the ceremonies of the mystery cults who worshiped the Great Mother, the goddess Isis, in order to understand "the universal mystery."
26. Christopher Partridge, *The Re-Enchantment of the West: Alternative Spiritualities, Sacralization, Popular Culture, and Occulture* (London: T&T Clark, 2004), 1:38–40.
27. Partridge, *Re-enchantment of the West*, 1:38–40
28. Richard Tarnas, *Cosmos and Psyche: Intimations of a New World* (New York: Penguin, 2006), xiii.
29. Richard Noll, *The Aryan Christ: The Secret Life of Carl Jung* (New York: Random House, 1997), 77.
30. These are choice phrases used by authors like Mary Daly, Professor of Theology at Boston College and author of *Pure Lust: Elemental Feminist Philosophy* (St. Paul, MN: Women's Press, 1998).
31. Daly, *Pure Lust*, 65.
32. Herbert Marcuse, *Eros and Civilization: A Philosophical Inquiry into Freud* (Boston: Beacon, 1955, 1966), xv, xix, 3.
33. Marcuse, *Eros and Civilization*, 147–48.
34. Marcuse, *Eros and Civilization*, xxvii.
35. Marcuse, *Eros and Civilization*, 201.

36. Alfred C. Kinsey, *Sexual Behavior in the Human Male* (Indiana University Press, 1948/1998), and *Sexual Behavior in the Human Female* (Indiana University Press, 1953/1998). See the critique of Kinsey and of his pseudoscientific methods by Judith A. Reisman, *Kinsey: Crimes and Consequences* (Crestwood, KY: The Institute for Media Education, 1998, 2000). Like Jung, Kinsey was greatly helped by the Rockefeller Foundation; see Reisman, *Kinsey*, 38–39.

37. UK homosexual activist Peter Tatchel stated in 2013: "The London Gay Liberation Front Manifesto 1971 transformed my consciousness and shaped modern LGBT identity. It gave us pride and vision. We dared to dream of a different, better world—with liberation for all of humanity." http://www.petertatchell.net/lgbt_rights/history/Gay-Liberation-Front-Manifesto-London-1971.htm.

38. Alan Sears and Craig Osten, *The Homosexual Agenda: Exposing the Principal Threat to Religious Freedom Today* (Nashville: Broadman & Holman, 2003); David Kupelian, *The Marketing of Evil* (Los Angeles: WND Books, 2005), 23.

39. Marshall Kirk and Hunter Madsen, *After the Ball: How America Will Conquer its Fear and Hatred of Gays in the 90s* (New York: Plume, 1990), 155.

40. Sears and Osten, *Homosexual Agenda*, 45.

41. Kirk and Madsen, *After the Ball*, 17.

42. See http://www.gallup.com/poll/147824/adults-estimate-americans-gay-lesbian.aspx.

43. Two other studies confirm low population percentages for homosexuals: a 2011 Williams Institute survey that found that 1.7 percent of the US adult population is gay or lesbian; and an older study by the Alan Guttmacher Institute, which "interviewed over 3,300 men throughout the country in 1991 [and] found that only 2.3 percent of those interviewed admit[ted] to a same-sex experience in the last ten years; only 1.1 percent say they have been exclusively gay." (Peter LaBarbera,"The '10% Gay' Myth Is Officially Dead," *Americans For Truth*, July 14, 2014).

44. Peter Montgomery, "Historic Pro-Gay Equality Shift Led by Millennials—Evangelicals Included," *Religion Dispatches* (August 30, 2011), http://religiondispatches.org/historic-pro-gay-equality-shift-led-by-millennials-evangelicals-included/

45. Anjana Sreedhar, "74% of Millennials Support Gay Marriage," *Policy.Mic* (March 25, 2013) http://mic.com/articles/30916/74-of-millennials-support-gay-marriage.

46. Sears and Osten, *The Homosexual Agenda*, 67.

47. Montgomery, "Historic Pro-Gay Equality Shift."

48. Kathryn C. Montgomery, *Target: Prime Time: Advocacy Groups and the Struggle over Entertainment Television* (New York: Oxford University Press, 1989), 78–79.

49. David Ehrenstein, "More than Friends," *Los Angeles Magazine* (May 1996).

50. Dr. Mary Klages, *Queer Theory: Definition & Literary Example* (Boulder, CO: University of Colorado, Fall 2005), quoted in a syllabus by Dr. Katherine Harris at http://www.sjsu.edu/faculty/harris/Eng101_QueerDef.pdf.

51. Noll, *Aryan Christ*.
52. Virginia Ramey Mollenkott, *Omnigender: A Trans-Religious Approach* (Cleveland, OH: Pilgrim Press, 2001), 41, 74.
53. I have included this list in previous books and publications, but its place here is nonetheless of value.
54. I list here a person with a rare medical abnormality of sexual organs, which does not mean an inherently bigendered identity. Nonetheless, this condition presents doctors and parents with difficult decisions that may lead to confusion as such an individual grows to adulthood.
55. Mollenkott, *Omnigender*, 69, proposes this as a useful temporary strategy for young people unsure of their sexuality.
56. Mollenkott, *Omnigender*, 70.
57. Surprisingly absent from this list is "polyamory," the love of more than one person at the same time—perhaps it was just assumed!
58. June Singer, *Androgyny: Toward a New Theory of Sexuality* (New York: Doubleday, 1976). See also Singer, *Boundaries of the Soul: The Practice of Jung's Psychology* (New York: Anchor, 1972, 1994).
59. Singer, *Androgyny*, 207.
60. Singer, *Androgyny*, 333.
61. Martii Nissinen, *Homoeroticism in the Biblical World: A Historical Perspective* (Minneapolis: Fortress, 1998), 28. For what follows of this older period, I am greatly indebted to this study. Nissinen's work is supported by Helmer Ringgren, *Religions of the Ancient Near East,* trans. John Sturdy (Philadelphia: Westminster, 1973), 25, who speaks of naked "eunuchs" associated with the cult to the Sumerian goddess Inanna (another name for Ishtar), that includes a *hieros gamos* rite.
62. Neal H. Walls, *The Goddess Anat in Ugaritic Myth*, SBL Dissertation Series 135 (Atlanta: Scholars Press, 1992): 83.
63. Cited in Turcan, *The Cults of the Roman Empire* (Hoboken, NJ: Wiley-Blackwell, 1997), 58. For more on the ancient concept of androgyny, see Peter Jones, "Androgyny: The Pagan Sexual Ideal," *Journal of Evangelical Theological Studies*, 43, no. 3 (Sept 2000): 443–69. See also chapter 4 of *The God of Sex: How Spirituality Defines Your Sexuality* (Escondido, CA: Main Entry Editions, 2006).
64. Singer, *Androgyny*, 333. Singer confirms what Mircea Eliade spoke of as "ritual androgyny" in shamanistic cults. See Eliade, *Patterns of Comparative Religions* (New York: New American Library, 1974), 420–21; *Myth, Dreams and Mysteries* (New York: Harper, 1974), 174–75; *Shamanism* (Princeton, NJ: Princeton University Press, 1964), 352.
65. Phillip Rieff, *The Triumph of the Therapeutic: Uses of Faith after Freud* (New York: HarperTorch, 1966).
66. Rod Dreher, "What Is 'Traditional Christianity,' Anyway?" (*The American Conservative*, July 24, 2014), http://www.theamericanconservative.com/dreher/what-is-traditional-christianity-anyway/.
67. Anthony Campolo, *Carpe Diem* (Dallas: Word, 1994), 85.

68. See Jenell Williams Paris, *The End of Sexual Identity* (Downers Grove, IL: InterVarsity Press, 2011).

69. Robert Reilly, *Making Gay Okay: How Rationalizing Homosexual Behavior Is Changing Everything* (San Francisco: Ignatius, 2014), 10.

Chapter 6: A Destructive Generation

1. Wayne Baker, *United America: The Surprising Truth about American Values, American Identity, and The Ten Beliefs that a Large Majority of Americans Hold Dear* (Canton, MI: Read the Spirit, 2014), 207.

2. Deroy Murdock, "The United States of Decline: America Unravels at an Increasingly Dizzying Pace" (*National Review Online*, February 17, 2014), http://www.nationalreview.com/article/371248/united-states-decline-deroy-murdock.

3. Patrick Buchanan, *The Death of the West: How Dying Populations and Immigrant Invasions Imperil Our Country and Civilization* (New York: St. Martin's, 2002), 145.

4. Buchanan, *Death of the West*, 2.

5. Mark Steyn, *America Alone: The End of the World as We Know It* (Washington, DC: Regnery, 2006), xvi, xiii, xix. This discouraging prediction is based on his observation of the Western refusal to have children.

6. Ben Velderman, "Pennsylvania mom of 7 dies in jail over unpaid school-related fines," EAGnews.org (Jun 13, 2014), http://eagnews.org/pennsylvania-mom-of-7-dies-in-jail-over-unpaid-school-related-fines/

7. David Kinnaman and Gabe Lyons, *UnChristian: What a New Generation Really Thinks about Christianity* (Grand Rapids: Baker, 2007).

8. Kinnaman and Lyons, *UnChristian*, 126.

9. Janice Shaw Crouse says that "we are in the midst of an STD epidemic with more than 20 million new STD cases every year—the majority of them affecting 15-25 year olds—triple the number just six years ago." See Crouse, "The Culture's War on Women," *The American Spectator* (2 Sept 2013), http://spectator.org/articles/54981/cultures-war-women.

10. Kinnaman and Lyons, *UnChristian*, 139.

11. Douglas Bond, "A Tragedy: Teens Unprepared For Life... And Eternity: Given the statistics, every Christian parent ought to be horrified at the prospect of sending their children off to college," review of *Preparing Your Teens for College* by Alex Chediak, *Aquila Report* (March 25, 2014), http://theaquilareport.com/a-tragedy-teens-unprepared-for-life-and-eternity/

12. Albert Mohler, "A Clear and Present Danger: Religious Liberty, Marriage, and the Family in the Late Modern Age," (lecture, Brigham Young University, Salt Lake City, October 21, 2013).

13. "Divorce in America (infographic)," *Daily Infographic*, October 24, 2013, http://dailyinfographic.com/divorce-in-america-infographic. According to the less dramatic figures of the American Psychological Association in 2014, about 40-50 percent of married couples in the United States get divorced; http://www.apa.org/topics/divorce/.

14. Aparna Mathur, Hao Fu, and Peter Hansen, "The Mysterious and Alarming Rise of Single Parenthood in America," *The Atlantic* (September

3, 2013), http://www.theatlantic.com/business/archive/2013/09/
the-mysterious-and-alarming-rise-of-single-parenthood-in-america/279203/

15. Crouse, "The Culture's War on Women."

16. Ben S. Carson, "MLK would be alarmed by black-on-black violence, lack of fam-ily values," *Washington Times*, August 28, 2013, http://www.washingtontimes.com/news/2013/aug/28/i-have-a-dream-50-years-later/#ixzz2dHLYuNnO.

17. Crouse, "The Culture's War on Women."

18. Cited by Peter Wehner, "America's Exodus from Marriage," *Commentary Magazine*, January 17, 2013, https://www.commentarymagazine.com/2013/01/17/americas-exodus-from-marriage/

19. Quoted in Wehner, "America's Exodus from Marriage."

20. Joe Boot, *The Mission of God: A Manifesto of Hope* (Ontario, CA: Freedom Press International, 2014), 380.

21. Boot, *Mission of God*, 380.

22. Sean Piccoli, "The Cheat Goes On at Harvard," *New York Post* (September 6, 2013), http://nypost.com/2013/09/06/the-cheat-goes-on-at-harvard/

23. Charlotte Miller, "Mobile adult subscription revenues to reach almost $1 billion by 2015" news release, Juniper Research, May 2, 2012, http://www. juniperre-search.com/viewpressrelease.php?pr=306

24. William M. Struthers, *Wired for Intimacy: How Pornography Hijacks the Male Brain* (Downers Grove, IL: InterVarsity Press, 2009), 43.

25. Struthers, *Wired for Intimacy*, 55.

26. Struthers, *Wired for Intimacy*, 59. See Al Mohler, "How Pornography Works: It Hijacks the Male Brain," review of *Wired for Intimacy*, by William Struthers, *AlbertMohler.com* (October 9, 2013), http://www.albertmohler.com/2013/10/09/how-pornography-works-it-hijacks-the-male-brain/

27. Struthers, *Wired for Intimacy*, 45.

28. Covenant Eyes, an Internet filtering and accountability program with Christian roots, has more on this troubling trend—and how to prevent it—on their blog. Visit www.covenanteyes.com.

29. Struthers, *Wired for Intimacy*, 59.

30. David Limbaugh, "Is this Still the America We Thought We Knew?" *Townhall.com*, September 20, 2013, http://townhall.com/columnists/davidlim-baugh/2013/09/20/is-this-still-the-america-we-thought-we-knew-n1704833/page/full.

31. Phillip Rieff, *The Triumph of the Therapeutic: Uses of Faith After Freud* (New York: HarperTorch, 1966).

32. Rod Dreher, "Sex After Christianity," *The American Conservative*, April 11, 2013, http://www.theamericanconservative.com/articles/sex-after-christianity/

33. Dreher, "Sex After Christianity."

34. Dreher, "Sex After Christianity."

35. Rebecca Downs, "Presbyterian Church USA Turns More Secular as it Strikes Down Pro-Life Principles," *Institute on Religion and Democracy*, June 27, 2014, http://juicyecumenism.com/author/rebecca-downs/

36. Jeff Walton, "National Cathedral 'Comes Out' With Transgender Preacher," *Institute on Religion and Democracy* (July 1, 2014), http://juicyecumenism. com/2014/06/25/national-cathedral-comes-out-with-transgender-preacher/

37. Charles Murray, *Coming Apart: The State of White America 1960–2010* (New York: Random House, 2012), 294–95.

38. Robert E. Webber, *Who Gets to Narrate the World? Contending for the Christian Story in an Age of Rivals* (Downers Grove, IL: InterVarsity Press, 2008).

39. Webber, *Who Gets to Narrate the World?*, 37.

40. Robert R. Reilly, *Making Gay Okay: How Rationalizing Homosexual Behavior Is Changing Everything* (San Francisco: Ignatius, 2014), 72.

41. John Adams, *Message from John Adams to the Officers of the First Brigade of the Third Division of the Militia of Massacusetts*, October 11, 1798, http://oll.liberty-fund.org/titles/2107

42. Cited in Eric Erickson, "Morning Briefing," *RedState*, August 28, 2013.

43. Cited in *The New American* (February 4, 2013), 9.

44. Bari Weiss, "Camille Paglia: A Feminist Defense of Masculine Virtues," *The New York Times*, December 28, 2013: "The military is out of fashion; Americans undervalue manual labor; schools neuter male students; [and] opinion-makers deny the biological differences between men and women."

45. Melanie Phillips, *The World Upside Down: The Global Battle Over God, Truth and Power* (New York: Encounter, 2010), 316.

46. Brian McLaren, *Finding Our Way Again: The Return of the Ancient* (Nashville: Thomas Nelson, 2008), 4–5.

47. Dianna Butler Bass, *Christianity After Religion: The End of the Church and the Birth of a New Spiritual Awakening* (New York: HarperOne, 2012), 30. For the opposing view, see Carl R. Trueman, *The Creedal Imperative* (Wheaton, IL: Crossway, 2012).

48. Bass, *Christianity After Religion*, 224.

49. Bass, *Christianity After Religion*, 1–2, citing William McLoughlin, *Revivals, Awakenings and Reform* (Chicago: University of Chicago Press, 1978). See also Bass, *Christianity After Religion*, 5, where she states: "What if the awakening is not exclusively a Christian affair, but rather that a certain form of Christianity is playing a significant role in forming the contours of a new kind of faith beyond conventional religious boundaries?"

50. Michael J. Boyle, "The Problem With 'Evil': The Moral Hazard of Calling ISIS a 'Cancer,'" *The New York Times* (August 22, 2014).

51. Cited in Penny Starr, "Panelist at Podesta Think Tank on Common Core: 'The Children Belong to All of Us,'" *CNS News*, February 3, 2014, http://cnsnews.com/news/article/penny-starr/panelist-podesta-think-tank-common-core-children-belong-all-us#sthash.4a1BcUkT.dpuf.

52. Rob Bell, *Love Wins: A Book about Heaven, Hell, and the Fate of Every Person Who Ever Lived* (San Francisco: HarperOne, 2011).

53. See Joe Boot's fascinating treatment of this subject, "The Oneist Utopia: Always a Dystopian Nightmare," in *The Coming Pagan Utopia: Christian Witness in Tough Times*, ed. Peter Jones (Escondido, CA: Main Entry Editions, 2014), 15–51. See

also Dennis Johnson's chapter in the same volume, titled "God's Final Eutopia," 239-59.

54. For an interesting treatment of transhumanism, see James Herrick's lecture on the subject at the 2014 truthXchange Think Tank: http://truthxchange.com/?s=transhumanism.

55. Cal Beisner, Newsletter, *Cornwall Alliance* (January 16, 2014).

56. Jenell Williams Paris, *The End of Sexual Identity* (Downers Grove, IL: InterVarsity Press, 2011), 97, 100, 109.

57. Beemyn and Rankin, "Can We Put an End to the Gender Binary?"

58. http://www.dartmouth.edu/livinglearning/communities/genderneutral.html.

59. Stephanie Chan, "Andreja Pejic Comes Out as a Transgender Woman," *Pret-a-Reporter* (July 25, 2014).

60. David Kupelian, *How Evil Works* (New York: Threshold, Editions, 2010), 171.

61. James Q. Wilson, *On Character* (Boulder, CO: AEI, 1995).

62. Brian Fitzpatrick, "Gay 'Marriage,' Distant Consequences," *Lambda Report on Homosexuality* (1996).

63. John N. Oswalt, *The Bible among the Myths* (Grand Rapids: Zondervan, 2009), 56–57.

64. See Dominic Lynch, "University to Offer 'Gender-Open' Restrooms," *College Fix* (July 30, 2014). It is already happening in certain hotels and on scores of college campuses.

Chapter 7: A Cosmology of Radical Egalitarianism

1. Tony Schwartz, *What Really Matters: Searching for Wisdom in America* (New York: Bantam, 1995), 431.

2. Arthur W. Hunt, *The Vanishing Word: The Veneration of Visual Imagery in the Postmodern World* (Eugene, OR: Wipf and Stock, 2013), 31.

3. http://www.imdb.com/title/tt0079470/quotes.

4. http://www.huffingtonpost.com/deepak-chopra/skepticism-and-a-million-_b_5522690.html.

5. My early publications were in French, since my first teaching appointment was in France.

6. Peter Jones, *The Gnostic Empire Strikes Back: An Old Heresy for the New Age* (Phillipsburg, NJ: P&R, 1992).

7. Steve Bruce, *God Is Dead: Secularization in the West* (Oxford: Blackwell, 2002), 156.

8. Cited by Bruce, *God Is Dead*, 74.

9. Christopher Partridge, *The Re-Enchantment of the West: Alternative Spiritualities, Sacralization, Popular Culture, and Occulture* (London: T&T Clark, 2004), 35.

10. On this, see chapter 9.

11. Andrew Cohen, "Is Your Ego Big Enough for God?" *Big Think,* http://bigthink.com/the-evolution-of-enlightenment/is-your-ego-big-enough-for-god.

12. Cited in Rod Dreher, "Sex After Christianity," *The American Conservative*, April 11, 2013, http://www.theamericanconservative.com/articles/sex-after-christianity/

13. Dreher, "Sex After Christianity."

14. June Singer, *Androgyny: Toward a New Theory of Sexuality* (New York: Doubleday, 1976), 237 [emphasis mine].

15. Mary Evelyn Tucker, "The Philosophy of *Ch'i* as an Ecological Cosmology," in *Confucianism and Ecology: The Interrelation of Heaven, Earth, and Humans*, ed. Mary Evelyn Tucker and John Berthrong (Cambridge, MA: Harvard University Center for the Study of World Religions, 1998), 187.

16. Thomas Berry, "Christianity's Role in the Earth Project," in *Christianity and Ecology: Seeking the Well-Being of Earth and Humans*, ed. Dieter T. Hessel and Rosemary Radford Ruether (Cambridge, MA: Harvard University Center for the Study of World Religions, 2000), 134.

17. Ken Wilber, *A Theory of Everything: An Integral Vision for Business, Politics, Science and Spirituality* (Boston: Shambhala, 2000).

18. Wilber, *A Theory of Everything*, xii.

19. Wilber, *A Theory of Everything*, ix, 37.

20. Wilber, *A Theory of Everything*, 83.

21. Bron Taylor, ed., *Encyclopedia of Religion and Nature* (London: Continuum, 2005), 164. The article speaks of "[Berry's] encounters with the ideas of Carl Jung and Mircea Eliade. Jung's understanding of the collective unconscious, his reflections on the power of archetypal symbols, and his sensitivity to religious processes made him an important influence on Berry's thinking. Moreover, Mircea Eliade's studies in the history of religions were influential in Berry's understanding of both Asian and indigenous traditions."

22. Ernest Sternberg, "Purifying the World: What the New Radical Ideology Stands For," *Orbis* 54, no. 1 (Winter 2010), 61–86.

23. Sternberg, "Purifying the World," 63.

24. Sternberg, "Purifying the World," 63.

25. Sternberg, "Purifying the World," 69.

26. Sternberg, "Purifying the World," 74.

27. Herbert Marcuse, *Eros and Civilization: A Philosophical Inquiry into Freud* (Boston: Beacon, 1955), xiii–xv.

28. Marcuse, *Eros and Civilization*, xix.

29. http://www.newsociety.com/Contributors/F/Farnish-Keith.

30. Keith Farnish, *Underminers: A Guide to Subverting the Machine* (Gabriola Island, BC: New Society Publishers, 2013), "Introduction."

31. Frances Goldin, Debby Smith and Michael Steven Smith, *Imagine: Living in a Socialist USA* (New York: Harper Perennial, 2014).

32. Paul Buhle, *Marxism in the United States: A History of the American Left* (Ann Arbor, MI: Verso, 1991).

33. Buhle, *Marxism*, front cover.

34. Please understand that I am not seeking to advocate for or excoriate any particular political party or agenda. However, because Oneist spirituality *must* function in a political realm, since its underlying assumptions refuse any realm other than the created one, Christians need to recognize Oneist influence wherever it appears.

35. David Horowitz, *Barack Obama's Rules for Revolution: The Alinsky Model* (Sherman Oaks, CA: David Horowitz Freedom Center, 2009), 26.

36. Paul Buhle, "Marxism, the United States, and the 20th-Century," *Monthly Review* (May 2009), 61, optimistically states: "The realities of a collapsing eco-system are as fearful as the threats of nuclear war in the first decade of *Monthly Review's* existence. Still, there are lots of prospects in front of us and around the corner. Marxism, always unfinished, is going to be a big help in figuring out what they are and what to do about them."

37. Buhle, *Marxism*, 100.

38. Buhle, *Marxism*, 100.

39. "Horowitz At Heritage Foundation: 'The Communist Party Is The Democratic Party,' " *Breibart News,* November 12, 2013, http://www.breitbart.com/Big-Journalism/2013/11/12/Horowitz-blasts-left-Heritage.

40. Paul Hawken, *Blessed Unrest: How the Largest Movement in the World Came Into Being and Why No One Saw It Coming* (London: Penguin, 2007), 2.

41. Hawken, *Blessed Unrest*, 4.

42. Hawken, *Blessed Unrest*, 22.

43. Michael Bastasch, "130 Environmental Groups Call for an End to Capitalism," *The Daily Caller* (July 23, 2014): "Environmentalists have declared that global warming can't be stopped without ending the 'hegemonic capitalist system,' saying that cap-and-trade systems and conservation efforts are 'false solu-tions. ... The structural causes of climate change are linked to the current capitalist hegemonic system.' "

44. Hawken, *Blessed Unrest*, 25.

45. See chapter 4, "The Perennial Philosophy—The Origin of Contemporary Spirituality."

46. Andrew Cohen, "A New Moral Context", as quoted on *2012: What's the "real" truth?,* May 24, 2012, https://jhaines6.wordpress.com/2012/05/24/a-new-moral-context-from-andrew-cohen/

47. See Boot, "Utopia: Always a Dystopian Nightmare," 15–51.

48. LGBTQQIAAP stands for Lesbian, Gay, Bisexual, Transgender, Queer, Questioning, Intersex, Asexual, Allies, and Pansexual, with nine other sexual identities camped out under the Queer umbrella.

49. Paula Ettelbrick, "Since When Is Marriage a Pathway to Liberation?" In Robert M. Baird, & Stuart Rosenbaum, *Same-Sex Marriage: The Moral and Legal Debate* (New York: Prometheus, 1997), 168.

50. "Michelle Obama and Eric Holder decry dangers to Sustainable Racism," *RedState* (May 18, 2014). Blogger Kira Davis, "Moving the Goalpost: The Left Redefines King's Color-blindness Ideal as Racism," *Currentsee* (May 2014) says: "To put it bluntly—some people just want someone to blame ... for everything. It's too painful to look inward to solve our problems, so we must find something else to explain our pain, our shortcomings, our struggles."

51. Paul Kivel, *Living in the Shadow of the Cross: Understanding and Resisting the Power and Privilege of Christian Hegemony* (Gabriola Island, BC: New Society Publishers, 2013), 2.

52. In the service of this neo-Marxist revival, "white guilt" is too good to be missed, especially in the light of the North American experience. Reaching deep into the complex question of the ambiguities of human relationships, "racism" is discovered to be ubiquitous (though objective proof is lacking). A psychological analysis has been developed that identifies "racial microaggressions," like "dismissive looks, gestures and tones," innocuous questions, like asking "an Asian person to help with a math or science problem," with the implied (insulting) racist message that "all Asians are intelligent..." See Derald Wing Sue, et al, "Racial Microaggressions in Everyday Life," *American Psychologist* vol. 62, no. 4 (May-June 2007): 271-86.

53. Paul Bond, "Dinesh D'Souza's 'America' to Explore Hillary Clinton's Teenage Years," *The Hollywood Reporter* (June 12, 2014).

54. Christian Gomez, "Working Together to Rewrite the Constitution," *New American* (9 June 2014). The article cites Harvard Law School Professor Lawrence Lessig, who states: "Perhaps ... it is time to rewrite our Constitution."

55. "Oppressed by the Ivy League," opinion article, *Wall Street Journal*, April 4, 2014, http://www.wsj.com/articles/SB100014240527023039870045794795011343 92562

56. Tracy Cuotto, "Psychology, Astrology and Carl Jung," *Metamorphosis* newsletter (Aug 2004).

57. Compare this with the basic views of Liberation Theology: "Marxism provides a scientific understanding of the mechanisms of oppression in the world, at local and national levels; It offers the vision of a new world which must be built as a socialist society, the first step to a classless society, where genuine brotherhood can be hopefully possible, and by which everything deserves sacrifice." Declaration of the Indian Theological Association (Delhi: Vidyajyoti College of Theology, April 1986).

58. Éliphas Lévi, *Transcendental Magic: Its Doctrine and Ritual,* trans. Arthur Edward Waite (London: Rider, 1968).

Chapter 8: Pagan Cosmology of Synthesis: The Joining of Reason and Spirit

1. Mike King, *Postsecularism: The Hidden Challenge to Extremism* (Cambridge: James Clark, 2009), 105.

2. King, *Postsecularism*, 105.

3. For other contemporary scholars who use the term "postsecular," see James K. A. Smith, "Secularity, Globalization, and the Re-enchantment of the World," chapter 1 in *After Modernity? Secularity, Globalization and the Re-enchantment of the World* (Waco, TX: Baylor University Press, 2008).

4. King, *Postsecularism*, 45, 47.

5. Dalai Lama, *Beyond Religion: Ethics for a Whole World* (New York: Houghton Mifflin Harcourt, 2011). See also Dalai Lama, *The Universe in a Single Atom: The Convergence of Science and Spirituality* (New York: Harmony, 2009).

6. Richard Tarnas, *The Passion of the Western Mind: Understanding the Ideas that Have Shaped Our World Views* (New York: Harmony, 1991), 435.

7. Tarnas, *Passion of the Western Mind*, 387.

8. Tarnas, *Passion of the Western Mind*, 405 [emphasis mine].

9. Tarnas, *Passion of the Western Mind*, 403.

10. Jeffrey Walton, "National Cathedral Hosts Muslim Friday Prayers," *Institute on Religion and Democracy*, November 14, 2014. See also Peter Jones, "'Christian' Liberalism Reveals Its Soul and Bares Its Fangs," *TruthXchange.com*, November 18, 2014.

11. King, *Postsecularism*, 147.

12. Tarnas, *Passion of the Western Mind*, 385, 387, makes the same point—that depth psychology joined science and psychic phenomena as an acceptable field of study.

13. Interestingly, there are only two opponents of the Christian faith represented by the theories of Grof; what he calls "monistic materialism" and what I would call "spiritual monism." They constitute the two possible sides of Oneism, which come together in the postsecular age. See the work of Mitchell Silver below.

14. Stanislav Grof, *Psychology of the Future: Lessons from Modern Consciousness Research* (Albany, NY: State University of New York Press, 2000), 209-10.

15. Richard Tarnas, "The Great Initiation," *Noetic Sciences Review* vol. 47 (Winter 1998): 24-31.

16. Richard Tarnas, *Cosmos and Psyche: Intimations of a New World* (New York: Penguin, 2006), 41.

17. Sean M. Kelly, *Individuation and the Absolute: Hegel, Jung and the Path toward Wholeness* (New York: Paulist, 1993), 3.

18. See *The Red Book*, back cover. On the place of the occult in this "new synthesis," see the following chapter.

19. On this, see *Malcolm Hollick, The Science of Oneness: A Worldview for the Twenty-First Century* (Ropley, Hampshire: John Hunt, 2006), as well as an older book by Fritjof Capra, *The Tao of Physics: An Exploration of the Parallels between Modern Physics and Eastern Mysticism* (Berkeley, CA: Shambhala, 1975).

20. King, *Postsecularism* 124-25.

21. King, *Postsecularism*, 131.

22. Fritjof Capra, *The Web of Life: A New Scientific Understanding of Living Systems* (New York: Anchor, 1996), 107. See also Capra, *The Tao of Physics*, and *The Turning Point: Science, Society and the Rising Culture* (New York: Simon and Schuster, 1982).

23. On this, see James A. Herrick, *The Making of the New Spirituality: The Eclipse of the Western Religious Tradition* (Downers Grove, IL: InterVarsity Press, 2003), 26.

24. Amit Goswami, *The Self-Aware Universe: How Consciousness Creates the Material World* (New York: Jeremy P. Tharcher, 1995), 11.

25. Frank Stootman, "The Spirituality of Quantum Mechanics," in *On Global Wizardry: Techniques of Pagan Spirituality and a Christian Response*, ed. Peter Jones (Escondido, CA: Main Entry Editions, 2010), 160.

26. Stootman, "Spirituality of Quantum Mechanics," 161. For an example of the interplay between science and spirituality, see Herrick, *The Making of the*

New Spirituality, chapter 5, "Science and Shifting Paradigms: Salvation in a New Cosmos."

27. Stootman, "Spirituality of Quantum Mechanics," 167.

28. Carter Phipps, *Evolutionaries: Unlocking the Spiritual and Cultural Potential of Science's Greatest Idea* (New York: Harper Perennial, 2012), 7. See also Ervin Laszlo, "Quantum Consciousness: Our Evolution, Our Salvation," *Huffington Post,* May 25, 2011, http://www.huffingtonpost.com/ervin-laszlo/quantum-consciousness-our_b_524054.html.

29. Phipps, *Evolutionaries,* 7.

30. Another element to this new science is the growing interest in "enhancement evolution," the merging of the human with the machine to produce the "transhuman." It is claimed that only in this way can we be sure of avoiding extinction. Technology will be the new magic, producing immortality. Inevitably, transhumanism is overtly Oneist, in the sense of requiring "a unified cooperative organization of living processes that spans and manages the universe as a whole." This sounds suspiciously like a human claim to divinity. See James Herrick, in *The Magician's Twin: C. S. Lewis on Science, Scientism, and Society,* ed. John West (Seattle: Discovery Institute, 2012), 251.

31. Tarnas, *Passion of the Western Mind,* quoted on the back cover.

32. William Blake, "London," in *Songs of Experience* (1794).

33. Tarnas, *Passion of the Western Mind,* 440.

34. Tarnas, *Passion of the Western Mind,* 411.

35. Tarnas, *Passion of the Western Mind,* 403.

36. Mitchell Silver, *A Plausible God: Secular Reflections on Liberal Jewish Theology* (New York: Fordham University Press, 2006), 7. For a similar discussion, see also Richard Dawkins, *The God Delusion* (New York: Houghton Mifflin Harcourt, 2006).

37. http://www.youtube.com/watch?v=g0B-cUSX57Q.

38. Silver, *A Plausible God.*

39. Silver, *A Plausible God,* 47.

40. Silver, *A Plausible God,* 105.

41. John P. Dourley, *The Psyche as Sacrament: A Comparative Study of C. G. Jung and Paul Tillich* (Toronto: Inner City Books, 2006), 65.

42. Wayne Teasdale, *The Mystic Heart* (Novato, CA: New World Library, 1999), 4.

43. Kurt Johnson and David Robert Ord, *The Coming Interspiritual Age* (Vancouver, Canada: Namaste, 2012).

44. Johnson and Ord, *The Coming Interspiritual Age,* 7.

45. This viewpoint is seeping into Evangelicalism, as the next chapter will show, but one case needs to be mentioned here. Johnson and Ord's *The Coming Interspiritual Age* is enthusiastically endorsed both by pagan philosopher Ken Wilber, and by Roman Catholic spirituality expert Richard Rohr. Rohr endorses both Wilber's books and his pagan "non-duality" and has taught "non-dual spirituality" to the DMin students at Fuller Theological Seminary in Pasadena, CA.

46. Andrew Cohen, "Editorial: Redefining spirituality for an evolving world," *What is Enlightenment,* 34 (Sept–Dec 2006), 16.

47. Andrew Cohen, "The Significance of Non Duality: There is Only One, Not Two" (lecture, EnlightenNext winter retreat, Tucson, AZ, Dec 27–Jan 6).

48. Jean Houston, "The Mything of the World: The Social Artist as Transcultural and Transpersonal Agent of Change," *ITC* (2004).

49. Houston, "The Mything of the World."

50. Virginia Lee, "Jean Houston: The Mystery of Human Consciousness: Exploring the Mystery of Human Consciousness: An Interview with Jean Houston," *Common Ground* (July 21, 2011).

51. Jean Houston, "A Stride of Soul: Shift Network on Global Oneness Day," *The Shift Network* (2012), http://light-of-consciousness.org/homepage-articles/stewards-of-time.html.

52. Jean Houston, "A Stride of Soul."

53. "Jean Houston, "Fractals and the Rise of the Shadow: Jean Houston Ph.D. Interview," by Alan Davidson, *Through Your Body* (2006), http://www.throughyourbody.com/members/newsletters/january2006/jeanhouston.html.

54. https://twitter.com/jbarro/status/492139917288693761

55. Joy Pullmann, "What's Happening to Gordon College is Just the Beginning," *The Federalist,* July 18, 2014, http://thefederalist.com/2014/07/18/whats-happening-to-gordon-college-is-just-the-beginning/

56. Al Mohler, "A Moral Revolution at Warp Speed—Now, It's Wedding Cakes," *AlbertMohler.com,* December 11, 2013, http://www.albertmohler.com/2013/12/11/a-moral-revolution-at-warp-speed-now-its-wedding-cakes/

57. Tony Perkins, "Help Us Stand Firm—Against the Lawlessness of the Obama Administration," *FRC* (July 21, 2014), http://christian-citizenship.com/?m=201407

58. Melanie Phillips, *The World Upside Down: The Global Battle over God, Truth and Power* (London: Encounter, 2011), 316.

Chapter 9: Salvation by Shaman

1. Jenny Hontz, "Yoga's Rock Stars," *Los Angeles Times,* August 21, 2006, http://articles.latimes.com/2006/aug/21/health/he-yogistars21

2. Steven G. Vegh, "Local yoga instructor infuses her classes with Christian worship," *The Virginian-Pilot,* May 30, 2006, http://hamptonroads.com/node/108171

3. See christianyoga.us.

4. Elizabeth Gilbert, *Eat, Pray, Love: One Woman's Search for Everything across Italy, India and Indonesia* (New York: Penguin, 2006).

5. "Modi means business with yoga focus," *The Straits Times Asia Report,* November 16, 2014, http://www.straitstimes.com/the-big-story/asia-report/india/story/modi-means-business-yoga-focus-20141116#sthash.GLQxgres.dpuf.

6. Jenny Hontz, "Yoga's rock stars."

7. Anne-Marie O'Connor, "Inner-Peace Movement," *Los Angeles Times,* March 25, 2004, http://articles.latimes.com/2004/mar/25/news/wk-cover25

8. See Pam Frost, "The Gospel According to Yoga" (lecture, TruthXchange Symposium, Raleigh, NC, October 31–Nov 1, 2014.)

9. Carl Jung, *Psychological Types: Or the Psychology of Individuation* (Princeton, NJ: Princeton University Press, 1921), 149–50.

10. Mark Gaffney, *Gnostic Secrets of the Naassenes: The Initiatory Teachings of the Last Supper* (Rochester, VT: Inner Traditions, 2004), 161.

11. Joel Stein, "Just Say Om," *Time Magazine* (27 July 2003).

12. See Edmund P. Clowney, *Christian Meditation* (Vancouver: Regent College Publishing, repr. 1979).

13. Swami Vivekananda, *Raja Yoga* (New York: Brentano, 1929), 51, 59.

14. Swami Sivananda Saraswati, "What Is Mind?" in *Bliss Divine* (Rishikesh, India: Divine Life Society, 2009).

15. Barry Long, *Meditation: A Foundation Course* (Los Angeles: Barry Long Books, 1996), 13.

16. Richard Wolin, *The Seduction of Unreason* (Princeton, NJ: Princeton University Press, 2006), 8–9.

17. Berry himself was a Jungian. See Thomas Berry, *The Great Work: Our Way into the Future* (New York: Bell Tower, 1999), 69, where he refers to the Jungian archetypes.

18. Timothy J. Leary, "Ancient Lessons of the Psyche: The Collective Unconscious and Shamanic Journeying," *Love Peace and Harmony*, July 26, 2013, http://lovepeaceandharmony.org/profiles/blogs/ancient-lessons-of-the-psyche-the-collective-unconscious-and-sham. See also C. J. Groesbeck., "C. G. Jung and the Shaman's Vision," *Journal of Analytical Psychology*, vol. 34, issue 3 (July 1989): 255.

19. C. Michael Smith, *Jung and Shamanism in Dialogue: Retrieving the Soul/Retrieving the Sacred* (New York: Paulist, 1997).

20. Smith, *Jung and Shamanism*, 6.

21. Smith, *Jung and Shamanism*, 3.

22. Jung provides a definition of *numinosum*: "...a dynamic agency or effect not caused by an arbitrary act of will. ... The *numinosum*—whatever its cause may be—is an experience of the subject independent of his will. ... The *numinosum* is either a quality belonging to a visible object or the influence of an invisible presence that causes a peculiar alteration of consciousness..." See his *Collected Works*, 11, paragraph 6.

23. John P. Dourley, *The Illness That We Are: A Jungian Critique of Christianity* (Toronto: Inner City Books, 1984), 50.

24. Richard Tarnas, *The Passion of the Western Mind: Understanding the Ideas that Have Shaped Our World Views* (New York: Harmony, 1991), 425.

25. Tarnas, *Passion of the Western Mind*, 425.

26. Stanislav Grof, *Psychology of the Future: Lessons from Modern Consciousness Research* (Albany, NY: State University of New York Press, 2000).

27. Lourdes is a town in southern France where miraculous healings are said to occur through appearances of the Virgin Mary.

28. See Grof, *Psychology of the Future*, 5, for a longer list of techniques.

29. Grof, *Psychology of the Future*, 4.
30. Grof, *Psychology of the Future*, 7.
31. Grof, *Psychology of the Future*, 5.
32. Grof, *Psychology of the Future*, xiii.
33. Grof, *Psychology of the Future*, 20. He calls this "identification with the Universal Mind and with the Supracosmic and Metacosmic Void."
34. Michael York, *Pagan Theology: Paganism as a World Religion* (New York University: NYU Press, 2003), 40.
35. Yusufu Turaki, "Foundations of African Traditional Religion and Worldview" in *On Global Wizardry: Techniques of Pagan Spirituality and a Christian Response*, ed. Peter Jones (Escondido, CA: Main Entry Editions, 2010), 115–30. It is intriguing that the techniques described here, from distinct cultures and countries, have an uncanny resemblance to one another.
36. Turaki, "Foundations of African Traditional Religion," 118–19.
37. Turaki, "Foundations of African Traditional Religion," 119–22.
38. Louis Sahagun, "Guru's Followers Mark Legacy of a Star's Teaching," *The Los Angeles Times*, August 6, 2006, http://articles.latimes.com/2006/aug/06/local/me-swami6
39. Berry, *The Great Work*, 106.
40. Berry, *The Great Work*, 2.
41. Berry, *The Great Work*, 168.
42. Berry, *The Great Work*, 73.
43. Berry, *The Great Work*, 88.
44. Berry, *The Great Work*, 22.
45. Berry, *The Great Work*, 18.
46. Walter Schwartz, "Thomas Berry obituary," *The Guardian*, September 27, 2009, describes Berry as "an influential Christian philosopher who sought to shift the focus of religion from individual salvation to care of the Earth and, indeed, the universe." Unfortunately Berry had abandoned any pretext of being Christian. As a "geologian," he effectively worshiped the earth.
47. Jean Houston, *Life Force: The Psycho-Historical Recovery of the Self* (New York: Delacorte, 1980), xxv, xviii, xix.
48. Richard Noll, *The Jung Cult: Origins of a Charismatic Movement* (Princeton, NJ: Princeton University Press, 1994), 137.
49. http://www.jeanhouston.org/Jean-Houston/
50. Jean Houston, "Social Artists," *New Connexion* (May–June, 2005).
51. On the *Beyond Awakening* Webinar in 2010, which I followed, Jean Houston addressed the subject, "A New Order Of Spirituality In Our Time." In the course of a live interview she was asked about her relationship with Mrs. Clinton, and Houston responded that she continued to have a relationship, "but under the radar," followed by a short laugh. She confirmed that "Hillary has a deep spiritual life," obviously "spiritual" in Houston's understanding of the term. However, on April 25, 2014, to 7,000 United Methodist women, Hillary Clinton gave her faith a Christian spin. Speaking of her liberal Christian background,

she declared: "I love that church. I love how it made me feel about myself ... I love the doors that it opened in my understanding of the world, I loved the way it helped to deepen my faith and ground it." See Adam Beam, "For Hillary Clinton, Faith Means Caring for Others," *Associated Press*, April 26, 2014; see also Robin Abcarian, "An Archetypical Analysis of Clinton," *Los Angeles Times*, May 12, 2008, http://articles.latimes.com/2008/may/12/nation/na-newage12

52. I am indebted to Rev. Dr. Ed Hird of Canada for some of these insights into the importance of Jean Houston. See "Jean Houston and the Labyrinth Movement," http://edhird.com/2010/08/26/dr-jean-houston-the-labyrinth-fad/

53. Jean Houston, *The Passion of Isis and Osiris: A Gateway to Transcendent Love* (New York: Ballantine, 1995), 2.

54. Houston, *The Passion of Isis and Osiris*, 2.

55. For more on this, see Peter Jones, "Androgyny: The Pagan Sexual Ideal," *Journal of the Evangelical Theological Society* (January 2000), in which I document the constant place of the homosexual shaman in pagan cults throughout time and space. For further reading, see Walter L. Williams, *the Spirit and the Flesh: Sexual Diversity in American Indian Cultures* (Boston: Beacon, 1986), 110–27.

56. Grof, *Psychology of the Future*, 67.

57. On these outer edges of "spirituality," where there is no recognition of the concept of "the image of God," we must also note the extreme expressions of sexuality. Scholars now speak of human beings having a "zoophilic orientation," that is, a deep psychological need for sexual relations with animals—see Gieri Bolliger and Antoine F. Goetschel, "Sexual Relations with Animals (Zoophilia): An Unrecognized Problem in Animal Welfare Legislation," in *Bestiality and Zoophilia: Sexual Relations with Animals*, 40. See also, Hani Miletski, *Is Zoophilia a Sexual Orientation? A Study in Bestiality and Zoophilia* (2005), 82, 95. There is really nothing to stop this perversion from being legalized as a self-evident civil right. An essay by a law student at Cornell University Law School argues that "the arguments deployed to support prohibitions against bestiality ... tend to break down, primarily because of what might be called irrational inconsistency. See Antonio Haynes, "'Dog on Man': Are Bestiality Laws Justifiable?" Cornell University Law School (Dec 5, 2012).

58. Grof, *Psychology of the Future*, 67.

59. Grof, *Psychology of the Future*, 68.

60. Berry, *The Great Work*, 159.

61. Helen A. Berger, Evan A. Leach, and Leigh Shafer, eds., *Voices from the Pagan Census: A National Survey of Witches and Neo-Pagans in the United States* (Columbia, SC: University of South Carolina Press, 2003), 40.

62. Berger et. al., *Voices*, 38.

63. See the *Burning Man* website [emphasis in the quote is mine].

64. Ken Wilber and Treya Killam Wilber, *Grace and Grit* (Boston: Shambhala, 1991), 77–88.

65. Josh Ellenbogen and Aaron Tugendhaft, eds., *Idol Anxiety* (Stanford, CA: Stanford University Press, 2001), 127.

66. James M. Robinson, ed., *Thunder, Perfect Mind* 13:19, 16:7; 19:15ff; 20:6–7, in *The Nag Hammadi Library in English*, rev. ed. (Leiden: Brill, 1996).

67. James M. Robinson, ed., *Gospel of Truth* 25:1–7, in *The Nag Hammadi Library in English*, rev. ed. (Leiden: Brill, 1996).

68. Alice Bailey states: "Christ and anti-Christ are the dualities of spirituality and materialism, both in the individual and in humanity as a whole." Bailey, *Externalisation of the Hierarchy* (New York: Lucis Trust, 1957), 136.

69. Carl Jung, *Collected Works*, ed. Gerhard Adler, trans. R. F. C. Hull (Princeton, NJ: Princeton University Press, 1970, 1975), 10:852, 11:295. Cited by Sean M. Kelly, *Individuation and the Absolute: Hegel, Jung and the Path toward Wholeness* (New York: Paulist, 1993), 18.

70. Kelly, *Individuation*, 18.

71. Kelly, *Individuation*, 18.

72. June Singer, *Androgyny: Toward a New Theory of Sexuality* (New York: Doubleday, 1976), 147.

73. Lynn Vincent, "Profile: Underestimating evil?" *World*, March 11, 2000, http://www.worldmag.com/2000/03/profile_underestimating_evil.

74. Noll, *The Jung Cult*, 268. See the comparison of Jung's theories with Buddhism in Radmila Moacanin, *The Essence of Jung's Psychology and Tibetan Buddhism: Western and Eastern Paths to the Heart* (Somerville, MA: Wisdom Publications, 2003).

75. Nietzsche, *Thus Spoke Zarathustra*, cited in Wolin, *Seduction of Unreason*, 50.

76. Noll, *The Jung Cult*, 264.

77. Friedrich Nietzsche, *Beyond Good and Evil: Prelude to a Future Philosophy*, trans. Helen Zimmern (1895).

78. Dourley, *The Illness That We Are*, 7.

79. Al Mohler, "'I Feel Super Great about Having an Abortion'—The Culture of Death Goes Viral," *AlbertMohler.com*, May 8, 2014, http://www.albertmohler.com/2014/05/08/i-feel-super-great-about-having-an-abortion-the-culture-of-death-goes-viral/

80. Mohler, "Super Great."

81. Mohler, "Super Great."

82. Berry, *The Great Work*, 174–75.

83. Berry, *The Great Work*, 165.

84. Jonathan Ott, "Shamanism," website of the Institute of Noetic Sciences.

85. Carl Jung, "The Undiscovered Self," in *Collected Works of Carl Gustav Jung*, vol. 10, trans. R. F. C. Hull, ed. H. Read *et al* (Princeton University Press, 1970), pars. 585–6.

86. Thomas Berry, *The Dream of the Earth* (San Francisco: Sierra Club Books, 1990), 211.

87. Berry, *Dream of the Earth*, 211.

88. Tarnas, *Passion of the Western Mind*, 411.

89. Tarnas, *Passion of the Western Mind*, 403 [emphasis mine].

90. Tarnas, *Cosmos and Psyche*.

91. C. G. Jung, *Memories, Dreams, Reflections*, cited in Tarnas, *Cosmos and Psyche*, 1. According to his biographer, Ronald Hayman, in *A Life of Jung* (New York: Norton and Company, 1999), 407, "Jung began to speak of archetypes as having a 'field of force' beyond the human psyche. He redefined them as transcendental 'arrangers of psychic forms inside and outside the psyche.'" His disciples in depth psychology find its ultimate grounding, then, in astrology. They believe astrology is able to reflect an infinity of archetypal experiences in relation to the natural cosmos.

92. John N. Oswalt, *The Bible among the Myths*, 14.

93. John Murray, *The Epistle to the Romans* (Grand Rapids: Eerdmans, 1959), 53.

94. Reilly, *Making Gay Okay*, 7.

95. Reilly, *Making Gay Okay*, 8.

96. Reilly, *Making Gay Okay*, 9.

97. Herbert Marcuse, *Eros and Civilization* (Boston: Beacon, 1955/1966). Plato would have denounced Jung, believing that "the liberation of Eros is not freedom but annihilation." Cited in Reilly, *Making Gay Okay*, 26.

Chapter 10: Christian Compromise with Culture

1. http://www.cbc.ca/news/canada/saskatchewan/u-s-anti-gay-activist-peter-labarbera-arrested-in-regina-1.2610123

2. David Kinnaman and Gabe Lyons, *UnChristian: What a New Generation Really Thinks about Christianity* (Grand Rapids: Baker, 2007).

3. I do not impugn the motives of these two sincere young men. I hope my contribution will be constructive.

4. Kinnaman and Lyons, *UnChristian*, 139.

5. Kinnaman and Lyons, *UnChristian*, 100.

6. https://web.archive.org/web/20141215111545/http://www.canainitiative.org/initiators.html.

7. From the poem "Wild Geese" by Mary Oliver. See Alexander Griswold, "Wild Goose Goes Gay: Drag Queen Edition," *Institute on Religion and Democracy*, July 15, 2014.

8. See Chelsen Vicari, "Why Liberal Evangelicals are Lying to Millennials," *The Blaze*, October 5, 2013, http://www.theblaze.com/contributions/why-liberal-evangelicals-are-lying-to-millennials/

9. As one example, *TIME* describes "the Reformation Project, a Wichita, Kans.-based effort by 24-year-old gay evangelical activist Matthew Vines to raise up LGBT-affirming voices in every evangelical church in the country. To reach that goal, he is training reformers in groups of 40 to 50 at regional leadership workshops. ... EastLake's Meeks is also planning an event in April, tentatively titled Sexuality, Inclusion and the Future of the Church and featuring British minister Steve Chalke, whose organization was kicked out of the U.K.'s Evangelical Alliance last summer for supporting the LGBT community" (Dias, "A Change of Heart," 46, 48).

10. Elizabeth Dias, "A Change of Heart: Inside the Evangelical Fight Over Gay Marriage," *TIME* (January 26, 2015), 44–48.

11. Dias, "A Change of Heart," 47.
12. Dias, "A Change of Heart," 46.
13. Rachel Held Evans, "Why Millennials Are Leaving the Church," *CNN Belief Blog*, July 27, 2013), http://religion.blogs.cnn.com/2013/07/27/why-millennials-are-leaving-the-church/
14. https://web.archive.org/web/20140715002349/http://www.canainitiative.org/initiatives.html.
15. http://www.patheos.com/blogs/christianpiatt/2013/10/what-is-the-cana-initiative-an-interview-with-mclaren-spellers-and-pagitt/ [emphasis mine]
16. Bass blogs for *The Huffington Post* and is associated with *Sojourners* magazine and the Red-Letter Christians movement—see http://sojo.net/biography/diana-butler-bass.
17. Bass, *Christianity After Religion*.
18. Endorsement in Bass, *Christianity After Religion*.
19. Bass, *Christianity After Religion*.
20. Bass, *Christianity After Religion*, 30.
21. Bass, *Christianity After Religion*, 7. Bass claims that "the 1970s were the beginning of the end of older forms of Christianity."
22. Bass, *Christianity After Religion*, 35, 96.
23. Bass, *Christianity After Religion*, citing James Forbes, "The Next Great Awakening," *Tikkum* (September–October 2010).
24. Bass, *Christianity After Religion*, 5. Bass describes the Sixties as "a spiritual hothouse, a garden of awakening," 223.
25. Bass, *Christianity After Religion*, 5.
26. Bass, *Christianity After Religion*, 224.
27. Bass, *Christianity After Religion*, citing with approval William McLoughlin, *Revivals, Awakenings and Reform* (Chicago: University of Chicago Press, 1978), 1–2. See also *Christianity After Religion*, 5, where Bass states: "What if the awakening is not exclusively a Christian affair, but rather that a certain form of Christianity is playing a significant role in forming the contours of a new kind of faith beyond conventional religious boundaries?"
28. Diana Butler Bass, "Contemplative Worship," *The Christian Century* (September 19, 2006): 25–9.
29. John P. Dourley, *The Illness That We Are: A Jungian Critique of Christianity* (Toronto: Inner City Books, 1984), 40.
30. I develop the contrast, in a variety of areas, between a gnostic view of Jesus and the Jesus presented in the canonical gospels in my book *Stolen Identity: The Conspiracy to Re-invent Jesus* (Colorado Springs: Cook Communications, 2006).
31. Bass, *Christianity After Religion*, 186.
32. Bass, *Christianity After Religion*, 189. On page 190, she states: "We belong to God because God is in each and every one of us."
33. Harvey Cox, in *The Future of Faith* (New York: HarperCollins, 2009) is also inspired by Gnosticism. For him, the gnostic texts show that a wide variety of different versions of Christianity, not just one, that flourished in the early

centuries, and they "offer an alternative spirituality that is attractive to many 21st century people" (*Future of Faith*, 16).

34. Bass, *Christianity After Religion*, 265.
35. Bass, *Christianity After Religion*, 18. She also mentions the important influence on her thought from Brian McLaren.
36. Phyllis Tickle, *The Great Emergence: How Christianity Is Changing and Why* (Grand Rapids: Baker, 2008), 28.
37. Tickle, *The Great Emergence*, 70. Jung's true self is a divine self-determining joiner of good and evil.
38. Tickle, *The Great Emergence*, 67.
39. I personally heard her say this at a public meeting.
40. https://web.archive.org/web/20090309125852/http://www.thevisionproject.org/Essays/mclaren_brian.html.
41. https://web.archive.org/web/20090309125852/http://www.thevisionproject.org/Essays/mclaren_brian.html.
42. See "Brian McLaren Calls Hell and the Cross 'False Advertising for God'—8 Jan 2006 and 12 Jan 2006" *Lighthouse Trails Research Project*, no date. Lest there be any ambiguity, McLaren endorsed a book by Episcopal priest Alan Jones, who in his *Reimagining Christianity*, calls "Penal substitution...[a] vile doctrine." See Alan Jones, *Reimagining Christianity: Reconnect Your Spirit without Disconnecting Your Mind* (Hoboken, NJ: Wiley, 2004), 168.
43. As, for example, in his course, "Action and Contemplation" (SP761, 8 units), Fuller DMin program, 2010.
44. Richard Rohr, "Creation as the Body of God," *The Huffington Post*, March 4, 2011.
45. Rohr, "Creation as the Body of God."
46. See the press release for the book at http://www.mmdnewswire.com/can-christians-be-saved-by-virginia-t-stephenson-buck-rhodes-27055.html.
47. Kester Brewin, *Signs of Emergence: A Vision for Church that Is Organic/Networked//bottomDecentralized/Bottom-up/Communal/Flexible/Always Evolving* (Grand Rapids: Baker, 2007), 53.
48. Brewin, *Signs of Emergence*, 104.
49. Brewin, *Signs of Emergence*, 128.

Chapter 11: A Whole or Holy Cosmos?

1. It also appears 182 times in the Roman Catholic Apocrypha.
2. David Tacey, *The Spirituality Revolution: The Emergence of Contemporary Spirituality* (London: Routledge, 2004), 128.
3. Huston Smith, *Beyond the Postmodern: The Place of Meaning in a Global Civilization* (Wheaton, IL: Quest Books, 2003), 222. "Quest" is the publishing arm of the Theosophical Society.
4. Mark Foreman, *Wholly Jesus: His Surprising Approach to Wholeness and Why It Matters Today* (Boise, ID: Ampelon, 2008), 39.
5. Jung similarly stated that "the Christ-symbol lacks wholeness in the modern psychological sense, since it does not include the dark side of things but specifically excludes it in the form of a Luciferian opponent." Cited in Jeffrey Satinover,

"The Gnostic Core of Jungian Psychology: Radiating Effects on the Moral Order," in James M. DuBois, ed., *Moral Issues in Psychology: Personalist Contributions to Selected Problems* (Lanham, MD: University Press of America Inc. 1997). 159.

6. Ethelbert Stauffer, "Hagios," in *Theological Dictionary of the New Testament* (Eerdmans, 1964) , 1:88.

7. Stauffer, "Hagios," 89.

8. Stauffer, "Hagios," 91.

9. Jeffrey Satinover, *Homosexuality and the Politics of Truth* (Grand Rapids: Baker, 1996), 240.

10. Roger Kimball, *The Perversions of M. Foucault* (New York: Simon and Schuster, 1993), cited by James Miller, "The Passion of Michel Foucault: A Review," *The New Criterion* (March 1993). http://www.newcriterion.com/articles.cfm/The-perversions-of-M--Foucault-4714

11. It is interesting to note that *kabod* (glory) and *qedesh* (holy) often appear together, because glory is sign of distinctiveness. Thus there are different kinds of glory, as Paul says, "There are heavenly bodies and earthly bodies, but the glory of the heavenly is of one kind, and the glory of the earthly is of another. There is one glory of the sun, and another glory of the moon, and another glory of the stars; for star differs from star in glory" (1 Cor 15:40–1).

12. Marc Byrd and Steve Hindalong, "God of Wonders," CCLI #3118757, 2000. Compact disc.

13. For a useful development of the being of God from this perspective, see my book, *The God of Sex: How Spirituality Defines Your Sexuality* (Escondido, CA: Main Entry Editions, 2013), 113–23.

14. Genesis 1:31. For a longer development of the creational process of separation and its holy character, see Jones, *The God of Sex*, 127–30.

15. According to rabbinic scholar Jacob Milgrom, in *Leviticus 1–16* (New York: Doubleday, 1991), 689: "Creation ... was the product of God making distinctions (Gen 1:4, 6, 7, 14, 18). This divine function is to be continued by Israel: The priests to teach it (Lev 10:10–11), and the people to practice it (Ezek 22:26), namely holiness.

16. Charles Fritsch, *The Book of Genesis: The Layman's Bible Commentary* (Richmond, VA: John Knox Press, 1959), 26.

17. Gerhard von Rad, *Genesis* (Philadelphia: Westminster, 1961), 59.

18. Amos 4:2 and Psalm 89:35: "Once for all I have sworn *by my holiness*; I will not lie to David."

19. Psalm 33:21: "For our heart is glad in him, because we trust in his holy name."

20. Exodus 22:31; Leviticus 20:7; 20:26; 21:8; Deuteronomy 7:6; 28:9.

21. See the parallel phrase spoken by Jesus: "Therefore you are to be perfect, as your heavenly Father is perfect," Matthew 5:48.

22. Romans 1:7. In Romans 15:16, Paul speaks of the Gentile converts as now "acceptable, sanctified [that is, made holy] by the Holy Spirit."

23. Common translation of the French, "*L'enfer, c'est les autres*," from Jean-Paul Sartre's play, *Huis Clos* (English: *No Exit*).

24. For the further use of *heteros* for "other," see "Let each of you look not only to his own interests, but also to the interests of others (*heteros*)" (Phil 2:4).

25. See Jones, *God of Sex*, 198-202.

26. Robert R. Reilly, *Making Gay Okay: How Rationalizing Homosexual Behavior Is Changing Everything* (San Francisco: Ignatius, 2014), 39, 41.

27. See the latest attempt by Matthew Vines, *God and the Gay Christian* (New York: Convergent Books, 2014), and the responses by Michael Brown *Can You Be Gay and Christian?: Responding With Love and Truth to Questions about Homosexuality* (Lake Mary, FL: Frontline, 2014) and Al Mohler, "God, the Gospel, and the Gay Challenge—A Response to Matthew Vines," *AlbertMohler.com*, April 22, 2014.

28. Sarah Ruden, *Paul Among the People: The Apostle Reinterpreted and Reimagined in His Own Time* (New York: Image Books, 2010), 138.

29. Reilly, *Making Gay Okay*, 45

30. Reilly, *Making Gay Okay*, 48.

31. Compare 2 Peter 3:10-11: "But the day of the Lord will come like a thief, and then the heavens will pass away with a roar, and the heavenly bodies will be burned up and dissolved, and the earth and the works that are done on it will be exposed. Since all these things are thus to be dissolved, what sort of people ought you to be in lives of holiness and godliness…"

32. David Horowitz, *The Black Book of the American Left* (New York: Encounter, 2013), 398.

Chapter 12: Blowing the Mind

1. I develop a sustained interpretation of that verse in *One or Two: Seeing a World of Difference* (Escondido, CA: Main Entry Editions, 2010).

2. John P. Dourley, *The Illness That We Are: A Jungian Critique of Christianity* (Toronto: Inner City Books, 1984), 158.

3. Cited in Dourley, *The Illness That We Are*, 23. "What one could almost call a systematic blindness is simply the effect of the prejudice that God is outside of man."

4. Brian Farmer, "The Holocaust: Denying the Deniers," *The New American*, March 25, 2014, http://www.thenewamerican.com/culture/history/item/17910-the-holocaust-denying-the-deniers.

5. Farmer, "The Holocaust," 35.

6. "The discerning mind" is the Greek δοκιμάζειν; "the undiscerning mind" is ἀδόκιμον.

7. Readers may wish to benefit from my lectures at the truthXchange Think Tanks, such as "Twoism and the Doctrine of God," http://truthxchange.com/section/media/audio/think-tank-2012-the-beauty-of-two/page/2/

8. Carl Jung, "Psychological Commentary on *The Tibetan Book of the Great Liberation*," in *Psychology and Religion*, Collected Works 11, 770—71.

9. Dourley, *The Illness That We Are*, 25.

10. For a useful understanding the systematic structure of God's revelation in the Bible, see R. C. Sproul, *Foundations: An Overview of Systematic Theology* (Orlando, FL: Ligonier Ministries, n.d.); Sproul, *Holy, Holy, Holy: Proclaiming the Perfections*

of God (Orlando, FL: Reformation Trust, 2010); Michael Horton, *The Christian Faith: A Systematic Theology for Pilgrims on the Way* (Grand Rapids: Zondervan, 2011); John Frame, *Systematic Theology: An Introduction to Christian Belief* (Phillipsburg, NJ: P&R, 2013); Sinclair Ferguson, *The Christian Life: A Doctrinal Introduction* (Orlando, FL: Ligonier Ministries, 2013); Joe Boot, *The Mission of God: A Manifesto of Hope* (St. Catherines, ON: Freedom Press International, 2014).

11. John Shelby Spong, *Rescuing the Bible from Fundamentalism: A Bishop Rethinks the Meaning of Scripture* (San Francisco: HarperCollins, 2009), 232.

12. William M. Struthers, *Wired for Intimacy: How Pornography Hijacks the Male Brain* (Downers Grove, IL: InterVarsity Press, 2009), 177.

13. Peter Jones, *The God of Sex: How Spirituality Defines Your Sexuality* (Escondido, CA: Main Entry Editions, 2013), 167.

14. Robert Sokolowski, *The God of Faith and Reason: Foundations of Christian Theology* (Washington, DC: Catholic University of America Press, 1995), 5.

15. Sokolowski, *The God of Faith and Reason*, x.

16. For access to this as-yet unpublished work, see http://carolinejones.com/wp-content/uploads/2014/01/Teaser.pdf.

17. Caroline Jones, *The Heart is Smart*, 5, 47. http://carolinejones.com/about-the-heart-is-smart/

18. Sokolowski, *The God of Faith and Reason*, x.

19. See Dourley, *The Illness That We Are*, 95.

Chapter 13: Gospel Power: A Given-Over Savior

1. This is clearly the problem of Islam, which is a false Twoism, in which God is an impersonal singularity and cannot enter into personal relationship with the other, namely creatures.

2. John P. Dourley, *The Illness That We Are: A Jungian Critique of Christianity* (Toronto: Inner City Books, 1984), 18, 50.

3. John Calvin, *Institutes of the Christian Religion*, 2.2.18.

4. Dourley, *The Illness That We Are*, 53.

5. Al-Qaeda in Iraq (AQI), now ISIS, after an October 31, 2010, attack on Baghdad's Our Lady of Salvation Church, murdered 2 priests and 44 congregants. It called Iraqi Christians "legitimate targets" and warned that the "killing sword will not be lifted." See Patrick Goodenough, "Iraq's Vulnerable Christians Further Imperiled by Jihadist Advance," *CNSnews.com*, June 13, 2014, http://www.cnsnews.com/news/article/patrick-goodenough/iraq-s-vulnerable-christians-further-imperiled-jihadist-advance.

6. Jordan D. Paper, *The Deities Are Many: A Polytheistic Theology* (Albany, NY: State University of New York Press, 2005), 10.

7. Stanislav Grof, *Psychology of the Future: Lessons from Modern Consciousness Research* (Albany, NY: State University of New York Press, 2000), 67.

8. Richard Tarnas, *Cosmos and Psyche: Intimations of a New World* (New York: Penguin, 2006).

9. By three different New Testament writers, Mark 1:14; Romans 1:1; 1 Peter 4:17.

10. See Gregory Beale, *The Morality of God in The Old Testament* (Phillipsburg, NJ: P&R, 2013).

11. Murray, *Romans*, 44.

12. In citing these verses, I've taken the liberty to emphasize the "For us" phrase by placing it first, so I have changed some of the sentence structure without changing the substance of the verse.

13. This is unambiguously clear in the Greek text where there is only one definite article that both terms, "God" and "Savior," share.

14. See also the use of this verb in: "Husbands, love your wives, as Christ loved the church and gave himself up" (*paredoken*) for her" (Eph 5:25).

15. "And walk in love, as Christ loved us and gave himself up (*paredoken*) for us, a fragrant offering and sacrifice to God" (Eph 5:2).

16. Jackie Hill Perry, "Love Letter to a Lesbian," *Desiring God*, May 16, 2013, http://www.desiringgod.org/blog/posts/love-letter-to-a-lesbian.

17. See chapter 11, " A Whole or Holy Cosmos?"

18. See also Ephesians 5:2: "And walk in love, as Christ loved us and gave himself up for us, a fragrant offering and sacrifice to God."

19. This verse has a slightly different form of the same verb.

20. Mark Foreman, *Wholly Jesus: His Surprising Approach to Wholeness and Why It Matters Today* (Boise, ID: Ampelon, 2008), 164.

SUBJECT AND NAME INDEX

SCRIPTURE INDEX

Old Testament

Printed in the United States
by Baker & Taylor Publisher Services